The
POWER
of
PRESENCE

A Guide to
Mindfulness Practices
in Early Childhood

Elizabeth Joy Erwin, EdD

Gryphon House
www.gryphonhouse.com

Published by Gryphon House, Inc.
P. O. Box 10, Lewisville, NC 27023
800.638.0928; 877.638.7576 (fax)
Visit us on the web at www.gryphonhouse.com.

Cover image used under license from Shutterstock.
Art by Liana Chetnik. Photographs by Alan Berger, Andrea Wesol, Bernardo Palomera, and Karen Connors

Library of Congress Control Number: 2020933572

Bulk Purchase
Gryphon House books are available for special premiums and sales promotions as well as for fund-raising use. Special editions or book excerpts also can be created to specifications. For details, call 800.638.0928.

Disclaimer
Gryphon House, Inc., cannot be held responsible for damage, mishap, or injury incurred during the use of or because of activities in this book. Appropriate and reasonable caution and adult supervision of children involved in activities and corresponding to the age and capability of each child involved are recommended at all times. Do not leave children unattended at any time. Observe safety and caution at all times.

For children everywhere
As we plant seeds of joy and justice together
World peace begins with us

Table of Contents

Preface ○ ○ ○

The unacceptable has now become acceptable. I had just returned from an annual international conference on equity and early childhood education and care—this time in Copenhagen—when it dawned on me that we have entered into uncharted territory. How has the unacceptable become so tolerable?

Those were the very first words for the original introduction to this book: "The unacceptable has now become acceptable." Who could have predicted that they would take on a whole new meaning when a global pandemic changed our planet forever? When I started writing this book, I had no idea a new reality would impact virtually every human being in the world just months later. At the time of printing, COVID-19 has required us to completely change the way in which we live. We work remotely (or not at all), schools are closed and classes are held online, nonessential travel has ceased, and public spaces are empty. People are grappling with how to feed their families and how to deal with a staggering loss of life within one's own inner circle.

At the same time, people are rising to meet the unexpected demands of this new reality together and with optimism and strength. People are finding creative ways of staying connected to loved ones virtually. There is an unprecedented outpouring of public appreciation for brave medical personnel, first responders, and other everyday heroes. We are seeing tremendous individual and collective generosity from within our communities and across the globe, reflecting, in my opinion, the heart and soul of humanity. I wonder if this global crisis has presented us with an unprecedented opportunity to turn our attention inward as we face uncharted waters and navigate them together. It seems like now is the time to slow down, invite silence, and to (re) mind ourselves that there is no place like home. The home to which I am referring is the place within ourselves where we can find comfort, ease, and inner peace despite what is happening all around us. It is my hope that the practices and ideas offered on the following pages will spark joy, elevate well-being, and promote a deeper sense of personal inquiry as we collectively and consciously plant seeds of mindfulness at home and around the world. It's about time.

Before COVID-19, one of the concerns I grappled with was how the education and care of young children has become utterly unrecognizable. As a mother for twenty-four years and a teacher educator for more than thirty years, I feel as if words are completely inadequate to describe the precious gifts that children are. And yet young children, who deserve to be the most protected and nourished, do not have the kinds of spaces, places, and positions they deserve in our schools, particularly in Western societies.

I remember visiting an early childhood center in Copenhagen and seeing the words for *kindergarten* in Danish beautifully handpainted on the wall. The words translate to "gardens where children grow." I recall smiling as I thought about how the early years of childhood are a celebration of unbridled joy, but then found myself wondering when such a party begins for children in the United States, given the increasing expectations placed on teachers to endorse standardization and conformity in their classrooms. The early years (from birth to age eight) are a magical time when wonder, curiosity, discovery, and creativity thrive. And yet teachers, families, and others knowledgeable about early childhood are increasingly facing pressures to remove the very pillars that make young children feel safe, joyful, confident, and competent.

The opportunity to write this book and confront many of these issues could not have come at a more perfect time. When the editors at Gryphon House approached me about writing a book to translate research into practice on the topic of mindfulness, I jumped at the invitation. At the same time, I recognized that addressing the concept of being present within an early childhood context requires an in-depth, critical examination of larger, complex issues in the world today. Luckily, the team at Gryphon House agreed, and *The Power of Presence* was conceived.

There seem to be numerous books on mindfulness and children flooding the internet and bookstores, but this is the first one (as far as I know) that offers an in-depth inquiry into mindfulness practices and early childhood education framed within a social-justice perspective. So, if you are curious to know even a little more or are a seasoned student (or teacher) of mindfulness practices, then it may be no accident this book has crossed your path.

The vision for this project is to deepen our lifelong journey of inquiry and to transform our teaching by exploring the practice of being present. The target audience is early childhood professionals, with a distinct focus on teachers of all backgrounds and experience levels, including global neighbors, who are invested in early childhood education and care.

Additionally, I hope this book will reach and appeal to other adults who care deeply about young children, including parents; grandparents; caregivers; practitioners across a variety of education-related disciplines, such as psychology, occupational therapy, nursing, and so on; yoga teachers; and university students. Especially in the West, teachers are encountering growing pressures inside the classroom with an increasing focus on academics and assessments. They are also facing pressures from outside the classroom as they engage in work that is undervalued in pay and esteem. This book has been designed for early childhood educators and others who are often faced with unrealistic demands that affect how they teach and take care of young children.

Many of the ideas are sparked by wisdom from ancient and native cultures, which I have learned through travel and teaching around the world. I wonder if one of the reasons there is growing interest in mindfulness is because people, particularly in the West, feel like they have lost their way. I imagine a world in which we would not need calming kits or quiet spaces in our early childhood settings because an understanding of mindfulness is deeply embedded into the fabric of daily living, as it has been in ancient traditions and contemplative practices for thousands of years. It is possible to challenge the unacceptable in early childhood. I remain optimistic that early childhood education and care can be the healthy and flourishing gardens for young children they were always intended to be.

My sense is that not only is this possible, it is nonnegotiable. It's about time.

Acknowledgments ⭘⭘⭘ ─────────────

It has been said that when the student is ready, the teacher appears. I have also heard that when the teacher is ready, the student appears. That is exactly what happened the day Andrea Wesol was hired as my graduate assistant. The impeccable timing, which coincided perfectly with the writing of this book, was no accident. We had wanted (and planned!) to work together two years earlier when Andrea first began her graduate studies at Montclair State University. As synchronicity would have it, things did not work out at the time, but fortunately everything fell into place when it needed to. Andrea was the perfect match for this project, given her passion for teaching, curiosity about early childhood, and her commitment to social action. She never missed a beat even though the pace was fast, the timelines were short, and the literature reviews dense. I relied on her meticulous research skills and attention to detail, while also appreciating her warmth, intelligence, dependability, and focus. Not only is Andrea a fast learner and a deep thinker, but she also openly shared her thoughtful insights and constructive criticism throughout all stages of the writing process. Deep gratitude goes to Andrea for all of this and so much more. I think of her now as a treasured friend.

I realize how fortunate I am to be surrounded by a wide circle of friends who inspire me through their own mindfulness practices. The diverse voices from the field, many from caring confidants and amazing former students, brought to life the chapters of this book and, I think, added an important personalized perspective. Heartfelt thanks goes to everyone who took the time to share their candid personal stories, which added a dimension of depth and clarity to this entire project: David Aveta, Alan Berger, Christina Bernal, Alyssa Blackman, Donna Bogart, Karen Carter, Bianca Fairley, Gabriella Gonzales, Corrine Harney, Sandra K., Alyssa Kovach, Yajaira Leon, Dana Lowe, Gabriella Martucci, Carissa Olivi, Minal Rosenblum, Ana Sanchez, Natalie Traverso, Sarah Veniero, and Andrea Wesol. Many thanks go to graduate assistant Lisa Bethel, who was a huge help in the final stages of editing and whose patience, perseverance, and good humor on Zoom calls were invaluable. The stunning artwork by Liana Chenik, also a former graduate student, impeccably brings to life the wonder, joy, and beauty of childhood. I am deeply honored that Liana chose to share her exquisite drawings with all of us in this way. Thank you, Liana. Wholehearted gratitude also goes to the longtime and trusted friends who were kind enough to offer feedback on early drafts of the manuscript or provided important original contributions on mindfulness practices for this book: Annie Bien, Donna Bogart, Gerry Costa, Lindsay Hilscher, Debby Kaminsky, Priya Lalvani, Susan Lederer, and Christer Ohlin. Thank you for your friendship and generosity in sharing your expertise so others can learn from you like I have.

Recognition is due to dear friends Leslie Soodak and Stephanie Teague, whose guidance nourished me when I needed it most. Were it not for the love, wisdom, and generosity of others whose friendship provided the perfect balance of support and care to carry me through this year, it is hard to imagine where I would be. Although too many to acknowledge by name, a gigantic and sincere thank you to the many circles that continue to nourish my soul: BEMER family; Ashtanga yoga community; academic and international colleagues; and, most importantly, the steadfast, loving, and dependable bonds of a wonderful extended family.

The road across one's lifetime is never driven alone, and so I wish to acknowledge all the wise teachers—past and present—who have helped me navigate and steer through triumphs, speedbumps, and everything in between. A special thank you to Eddie Stern and Jeffrey Lally. The well of gratitude is not deep enough to express what their teachings and inspiration have meant to me for more than a decade. And to the many graduate students along the way who have served as copilots during the journey—a warm and sincere thank you.

Working with Gryphon House has been exceptionally smooth, exhilarating, and a delightful experience. Of particular note, Executive Editor Stephanie Roselli was simply first-rate. Not only was she incredibly knowledgeable, efficient, and responsive, Stephanie also provided everything an author could ever want. Whether it was resources, guidance, clarity, and much more, Stephanie always delivered with warmth and a sense of humor. I feel extremely fortunate to have had this incredible opportunity to work with Stephanie and the amazing team at Gryphon House.

Although unconventional, I would be remiss if I did not acknowledge the musical sensation Train for the powerful reminder that no one travels alone on this planet. So when I look to the sky—thank you to Mom and Dad for their loving presence, then and now. Profound gratitude goes to Michael's love for making me smile and Bill's gift for always showing up and lending a helping hand. Bill is my hero because most run from burning buildings, but Bill runs toward them. It is a total privilege to have in my life a daughter like Alyssa Beatrice Blackman. I appreciate her brutally honest feedback and tremendous encouragement (YGTM) throughout the writing of this book. Our shared love of teaching, learning, travel, yoga, children, books, culinary adventures, and much more has brought magical moments of laughter and tears of joy, and for that I am eternally grateful.

Introduction ○○○

How This Book Is Organized

The central organizing idea for this book is time. The following anchoring principles are deliberately, yet delicately, threaded throughout each chapter:

- Mindfulness is a practice, an ongoing journey, not an end goal or destination.

- Teaching and learning are intricately connected; there cannot be one without the other.

- Reflective personal inquiry is an integral part of any mindfulness practice in which beliefs, thoughts, and questions are critically examined and reexamined.

- It is not possible to teach mindfulness practices to young children if we do not have our own personal mindfulness practice, but it is best to learn about being present from young children themselves.

- Families are the most important and steady aspect of a young child's life. Home-school partnerships are at the very heart of early childhood education and care.

- The term *classroom* is used throughout this book as a metaphor for where young children learn and grow. The classroom is not meant to be narrowly conceptualized as only the four walls in a school, but rather as representative of the larger world in which children learn and grow.

- Young children live in a state of presence and joy when they are nurtured and loved.

The Power of Presence is organized in eight chapters within three distinct sections. Although each chapter can be read and understood on its own, I suggest you read the book sequentially because each chapter sheds new light on key ideas. At the beginning of each chapter, a special quote introduces the chapter content and inspires questions about what is to come. Each quote has been purposely selected based on the personal meaning it holds in my life, as well as the intersecting connections it has to concepts and ideas presented in the chapter.

Throughout each chapter, I offer an original and authentic perspective on being present. I translate research into practical applications and highlight diverse voices from the field about the intersection of mindfulness, teaching, and learning. Chapters also include a compilation of recommended resources, a menu of options for teaching inclusively, mindfully, and equitably:

 Children's Corner: children's books to inspire, elevate, and educate young learners throughout the early years through the use of children's literature

 Caregivers' Corner: a treasure chest of resources and tools geared to families, teachers, and others who care about the well-being of children

Take It to the Classroom: simple child-tested ideas that can be easily implemented and adapted for home or classroom use

These resources provide a wide variety of practical teaching ideas and innovations and correspond to chapter content.

This book is an invitation to embark on a journey together—a journey of being present for and with young children. When we broaden our understanding of the complex landscape of early childhood education and care, we inform our teaching and mindfulness practices. As we recognize what is at stake, we can (re)turn to what really matters.

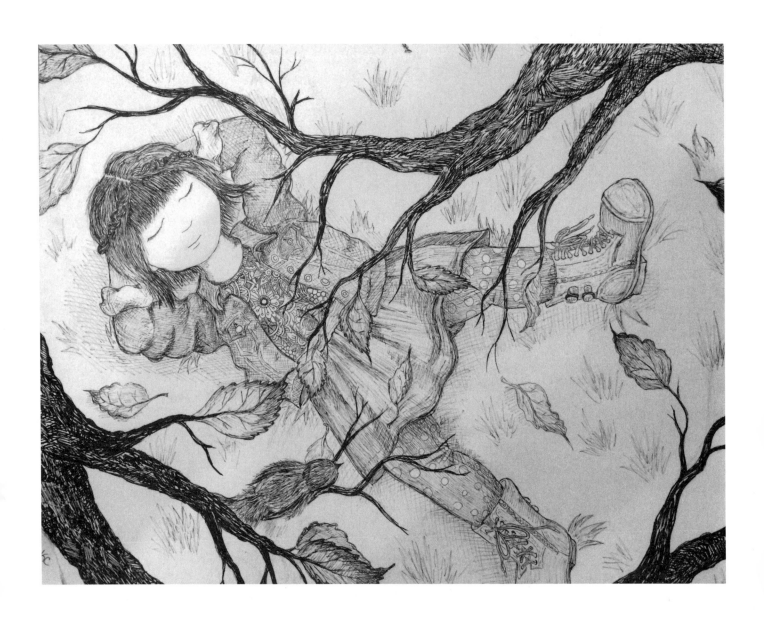

PART I

The Urgency to Know—Why It Matters More Than We Think

In part I, we critically examine the notion of mindfulness, what the research says, and how mindfulness connects with affirming the dignity in ourselves and others. We explore the increasing focus on being present in early childhood settings, and why mindfulness matters in the lives of young children and the adults who care about them.

CHAPTER 1

If Not Now, When?
Being Present for Young Children

> **"It's like breathing in blue skies and breathing out stormy clouds."**
> —Second grader

I was getting ready for class when I thought about how unusually busy and unpredictable the semester had been for one of the graduate courses I teach. Like so many educators, I noticed how I was starting to feel a twinge of pressure because the class was behind schedule. I wanted the students to be well prepared for an upcoming field-based assignment, so there was no room for any diversion.

Well, you can likely guess what happened next. Right from the start of class we had one interruption after another. Just when I thought it could not get any worse, the piercing fire alarm sounded, jolting us all with a rush of adrenaline. Needless to say, it was as if everything was lining up—and not in our favor.

Luckily, this fire alarm turned out to be a false alarm. I was keenly aware that the inner alarm inside of me could have also sounded off, given the way the evening was turning out. But for some reason my mind was quiet—no inner messages such as "There won't be enough time to cover the material" or "Students are going to be anxious and upset if they don't have all the information." I felt an inner sense of peace despite having significantly less time for the course material that needed to be covered. As we returned to our classroom, I was joking even though I had no clue how to teach the enormous amount of content in the limited amount of time we had left.

This is how practicing mindfulness can make all the difference in the world.

Just a few years ago, far less would have caused me to feel anxious. Although I have been practicing mindfulness for many years, I continue to notice how the cumulative effects grow stronger and more consistent over time. Practicing mindfulness on a regular basis means you have more tools, experiences, and insights readily available. Many people, myself included, can more easily recover from a stressful event because a daily mindfulness practice helps to maintain a state of inner peace and restore a sense of ease, even when triggers are set off. It's not that I never feel stressed, annoyed, impatient, or upset. Trust me—I can get pretty cranky. But that happens less often these days, and I am able to quickly regain a sense of calm.

So, as our class settled back in after the fire-drill commotion, I made a few adjustments as teachers naturally do when their plans don't work out. When class ended, the students walked out seemingly confident and comfortable about what they were expected to do to start their projects. This was a good reminder for me about how, when mindfulness is practiced in an intentional and sustained way, we can more easily experience a sense of calm and focus inside of us, notwithstanding what may be happening on the outside. And it is up to us to show children this way.

The beautiful quote at the beginning of this chapter are the wise words from a second grader about what it is like to meditate. I found this quote to be such a clear and poetic way to describe what mindfulness is like for her. The quote, "It's like breathing in blue skies and breathing out stormy clouds," actually served as the title for an article on mindfulness practices in early childhood that I coauthored with current and former graduate students at my university. Despite studying mindfulness on my own for many years, working on that article ignited a spark in me to engage in a more formal inquiry into the meaning of being present in early childhood. My intention in this chapter is to deliver an overview of what I have discovered over time—personally and professionally— about mindfulness during the early years.

What It Means to Be Present and to Quiet the Mind

When we meditate or engage in any mindfulness practice, we teach our minds to become quiet. This is the essence of mindfulness, quieting the mind. When the mind becomes quiet and relaxed, a deep awareness about being in the present moment occurs. The significance of being present is rooted in ancient wisdom.

One of the most prolific teachers on mindfulness, Jon Kabat-Zinn, founder and director of the Stress Reduction Clinic at the University of Massachusetts Medical Center, explains in his book *Wherever You Go, There You Are: Mindfulness Meditation in Everyday Life* how mindfulness is "awareness, cultivated by paying attention in a sustained and particular way: on purpose, in the present moment, and non-judgmentally." In essence, our mind becomes quiet and we experience a sense of calm when we stay open to the beauty, complexities, and contradictions of being human—with no judgment—moment after moment. Mindfulness is about deliberately paying attention to or witnessing sensations, feelings, and thoughts without interpretation or commentary.

When we are fully present, we live now. One of my favorite poets, internationally acclaimed activist and author Maya Angelou, articulates the treasure of the "now" at the beginning of her poem "Wonder."

> A day
>
> drunk with the nectar of
>
> nowness
>
> weaves its way between
>
> the years . . .

When we are present and living in the here and now, we live in harmony with nature. We also acknowledge a deep appreciation not only for being alive but also for the connection to the world around us. Young children generally live with a sense of wonder and delight. This natural sense of mindfulness during the early years can be eventually replaced by a sense of busyness, distraction, or mindlessness—often learned within the contexts in which young children live and play.

This may be why educators are becoming increasingly interested in learning more about the power of presence in the classroom and how to deepen their own mindfulness practice. In his book *The Way of Mindful Education: Cultivating Well-Being in Teachers and Students*, Daniel Rechtschaffen offers this simple explanation: "Mindfulness invites us back to the preciousness of the present moment." He poses several questions to help us consider specific times when we have experienced a deep awareness grounded in the moment:

- Have you ever been playing sports, making music, or creating art when all of your thoughts seemed to move into the background and you were totally absorbed in the present activity?

- Have you ever been in a dangerous situation where your senses became highly attuned and your attention was laser focused?

- Have you ever looked into the eyes of a baby and felt yourself dumbstruck with love and wonder?

These experiences of being fully present and deeply aware in the moment are unmistakable. They occur when our mind is quiet and not filled with endless chatter, thoughts, judgments, contrasts, justifications, comparisons, and contradictions. It is not that our thoughts are harmful. The challenge, however, is that our minds are continuously running.

The Path of Mindfulness Practice

Mindfulness is a practice, not a goal to be achieved. Early childhood educators have long understood how the process is more important than the final product in children's learning. Mindfulness can be thought of in the same way—being aware of being present is a lifelong process.

- Mindfulness can be thought of as a journey as opposed to arriving at a specific destination.

- Mindfulness is a fascinating and winding adventure of deep inquiry.

- Mindfulness is about being here rather than wanting to be over there and having no judgment or expectation either way.

- Mindfulness is an ongoing practice as opposed to an end goal or outcome.

In his book *Silence: The Power of Quiet in a World Full of Noise*, Thích Nhất Hạnh, the world-renowned Vietnamese poet, scholar, and teacher who was nominated for the Nobel Peace Prize by Dr. Martin Luther King Jr., characterizes mindfulness as "the practice that quiets the noise inside us." He describes how we can get distracted by the future when we focus on fear or stress about the unknown. Likewise, he suggests that we can be dragged into our past by focusing on grief, disappointment, and guilt that we keep recreating and reliving in an endless cycle. According to Thích Nhất Hạnh, we get caught in the prison of the past or the prison of the future.

Take a moment to think over how much energy you devote to thinking about the past or projecting into the future in the course of a day. Can you calculate the actual amount of time spent?

If we take a moment to seriously consider how much time we waste dwelling in the past or anticipating the future, we realize how very little time is spent being fully present in each precious moment that we are alive. It is almost as if our minds are in a constant state of chattering about the past or the future. Thích Nhất Hạnh further explains that "even if we are not talking with others, reading, listening to the radio, watching television, or interacting online, most of us don't feel settled or quiet. This is because we're still tuned to an internal radio station, Radio NST (Non-Stop Thinking)." This non-stop thinking consumes much of our waking moments, even when we are silent and not moving. That is why mindfulness is often referred to as quieting the mind. It is about tuning out the noise or clearing the clutter. It is no accident, therefore, that mindfulness is commonly understood as a practice. Mindfulness is essentially a deliberate and conscious choice we make over and over and over again. My yoga teacher, Eddie Stern, recently said that mindfulness is not difficult at all—the challenge is being mindful continuously!

Mindfulness as a Cliché

When I started noticing an escalating interest in mindfulness in the field of education several years ago, it made me uncomfortable and I wasn't quite sure why. I was eventually able to make sense of the strong reaction I was experiencing. The idea of mindfulness was sounding more like a cliché—superficial and trivial—as opposed to the deep practice that I have known it to be. In addition, I felt as if the commercialization of education was (once again) happening and children were positioned as a commodity. I observed, for example, how the notion of mindfulness was becoming (and still is) a hot trend in education, thereby producing enormous economic gains, primarily for large corporations, most of whom lack any experience or genuine interest in education. Suddenly there was a new marketing, advertising, and merchandizing "business" around mindfulness in schools.

I recall a time not too long ago when yoga mats, bags, and clothing did not exist; now they seem to be everywhere. The contradiction surrounding marketing and selling mindfulness is quite striking. In his book *One Simple Thing: A New Look at the Science of Yoga and How It Can Transform Your Life*, Eddie Stern describes the phenomenon he witnessed as the West began to learn about yoga. Stern writes, "It's now more like West gobbles up the East. . . . veer[ing] into a head-on collision with consumerism—exactly the opposite of what yoga was supposed to promise and deliver." The unapologetic consumerism in Western cultures is a reason why there is cause for alarm regarding the mindfulness explosion in education. I am deeply troubled when children are targeted and groomed intentionally for economic gain. This is not to suggest that we should not pursue mindfulness in schools. Instead, we have an opportunity to be acutely aware of and outspoken about how children and schools are positioned as consumers and explicitly pursued for economic profits.

The movement—led by teachers, families, and others committed to education—to embed mindful practices into schools is transforming children's lives. Teaching children how to be more mindful in everyday life is indeed important. The intensifying interest in mindfulness over the past several years, particularly from an educational, cross-disciplinary (occupational therapy, psychology, and social work) perspective, has generated new understandings, innovative paradigms, and healthy discourse. However, given that the concept of mindfulness is sometimes presented in a shallow, cursory way or driven by commercialization, I feel more comfortable referring to mindfulness as being present or being conscious and will do so more often in the pages that follow.

The Hurried Life: Why Slowing Down Matters

If being present is a practice, as opposed to a goal or outcome, and we decide to be fully in touch in our daily lives, what does this actually look like? Being present does not just happen on weekends or in yoga class or first thing in the morning before heading to school or work. Being present is not about conquering the mind. Being present or conscious can be thought of as simply a way of living. To engage in the practice of being present, we decide—again and again—to quiet the mind. This is a practice that occurs throughout our lifetimes.

But how does one even begin? In her best-selling book *My Stroke of Insight: A Brain Scientist's Personal Journey*, Jill Bolte Taylor, a Harvard-trained brain scientist, describes in meticulous detail her extraordinary eight-year recovery from a serious traumatic brain injury. Taylor describes how becoming aware of the present moment is about first acknowledging our thoughts and beliefs and then pressing the pause button to silence them for the moment. Although our thoughts and beliefs serve a function by helping us navigate daily life in the world, the incessant chatter takes us away from being fully aware. To return to the present moment, Taylor explains, "We must consciously slow down our minds. To do this, first decide you are not in a hurry."

Not in a hurry? It is almost as if everything these days is moving faster than ever, particularly in the West. "Busy" has become almost a rote response when people greet each other and ask, "How are you?" Even though every human being has the same twenty-four hours in a day, it appears as if people are packing more into a day than ever before. I can't recall the last time I met a teacher who said there was enough time in the day to "get it all done." It is commonplace these days for me to take an elevator and be the only person who is not using a cell phone or devouring food in between floors. Take a moment to notice how a sense of hurrying shows up in your own life.

It seems to me that we are in a constant state of hurrying. It is as if a hurried, busy life, for children as well as adults, has become the norm. And yet, the idea of hurrying, particularly during the early years, is not a new concern: "Today's child has become the unwilling, unintended victim of overwhelming stress—the stress born of rapid, bewildering social change and constantly rising expectations." This quote, which still rings true today, was written decades ago by David Elkind as he examined the issue of hurrying in his highly esteemed book *The Hurried Child*. Has much changed since the early 1980s? Well, yes and no.

We either want to pack more in or do less so we can have more time. Have you noticed a steady, relentless stream of new or improved products to make personal communication quicker or household cleaning easier? Food is packaged for our convenience so that we can grab a meal on the go. Modern convenience foods first appeared generations ago, offering food not in its natural state but canned or frozen to make meal preparation easier. The purpose behind these "innovations" was having more time. If we have less preparation and cleanup around mealtime, then we can spend that time doing something else. In short, hurrying is really about accumulation and the pursuit of more. This Western focus on accumulation is not solely restricted to time. We are in relentless pursuit of accumulating things we can hold, touch, smell, taste, and see. And there is also the accumulation of abstract or intangible things, such as power, information, experiences, and outcomes. A sense of hurrying still prevails but extends well beyond time. The core beliefs behind a sense of hurrying are about having more, doing more, and being more.

Darcey Dachyshyn, author of the compelling journal article "Being Mindful, Heartful, and Ecological in Early Years Care and Education," is a parent raising a child with indigenous

Canadian origins as well as an instructor of master's level students in Dar es Salaam, Tanzania. In her article she describes a continuous "busyness" around doing observed in Western cultures. She explains that this incessant doing is like being on a treadmill on which we lose sight of the here and now. Dachyshyn warns about the constant busyness of doing, even when the outcome may be beneficial within the field of early education and care: "I think this can be true even of doing good deeds, doing critical thinking, doing social justice, or doing that which might make the world more equitable." Despite noble intentions, the constant need for and pursuit of accumulation distracts us from being fully engaged and aware in the moment, especially when we are in the presence of young children. And because young children naturally follow the adults in their lives, we are teaching them to do the same.

It has become a popular joke these days to acknowledge how we are slowly transforming into human doings as opposed to human beings; however, the joke is actually on us. Because we are incessantly doing more and more, we are gradually losing touch of who we are. Mark Nepo, poet, philosopher, and author of *The Book of Awakening: Having the Life You Want by Being Present to the Life You Have*, describes so perfectly the essence of our constant quest for accumulation: "The greedy one gathered all the cherries, while the simple one tasted all the cherries in one." If we are not fully present or conscious, how can we genuinely show up for young children? Actually, I believe we should be asking a different question altogether: What can adults learn from children about being present?

Breathing in Blue Skies and Breathing out Stormy Clouds: What We Can Learn from Young Children about Being Present

Like it was yesterday, I recall the fascination my (now adult) daughter had about the world as she posed questions such as "Why is water always wet?" or "Why do cars drive on the parkway and park in the driveway?" Young children have spectacular imaginations, and I smile every time I think of Alyssa stating, at age three, "I wish I had magical powers so I could fly anywhere I wanted," as well as declaring, "I like wearing short sleeves so I can feel a cool breeze on my arms." Young children live in the moment as they wonder, ponder, and notice ordinary treasures in everyday life that adults can so easily take for granted. When we take the time to pause, we realize children have much to teach us.

When families, caregivers, and teachers genuinely perceive young children as the wise beings they are, we are better able to notice and to contemplate what we can learn from and alongside them. When Alyssa was born, I decided that she was going to be my teacher, not the other way around. Obviously, I was going to protect her from harm and provide safe spaces and nourishment so she could thrive, but I also realized that she had as much to teach me as I had to teach her. It was years later at a conference in New Zealand when I heard a term that reflected my intentions as a parent—I wanted to be *power-sharing* instead of *power-bearing*. I did not want to make every decision about Alyssa's life because I was the adult or the parent; instead, I recognized that she had an important, equal status as a human being in our family.

In essence, when I released the expectations of what I thought Alyssa had to learn or what she should be doing, I was more present for her and could see what she needed from me. When I was fully aware in the present moment during those early years, I could see my daughter as a human being and understand all the complexities that made her a unique individual within our family structure. Instead of focusing on my own agenda for Alyssa's future, I was more open to receive the countless lessons and gifts that she brought daily into my life. When I was present in the moment, I could receive what Alyssa had to teach me about the world regarding beauty, wonder, patience, equity, kindness, joy, and so much more. When I focused on my list that had to be accomplished that day or other expectations that cluttered my mind, I simply could not be as present for my daughter and, therefore, missed opportunities to fully engage with her. Being present in each moment is still an ongoing journey with many twists and turns, which is why mindfulness is a humbling daily practice for anyone.

Mindfulness and the Partnership between Home and School

In the multiple roles we play as humans, I consider that the most meaningful is the one we assume when there are children in our lives. It is no surprise that the family is the primary and most influential teacher in a young child's life. If educators are not actively engaged in partnerships with the families of the children we teach, we cannot teach well. Maintaining consistent and clear communication with families in the classroom and beyond can provide critical support, guidance, and information, especially when it comes to mindfulness.

Carissa Olivi, a teacher at a public elementary school, has developed a deep personal and meditation practice. Several years ago, she began cultivating mindfulness with her young students, being present for them in a meaningful way and teaching them how to begin to do the same.

> I am more skilled now than I was in the past few years when I simply taught sitting still and quietly, listening to our surroundings. Now I teach them about their brains. We practice mindful breathing and mindful listening. We pay attention to our breath.
>
> A parent, just the other day, told me she took her son to the Museum of Natural History and it was very crowded. Her son sat down on the side and did a mindful minute before moving on. (He felt overwhelmed. He noticed that. He responded mindfully. Wow!)

What does communication in an early childhood classroom actually look like? Here is a snapshot between one parent and the teacher, illustrating the significant and positive influence that mindfulness practices can make. Karen Carter's son was in Olivi's kindergarten class a few years ago. Here is what Carter had to say:

Ms. Olivi's focus on mindfulness [in school] definitely helped my son. He has a ton of energy. (When presented with the option to develop a sense of quiet, he kind of accepted that invitation. It was a new world for him but a world that has become very important for him.)

A while ago we were in a busy area, and he just sat down in front of a fountain and started doing a mindful minute. Everyone was staring at this kid sitting silently, breathing slowly with his eyes closed in the middle of chaos. But he knew what he needed in that moment. (Two years after being in class with Ms. Olivi, he has that in his toolkit. He reaches for it when he needs it.)

I think a huge part of part of mindfulness for my son has been connecting to something bigger than himself. Kids start out in this world as very self-focused. (That's kind of the point of childhood. They need to learn about their own experience before tackling the bigger world.) But mindfulness offers them the chance to stop the never-ending activity and develop a sense of awareness about how they fit in the world and with other people. Ms. Olivi's mindful approach, particularly regarding conflict resolution, is all about this. She teaches the kids to consider the sources of their feelings when they feel wronged by another child and to think about what they can do together to solve the problem.

Home-school connection is another amazing part of this. I like knowing techniques that work for him. He teaches me. One day, driving home from school, I was asking him all sorts of questions. He wasn't answering me. "Are you listening to me?" I asked. "I'm having a mindful moment, Mom," he said. Okay, my kid is now taking some time to connect and reflect after a busy day at school. And is expressing that to me. I can support that.

Given the opportunity and the tools, young children can practice mindfulness anytime and anywhere. The ongoing practice of being present is meant to be shared between home and school. Families and teachers can share critical information about how a child learns best or what he needs to feel safe and engaged. This communication essentially guides adults on how to provide the necessary continuity between the two of the most important places in a child's life: home and school.

Many of the recommendations and mindfulness strategies explored in this book are purposely designed to be carried out at school or at home. Keeping this in mind, the journey of mindfulness during the early years is more than simply practicing mindfulness, although this is a terrific way to begin! It is also about teaching others about the practice and process of being present. It is not enough, therefore, for teachers to simply inform families about the mindfulness discussions or activities that are engaged in during the school day. Sending home letters about mindfulness without thoughtful explanation or descriptions is not reflective of the deep practice that being present is all about.

When teachers take the time to thoughtfully explain, explore, and reflect with families how mindfulness practices are essential in young children's lives, they can strengthen the partnerships between home and school. Likewise, families may have much to share with educators too, particularly if families already thread the concept of mindfulness into their home lives. On page 22, you will find a list of recommended books that families may wish to use to deepen their understanding about being present with children.

Children Are Naturally Curious, Mindful, and Joyful

After decades of inquiry, what I have come to understand about presence is this: young children tend to naturally "be" in a state of mindfulness. I believe this is because they embrace joy in the ordinary moments of life. Consider the way a toddler giggles as the family dog licks his face, or how a baby works diligently to find his favorite toy now buried within the cushions of the family couch. Even for children who are living in extreme or harsh circumstances, the very young understand the sparkle in a grandparent's eyes or the warmth of a hug or the delicious taste of a blueberry. Children naturally notice and enjoy the simple and the ordinary, which is why they experience curiosity, delight, and wonder every day. I believe that it is not humanly possible to be in a state of joy without also being present in the moment. When we are joyful, we are naturally anchored in the present moment. Tears are, in my opinion, the ultimate expression of joy. It is as if words and thoughts cannot adequately convey the depth of the unbridled joy felt in that very moment.

Ingrid Fetell Lee, author of the recently published book *Joyful: The Surprising Power of Ordinary Things to Create Extraordinary Happiness*, notes, "Joy isn't hard to find at all. In fact, it's all around us." Infants, toddlers, and young children seem to find joy pretty much everywhere. It seems to me that the young live in a state of joy-full-ness—they are literally full of joy—at virtually every turn. Perhaps this is one reason behind the growing interest in mindfulness around the world. I believe that many adults, particularly in Western society, seem to have lost the connection to unbridled joy. There may be fleeting moments in the beauty of a spectacular sunset or the aroma and taste of a favorite childhood dish, but it seems that joy has been replaced by distraction, anxiety, and stress from ordinary everyday living. But this is not a book about how stressed teachers and children are or how mindfulness can relieve stress. Even though mindfulness can be a powerful tool to help manage stress and anxiety, it is more like a state of being. Mindfulness and being present reflect a basic choice we make about how to approach each moment.

To better understand how present or absent we may be from life, I believe it's worth knowing the joy that exists in the spaces we inhabit. In her book, Lee invites us to ponder:

- How often do you laugh?

- When was the last time you felt a true, unfettered moment of joy?

- What emotions do you feel when you walk into your home at the end of the day? When you enter each room?

- What activities bring you the most joy? How often do you engage in them?

- What are your happy places? When was the last time you visited one?

These questions can be barometers to help us identify where joy exists (or may be absent) in our day-to-day surroundings.

Let us take a moment to consider these same questions from a child's point of view. Think about a young child in your life. Imagine that you are seeing the world through that child's eyes. Reimagine Lee's questions within the context of your classroom and/or home environment. Reflect on how a child who inhabits those spaces might respond to each question. Answer the questions as the child would. This is a great tool for adults to use with children of any age—from an infant who may spend time in a child-care arrangement to a student attending elementary school. Even though infants would not be able to verbally articulate answers, based on what you know about them, their behavior, and the climate of the environment you are reflecting upon, seriously consider how you think they would respond:

- How often does the child laugh? In what part of the classroom (or home) does the child laugh the most? the least?

- When was the last time the child experienced a true, unfettered moment of joy?

- What emotions do you think the child feels when he walks into the classroom (or home) every day? Would the emotions change across different times of the day? different days of the week?

- What activities bring the child the most joy? How often does the child engage in them?

- What are the child's happy places? How often and how long is the child able to spend time there?

Reflecting on these questions for children could be beneficial at different points in the year. Additionally, answering them thoughtfully could potentially provide fresh insight about a child you struggle to understand. When a young child is not naturally or consistently expressing joy—as demonstrated by a curiosity, delight, and fascination with the world—I often wonder if it is because the surroundings and/or people that the child spends most of the time with may not be well suited for one another. Perhaps a young learner shows great enthusiasm for music but has very limited access to music and only in a very structured way one time each week. Or maybe the fifteen-month-old spends each weekday morning in a highly unpredictable child-care situation outside the home.

Erika Christakis, author of *The Importance of Being Little: What Young Children Really Need from Grownups*, proposes that "in our urge to 'adultify' young children and their surroundings . . . we ask them to conform to our timetables and tastes." This approach completely disregards who young children are and the critical importance of the early years. She furthers warns that simply limiting children's screen activities or adding more blocks to their play is not enough to repair the harm done when we adultify young children and place expectations on and provide experiences to them that are actually suitable for adults. Whether we realize it or not, our adult expectations, behavior, environments, and discourses shape young children's lives at home, school, and everywhere in between. As trusted adults, we can do a better job to protect infants, toddlers, and young children by fiercely preserving their right to be present. My sense is that we have fallen short.

So it's about time. As educators, we can individually decide every day to teach mindfulness. However, we can't authentically teach young children about being present if we are not practicing what we teach. We must also be learners of mindfulness.

Concluding Thoughts

As long as I can remember, my wisest teachers have been young children who naturally possess a genuine joy, insatiable curiosity, and profound wisdom about the world. When our focus is on accumulating more, we cannot be fully present in the moment. In the next chapter, I provide a foundation for understanding what we can learn from research and what we cannot, and how research on mindfulness and children can shape our teaching practices.

I believe that true teaching cannot occur until we become present in the mosaic of moments that illuminate our daily lives. And the only way to begin on the path of mindfulness is by committing to the practice every day. Mindfulness is an unfolding practice of being present in the moment. To return to the words of a wise second grader, I wonder what kind of transformation would occur if educators all over the world practiced with young children to "breathe in blue skies and breathe out stormy clouds."

A Menu of Options for Teaching Inclusively, Mindfully, and Equitably

 Children's Corner

It has been said that children learn mostly by how we make them feel. When we are calm and focused, we set an example. If you want to build or expand a mindfulness-based children's library, or if you simply want to plant seeds about the importance of being present and grateful, here are a few excellent choices for young children.

Adams, Jennifer. 2018. *I Am a Warrior Goddess*. Louisville, CO: Sounds True.

Gibson, Amy. 2014. *By Day, by Night*. Westminster, MD: Boyds Mills.

Grimes, Nikki. 2006. *Thanks a Million*. New York: Greenwillow.

Hạnh, Thích Nhất. 2011. *Planting Seeds: Practicing Mindfulness with Children*. Berkeley, CA: Parallax.

Mora, Pat. 2009. *Gracias/Thanks*. New York: Lee and Low.

Verde, Susan. 2017. *I Am Peace: A Book of Mindfulness*. New York: Abrams.

Caregivers' Corner

Deciding to start or continue a contemplative practice is often the hardest part. After that, all you have to do is to show up! In the spirit of transparency, I want to remind you that I am not a yoga instructor or meditation teacher. I am simply a student, as you are. It is my hope that the experiences, knowledge, and lessons garnered over my many years of a steady mindfulness practice will be helpful as you start or continue on your own path. The truth is that much of the time I feel like a beginner, as the practice of mindfulness never ceases to bring a sense of humility and openness.

In mindfulness practice, as in life, there are shifts, struggles, speed bumps, and transformations. The one thing that has made all the difference for me is perseverance. I just show up, even when I least feel like it and even when conditions are not conducive for practice. For more ideas about a daily mindfulness practice, see the appendix on page 183.

In *Mindfulness for Beginners: Reclaiming the Present Moment—and Your Life*, Jon Kabat-Zinn provides four simple suggestions for establishing a formal mindfulness and meditation practice:

1. **Posture:** Sit on the floor, a cushion, or a chair with your back straight and relaxed. Rest your hands on your lap or knees.

2. **Eyes:** Your eyes may be open or closed. If you choose to keep your eyes open, make your gaze relaxed and unfocused.

3. **Sleepiness:** It is best to meditate during the day, such as early morning, when you are likely to feel fully awake.

4. **Protecting this time:** Choose a time when you are unlikely to be interrupted. Close your door, and turn off all devices.

Sharon Salzberg, founder of the Insight Meditation Society in Massachusetts, best-selling author, and acclaimed international speaker, shares in her book *Lovingkindness: The Revolutionary Art of Happiness* how to begin a lovingkindness practice by uniting the self and the greater community.

1. Sit in a comfortable position with your eyes closed. Take a few deep breaths to relax your body.

2. Reflect upon these four traditional phrases, which you can adjust so they are meaningful and comfortable for you. You will softly repeat them.

   • May I be safe.

   • May I be happy.

- May I be healthy.

- May I have ease of well-being.

3. Let your mind rest in these phrases. Allow your feelings to come and go.

4. Think of people in your life, and repeat the four phrases as you direct your lovingkindness to each person in turn.

This meditation is a long-term practice; beginners may want to start with themselves only. When you feel ready, add on another part of this meditation as you see fit.

Include people who have been kind to you, people for whom you do not have strong feelings (whether positive or negative), and people with whom you have felt uncomfortable or challenged. Then expand your thoughts to consider groups of people, the multiplicity of humanity, or the entire universe.

Thích Nhất Hạnh offers the following advice in his book *Silence*:

- At the beginning, regaining your attention for even ten breaths can be challenging. With steady practice, you can enhance your ability to simply be.

- Sit quietly and just notice how your thoughts rush in. No need to focus on them but rather just observe and let them come and go.

- Find a few minutes for yourself to find stillness and calm.

- "The joy of true quiet becomes a daily healing food."

Take It to the Classroom

Since 2009, the innovative Newark Yoga Movement has taught yoga and mindfulness practices to thousands of children and educators in Newark, New Jersey. In 2014, founder Debby Kaminsky developed Instant Calm in response to the growing stress she observed around standardized testing. Instant Calm is a three-minute script guiding breathing, movement, and relaxation, which can be read over the public-address systems of schools before standardized testing. Because no lesson or curriculum is ever interrupted, Instant Calm is currently used in ten Newark Public Schools, reaching and teaching thousands of students.

This Instant Calm script includes three key parts: centering/breath, movement, and relaxation. At the end of each of the three parts, there is a moment to pause for two breaths. When used in a classroom situation, educators can read the entire script verbatim or just one part at a time. I encourage you to try out this script on colleagues before sharing it with children.

Part 1

It's time for Instant Calm. It's a fun way to help you feel calm, focused, and peaceful.

(Optional: Ring a chime or bell.)

Please stand. (Pause for five seconds.) Breathing is key to this practice.

Breathe in and out through your nose. Stand tall with your arms at your sides. This is called *mountain pose*.

Breathe in through your nose, and imagine you are blowing up a balloon in your belly. Breathe in through your nose and fill the balloon with air.

Breathe out through your nose, and let the air out of the balloon.

Try it again. Inhale. Exhale. Inhale. Exhale, and let your shoulders move away from your ears.

Gaze down at your feet, and see if you can make them look like the number eleven.

Breathe in and stand a little taller.

Breathe out. Feel your feet planted on the floor. Continue breathing. (Pause for two breaths.)

Part 2

Inhale and lift your arms up. Interlock your hands together.

Turn your palms up toward the sky. Exhale and bend to the right for a side stretch.

Stay there and breathe as you stretch your arms.

Inhale and come back to center with your arms overhead.

Exhale and bend to the left. Can you feel the stretch?

Inhale back to center.

Exhale and release your arms back to your sides.

Please sit down. (Pause for two full breaths.)

Part 3

Place your feet flat on the floor as you prepare to do a seated twist.

Bring your hands to your shoulders. Inhale and sit up tall.

Exhale, and twist your belly button, shoulders, and chin to the left.

Inhale. Exhale.

Inhale back to center, keeping your hands on your shoulders.

Exhale and twist to the right. Breathe.

Inhale back to center.

Exhale and rest your hands comfortably on your lap.

Inhale and sit up nice and tall.

Exhale and keep your spine in a tall line. You may close your eyes or just make your focus soft and fuzzy as you gaze downward. Breathe slowly in and out of your nose for the next few breaths. Relax your shoulders. (Pause for five full breaths.)

Inhale. Exhale. Gently lower your chin. Breathe. Inhale. Exhale.

Continue breathing. Can you slow your breath down? (Pause for five full breaths.)

Inhale, slowly open your eyes, and lift your chin. Bring your palms together to your chest.

(Pause for two breaths.)

CHAPTER 2

Being Present—What the Research Says about Mindfulness in Education

> **"Any teacher knows, when a student feels safe, relaxed, and attentive, learning comes naturally."**
> —Daniel Rechtschaffen, *The Way of Mindful Education*

To feel safe and at ease is every child's fundamental right. It is not a privilege reserved for some or a reward to be earned. Early childhood educators are well aware that learning occurs naturally and joyfully when young children feel safe, understood, and focused. It seems to me that the very same holds true about teaching. When our basic needs for safety, ease, and engagement are met, teaching comes naturally. When teachers engage in the joy of teaching, children engage in the joy of learning.

I seriously doubt that any teacher would say she chose the teaching profession because she was excited to teach from a worksheet or eager to follow a prescribed curriculum to help young learners take a standardized assessment. When people ask him why he decided to work in an elementary school of all places, David Aveta, a first-grade teacher in an underserved, economically challenged school district, replies:

> As a male in a primarily female profession, I often get asked, "Why?" My answer has been consistent: "I love what I do, and I do what I love." I have a deep connection where I work and the people I work with.
>
> I chose to work where I do because I am a product of this district's educational system. I choose to give back to the district that played a role in who I am today. . . I want each student to see how an education obtained from this district can help them achieve their dreams. As a male teacher, I want to bridge the gap and break those "old school" stereotypes built around the profession while also opening the door of possibilities for young boys to recognize that a career in elementary education is a possible route for them to take. It warms my heart to hear, "Mr. Aveta, I want to be a teacher just like you!"

The Role of Research in Understanding Mindfulness

In this chapter, we will learn about mindfulness from a broader perspective. What role does research play in understanding mindfulness in schools? What can research tell us about mindfulness and learning? The daily contemplative practice that you (hopefully!) are engaging in will serve as a sturdy foundation to explore what the research says—and does not say—about mindfulness and early childhood education. In my opinion, we cannot critically examine the research base about mindfulness if we do not have direct and personal experience to draw upon. It is highly beneficial to have a private, individualized mindfulness practice as we examine the body of educational research about being present. This is because both the individual and collective perspectives inform one another, just as teaching and learning do. As we investigate the role and promise mindfulness plays in education, consider the educational environments (school or otherwise) in which we situate ourselves.

• What has been your experience with research?

• Has research informed your teaching practice? How so? If not, why not?

Consider the wise words about the connection between research and teaching from the late Brazilian educator Paulo Freire. Widely respected worldwide for his activism and philosophy, Freire explained the inseparable connection between research and teaching. Freire and the significant body of work he produced across his lifetime demonstrate an "unfinished" example of what it means to be present and conscious in education—and in life. In one of his most influential books, *Pedagogy of Freedom: Ethics, Democracy, and Civic Courage*, Freire notes:

> As I teach, I continue to search and re-search. I teach because I search,
> because I question, and because I submit myself to questioning. I research
> because I notice things, take cognizance of them. And in so doing, I intervene.
> And intervening, I educate and educate myself. I do research so as to know
> what I do not yet know and to communicate and proclaim what I discover.

Freire understood the dynamic nature between teaching and researching because he held deep respect for the role that inquiry, action, and reflection play in the lives of educators. Our need for deeper inquiry is inexplicably linked to the work we do. Quite simply, there can be no teaching without (re)search.

As a researcher and teacher educator, I believe all research must be widely available and presented in accessible, diverse formats, especially for stakeholders. Stakeholders are those who are directly affected by and could benefit from research findings. Stakeholders include families, teachers, practitioners, and children (who are not generally considered consumers of research but could be). I think that practice and research must inform and shape one another.

We know much more now than we did ten years ago. The body of research on mindfulness in early childhood education and care is young and emerging. On the other hand, there is a robust knowledge base on the benefits and applications of mindfulness for adults and youth as well as an ever-expanding reservoir of research in education. The growing movement to explore mindfulness practices in schools over the past two decades has produced a distinct new generation of knowledge. This section will explore how research on mindfulness can inform our teaching practice.

Emerging Research in Early Childhood

The existing studies on mindfulness and education generally focus on elementary-age and older students. The topic continues to gain considerable attention in the early childhood field through scholarly and practitioner discourses in professional journals. However, research conducted on mindfulness in early childhood education and care remains limited. The small but growing number of studies examining mindfulness-based programs or interventions with young children are showing promising findings. The research is focused on specific practices, such as yoga, meditation, relaxation, and breathing, taught to young learners and embedded into the school day.

In studies examining preschoolers and the effects of mindfulness-based interventions, Lisa Flook and her colleagues at the Center for Healthy Minds at the University of Wisconsin–Madison found positive outcomes associated with social competence, learning, health, and social-emotional growth. Researchers Xinyi Lim and Li Qu discovered an increase in children's attention. Rachel Razza and colleagues reported an improvement in preschoolers' self-regulation. In a two-year study examining a mindfulness-based intervention, Karen Thierry and colleagues observed that preschoolers demonstrated gains in academic and executive functioning skills.

Why do these outcomes that relate to social competence, social-emotional development, attention, self-regulation, and executive functioning matter? These skills are the essential foundational skills that young children use as they navigate social, emotional, physical, and cognitive domains in the learning process. I became curious to learn more as I started to notice a growing number of publications related to mindfulness and young children. The body of knowledge suggests the very positive and promising benefits of using a mindfulness-based program with young children.

I started to wonder what the collective body of research says on mindfulness in early childhood education and decided to conduct an extensive review to find out. In 2015, I coauthored an article titled "The Joy of Being: Making Way for Young Children's Natural Mindfulness." Here are highlights of this research review:

- Only twelve articles met our research criteria related to soundness, clarity, and peer review; eight of these articles were conducted in the United States, and the rest originated from Australia, India, Malaysia, and South Korea.

- Mindfulness practices resulted in favorable outcomes and advantages in all twelve studies, including benefits such as focus, attention, self-regulation, and physical and social-emotional growth.

- In most of the studies conducted outside the United States, mindfulness practices were part of the larger social, cultural, or environmental context and consistently embedded into classroom and/or school routines.

- Two-thirds of the studies were conducted by a discipline other than education, such as occupational therapy, psychology, child development, and family studies.

- Several studies demonstrated how the focus on mindfulness reflects a broader holistic perspective, which encompasses a deep concern over environmental sustainability, ecology, and nature.

- Half the studies reviewed positioned mindfulness as a tool to promote overall health and wellness. The other six articles depicted mindfulness as prescriptive and/or a way to remediate skills or "fix" an issue, such as a child's perceived undesirable behaviors.

Although this was an initial inquiry, our preliminary impressions suggest that the larger sociocultural climate generally determines how mindfulness is practiced or valued within a particular educational setting. For example, by focusing solely on changing a child's behavior that we deem undesirable or noncompliant without taking adequate time to fully understand or discover what the cause is behind the behaviors, adults generally cannot fully realize the essence of who a young child is, especially her individual, unique ways of being and learning in the world. Children do not need to be changed, but often their environments do.

Consider that when a five-year-old is taught to breathe deeply when she is visibly upset, we may not learn that she is actually hungry or the noise level in the classroom feels too loud for her during transitions. Of course, teaching children to breathe deeply can be beneficial, but there is an inherent danger when mindfulness practices are perceived only as a quick fix or a means to an end or are encouraged by adults who do not "get" young children or mindfulness practices. One simple but profound reminder from our research review is that young children are naturally inquisitive and filled with joy. Young learners also tend to be absorbed in each moment, so it is the adults who need to step aside and move out of their way. We can inadvertently teach children how to be overstimulated, distracted, or anxious by the example we set or the atmosphere we create.

Mindfulness and Children Labeled with Disabilities

There is growing body of mindfulness research on students who have been identified or labeled by schools in some way, with some of these studies focusing on children during the early childhood and elementary years. Consider the following:

- Jeremy Fox and colleagues investigated preschoolers exhibiting anxiety. After implementing an intervention for both the children and their parents, they reported a decrease in children's anxiety and an increase in the parents' estimation of their children's reactions to anxiety.

- In another study, Melanie Viglas and Michal Perlman implemented a research-based mindfulness program with kindergarteners ages four to six years old. While all children experienced improved self-regulation and prosocial behavior, as well as decreased hyperactivity, children with hyperactive tendencies improved the most on all three measures.

- Kristie Koenig and colleagues introduced a yoga program to elementary students identified as having autism spectrum disorders. Teachers reported more prosocial behavior, less lethargy, and less irritable behavior from the students after the program. Notably, the authors remarked how yoga was a fitting activity for students on the autism spectrum, as it inherently lends itself to visual instruction. Students required minimal prompts, if any, to do the practices by the end of the intervention.

Mindfulness practices appear to be an accessible and engaging experience that yields benefits for children categorized as having a diagnosis or label. This young body of research, however, should be interpreted with caution, particularly during children's early years. Many studies conducted on children with disabilities include students from a wide age range, so it can be difficult to get a clear or general sense about the specific implications. Even when studies focus exclusively on young children within a certain age range, expectations and understandings of children must be culturally and contextually driven. Therefore, these research findings may have limited application or generalization across cultures, class, and geographic regions.

Another reason educators should consider reading this research with caution is because the only factor the children in the study may have in common is their diagnosis. A label reveals very little, if anything, about a child's individual learning style, strengths, preferences, interests, challenges, and talents. The differences among children who have been given a clinical label, such as Down syndrome, a visual impairment, or a learning disability, are vast.

Children's Voices in Mindfulness Research

We are beginning to learn directly from children themselves about mindfulness in schools. Julia Keller and colleagues were among the first to study the perspectives of students involved in a school-based mindfulness intervention. They studied fourth graders from economically and culturally diverse backgrounds. One student in this study summed up the mindfulness experience in a profound way: "To me, mindfulness breathing means it gives your stress to happiness. When your stress comes, your brain will become a storm, but when you do mindful breathing your brain becomes a rainbow." I find this to be an incredibly insightful way to describe mindfulness.

Researcher Daniel Devcich and colleagues in New Zealand discovered via elementary-aged students' self-reporting that the children's well-being showed dramatic and sustained improvements after a mindfulness intervention. The research team asked children how much they enjoyed the mindfulness practices, how much they felt the practices helped them personally, and whether they practiced mindfulness outside of the classroom. Children agreed that they liked participating and found the practice helpful. Eighty-seven percent of participating students responded that they continued to practice mindfulness outside of school three months after the program ended. The focus on student-generated data marks an important early trend in the inquiry of children's voices and mindfulness in the classroom. Future research must ensure children's perceptions, firsthand accounts, and voices across all aspects of diversity are well represented.

Mindfulness and the Connection to Families

Similar to the recent attention to mindfulness research in schools, there is also growing attention to these promising practices at home. Interestingly, the majority of studies examining parents and mindfulness focused on families who have a child with disabilities. Here are a few highlights:

- Nirbhay Singh and colleagues conducted some of the earliest work on mindfulness in the parent-child relationship. They developed a two-pronged mindfulness intervention focusing on children with attention-deficit/hyperactivity disorder (ADHD) and their mothers. The children's compliance increased after their mothers' initial mindfulness practice, then further increased after the children received mindfulness training. This amplifying effect points to the promise of wraparound mindfulness for the whole family.

- Elaine MacDonald and Richard Hastings reported a relationship between Irish fathers' level of mindfulness and the fathers' involvement with their children with intellectual disabilities: the more mindful the father, the more involved they were in the care. The researchers suggested that mindfulness training may increase the amount of caregiving offered by fathers.

- As reported in the *Journal of Applied Research in Intellectual Disabilities*, Cameron Neece conducted a mindfulness-based stress-reduction intervention for parents of children with developmental delays and reported that these parents subsequently had fewer feelings of anxiety and depression, improved stress management, and higher satisfaction with parent-child relationships. Neece's work underscores the link between a parent's feelings of stress and child behavior; when parents become more mindful, the entire family benefits.

Although this summary provides only a few highlights, the growing body of research demonstrates that mindfulness practices offer support for families who have a child who is labeled with a disability.

Mindfulness Research and Professionals in the School Community

The research on mindfulness in schools is still relatively young, but early studies are pointing to the wide-ranging potential benefits for children as well as adults. Robert Roeser and colleagues investigated the effects of mindfulness training on teacher stress.

They reported that teachers experienced less stress and feelings of burnout after being trained in mindfulness practices. Furthermore, they posited that the heightened mindfulness and self-compassion that resulted from this training served as vital factors to help teachers better manage stress going forward. In the first investigation on examining the effects of mindfulness-based interventions on teachers (preschool to twelfth grade), David Klingbiel and Tyler Renshaw's meta-analysis reinforced these findings and noted that teachers experienced positive outcomes.

The growing inquiry into mindfulness and schools is also producing a fair amount of research from education-related professional disciplines, such as school psychology, nursing, counseling, occupational therapy, speech-language therapy, and physical therapy. In a 2017 article published in *Contemporary School Psychology*, Uma Alahari suggests that mindful breathing could facilitate school psychologists' increased presence in their interactions with children and indicates that greater focus enables more attuned listening to children. Joshua Felver and colleagues at the University of Oregon conducted an in-depth analysis of the potential applications that mindfulness offers in school psychology. They discovered the practice may help school psychologists improve how they serve students and also noted the promise of sharing these mindfulness practices with students.

Based on the growing research on mindfulness interventions in education, some occupational therapists have begun to incorporate these practices into their work with children. Klatt and colleagues conducted a feasibility study to investigate the effects of a mindfulness intervention in a third-grade classroom. This particular project emphasized mindful breathing, movement exercises, guided meditation, and art-based reflection. One classroom teacher involved in this study reported, "I think they learned how to relax. There were some times when they would be all worked up, and I would tell them to remember just to breathe and let it go, and I think they learned how to do that."

The interest continues to grow among teachers and therapists across various disciplines in mindfulness applications in educational settings. Susan Lederer, a professor of communication sciences and disorders at Adelphi University, has made several presentations at the American Speech-Language-Hearing Association conferences about the promise of mindfulness research and practice for children. I am intrigued by this emerging body of work in education-related disciplines about mindfulness applications with children and adults.

Making Sense of the Research on Mindfulness: Insights and Implications for Early Childhood Education and Care

Even in these early stages, research on mindfulness in education has become a widely sought-after area of inquiry. Researchers from all over the globe and across a wide variety of disciplines are studying the effects and implications of mindfulness in schools. However, when examining the collective body of research, we must analyze what the studies demonstrate or do not demonstrate, what is not noticed, and whose voices are missing. There is also the question of accessibility: who has ready access to research and who does not.

In early childhood education and care, for example, stakeholders such as practitioners and families do not often have timely, affordable, or easy access to key research studies. Without such access, educators are at a significant disadvantage because they are unable to integrate the latest and most innovative ideas, technology, pedagogy, and trends into their teaching practice. Here are some of my additional impressions about the mindfulness research base.

Mindfulness Research and the Lack of Racial and Cultural Diversity

Although mindfulness is being studied worldwide, there is not an adequate or consistent focus on children across social classes, abilities, religions, languages, gender identities, cultures, and races. Additionally, much of the research is done *on* participants who agree to be involved in a study as opposed to *with* them. Research partnerships with families or teachers, for example, might involve all members of the research team in collectively identifying a research question or determining what, how, and when data will be collected. Study participants can be invited to serve as partners in all stages of the research process.

There is a noticeable dearth of research related to teachers and other education-related professionals representing cultural, racial, economic, ethnic, and other diversity. One reason is because people across various aspects of diversity are not invited to participate in the research, even though they are stakeholders who would benefit directly and immediately from the research findings. In Western societies, we are only beginning to understand mindfulness through a lens of cultural, ethnic, and racial diversity even though mindfulness is deeply rooted in indigenous cultures and traditions.

Researchers Sandi Tenfelde, Lena Hatchett, and Karen Saban investigated Black women's perceptions of mindfulness. Although women of color who participated in this study had limited understanding or experience with mindfulness practices such as yoga, the researchers discovered that the women were interested in and willing to learn about its benefits. One woman reported, "I don't have any negative connotations about it at all. I just have never done it. I have someone I know now that is getting into yoga and [in]to meditation, and they're . . . getting a lot of enjoyment out of it." The researchers also identified obstacles to Black women's participation, such as limited availability and accessibility to community mindfulness experiences, the expense of yoga classes and clothes, sociocultural understandings about body image, and perceptions of yoga practitioners. The researchers offered recommendations about how to make yoga and other mindfulness practices more accessible and culturally relevant to Black women. For example, they suggest engaging in widespread and inclusive discourse about yoga and creating new marketing, advertising, and recruitment tools. The need to explore availability, barriers, and solutions for social and community engagement is crucial, so everyone who would like to access mindfulness-related experiences can easily do so.

In another study addressing cultural diversity, Devon Hinton and his team adapted mindfulness techniques to correspond to the cultural experiences of people with post-traumatic stress disorder (PTSD). Hinton and colleagues personalized imagery for a meditation exercise to fit two patients' respective cultural identities. For a Puerto Rican woman, they suggested the image of a heart exuding warm light (familiar and sacred to many as the *Sagrado Corazón de Jesús* [Sacred Heart of Jesus]). For a Cambodian woman, they used streaming cool water, which symbolizes freedom from negative feelings in the Buddhist tradition. This type of sensitive cultural adaptation is vital in providing meaningful connections to mindfulness practices for diverse populations.

Additionally, researchers led by Javier García-Campayo explored mindfulness within Latino cultures. They emphasized that certain cultural characteristics, such as the strength of family ties and the comfort in physicality, can bolster mindfulness outreach. Other characteristics, such as the dominance of the Roman Catholic Church and the time commitment and demands of employment, can complicate this outreach. These studies, which are nuanced and responsive to diverse communities, are virtually absent yet sorely needed in early childhood education and care.

An article recently published in *Zero to Three*, a well-respected journal on topics related to the well-being and nurturing of infants and toddlers, focused on how to incorporate mindfulness for very young children and the families and professionals in their lives. Coauthors Rebecca Shahmoon-Shanok and Howard Carlton Stevenson explore how the concept of mindfulness is perceived, articulated, and experienced in unique ways across various cultures, religions, and races. Shahmoon-Shanok and Stevenson suggest that the central tenets of mindfulness—focus and nonjudgment—can anchor a shared under-standing of mindfulness during the early years.

Given the cultural and contextually driven nature of being present in early childhood education and care, any inquiry should mirror the voices, representations, understandings, and expressions of what it means to be mindful. When introducing mindfulness practices into the lives of young children and families, practitioners should keep in mind that there is not just one path. Instead, we should incorporate a broader understanding about how these practices can be culturally relevant, meaningful, and accessible for everyone.

A Narrow Focus on Mindfulness Research with Children with Disabilities

A robust and steadily growing body of mindfulness research focuses on children under the age of ten years who have been labeled with a disability. The majority of this research, however, emphasizes increasing desirable behaviors and skills or decreasing undesirable behaviors and presents mindfulness practices as a solution to change a child's behavior or teach a particular skill.

Viewing mindfulness through the narrow lens of "fixing" behaviors can be complicated and even oppressive for many reasons. First, there is a tendency—as unconscious as it may be—to perceive the child in a negative, limiting way. Sometimes the child is con-sidered "the problem." Recently, I heard an early childhood teacher ask about a child with a disability, "What's wrong with him?" There is nothing wrong with any child. And children are never "the problem." When a disability or any aspect of diversity is viewed from a deficit-oriented perspective, adults believe that there is a deficiency that needs to be remediated, fixed, or eliminated.

Consider that a disability is one facet of human diversity in the same way gender, social class, or race are aspects of human variation. The way that diversity is depicted in a collective body of research will generally reflect how diversity is perceived by contemporary society. Although we live in a diverse world where people coexist with many different identities, we do not yet widely celebrate a disability identity as a positive marker.

Further, practitioners and family members can misjudge or misinterpret behavior, particularly in children categorized with a disability label, and attempt to correct or change the behavior even though it may not need fixing. For example, a child's behavior may be labeled by adults as troubling or socially inappropriate but might actually be a child's unique way of interacting with or adapting to the world. Consider the child who does not make eye contact during an interpersonal exchange. It just may be that direct eye contact is too overstimulating, and so she skillfully learns to engage in the interaction by looking peripherally at the person. Think about certain classroom expectations that require all children to sit quietly during the entire circle time. Young children—with or without a disability label—need frequent breaks or may prefer to sit in a defined space, such as a beanbag chair or on a carpet square. The point is that when adults perceive a child's behavior or learning as negative, nonconforming, noncompliant, or problematic, we fail to see the wholeness and essence of who the child is and, therefore, will likely miss the child's unique qualities, interests, fascinations, strengths, talents, and preferences.

The research focus on children with disabilities is not an issue; rather, how the study of children and mindfulness is emerging is an issue. The majority of research studies targeting children with disabilities is based on interventions to determine whether mindfulness practices are effective in eliciting some type of "improvement" in the child. Of course, supporting children in using mindfulness tools that will make them feel joyful, confident, focused, self-regulated, and safe is highly desirable. But if mindfulness practices with children with disabilities are studied solely as a means to reach an end result, then the concept of mindfulness can become too outcome driven, which is the exact opposite of being present in the moment. The long-term, unintentional effects of approaching children from a deficit-based point of view could leave enduring harmful imprints as children perceive an adult world where compliance and conformity matter and difference is not welcomed.

A New Agenda for Mindfulness Research in Early Childhood Education and Care

I wonder about another kind of research agenda, one that focuses on mindfulness embedded into the fabric of society, starting with schools. Possible research questions on mindfulness from a social-justice perspective in classrooms and schools might include the following:

- How can the concept of being present be valued across an entire school system?

- How can educators use mindfulness practices to disrupt a culture of exclusion or inequity in a school?

- When it comes to mindfulness, what do families, teachers, and children want to know more about, and why?

- What are the most collaborative ways teachers and children can work together to embed mindfulness into the classroom climate?

- What are some institutional challenges that are causing children and/or teachers to feel stressed and anxious, and what role can mindfulness practices play in alleviating that stress?

Additional questions for deeper inquiry and contemplation might focus on how, where, or when children can learn about the lifelong practice of mindfulness:

- When can mindfulness practices be used to support a child's interests, fascinations, or talent?

- What mindfulness practices are already working in a child's life? How can they be further expanded upon?

- How does a child learn to not be mindful?

- When could mindfulness practices be used to foster a child's confidence?

Another impression about the existing body of studies on mindfulness is that research tends to be conducted *on* children as opposed to *with* them. Young children's active engagement in designing, conducting, and analyzing research can play a meaningful role in deepening an understanding about being present during the early years by honoring their voices as coresearchers. Consider what the research process might look like when young children are coresearchers with teachers (and families) in studying mindfulness. How could teachers work with children to identify what research questions to investigate or to determine how to study what mindfulness looks like in the classroom? Teachers can start planting seeds by sparking conversations about mindfulness-related ideas, such as peace, breathing, and stillness, that may eventually turn into an investigation with children as coresearchers. Children can play a meaningful role as coresearchers by harvesting the seeds that they have planted. In other words, based on children's interests and questions related to mindfulness, the teacher might further guide the class in making a collective decision about how they can learn even more about a topic of interest. An ongoing, in-depth investigation begins to emerge, driven predominantly by children's curiosity about how, where, when, and what to investigate.

These and other ideas can serve as an important foundation for engaging in social justice with young children, a topic we will explore in chapter 3. The small but growing number of studies related to mindfulness during the early years consistently point to benefits to both young children and the adults who care for them. But exercise caution when examining individual studies or the collective body of work, because this research base is still in its infancy and currently offers only a partial glimpse into mindfulness and the early years. The current body of research, however, has played an unquestionable role in bringing mindfulness into the public eye, and interest is steadily growing across all sectors of the population. Even though the concept of mindfulness is deeply rooted in indigenous cultures and ancient traditions, Western society still requires confirmation through logic and scientific evidence. As the body of research continues to expand, mindfulness may also become more widely respected, trusted, and embedded into the fabric of daily life in Western societies.

 ## Concluding Thoughts ·

In this chapter, we took a snapshot of the growing body of research on mindfulness and schools, and critically analyzed the research base and related implications in early childhood education and care. We also explored possibilities for a new mindfulness research agenda in early childhood, including opportunities for social action. The next chapter delves into the intersections of mindfulness practices and recognition of the dignity of all people, and how those ideas can play out in the early childhood classroom.

· ·

A Menu of Options for Teaching Inclusively, Mindfully, and Equitably

 ## Caregivers' Corner

Here is a collection of online resources about the philosophy, practice, and pedagogy of mindfulness. Take the time to notice which ones call to you. More resources on this topic are appearing all the time, and the following suggestions are just the tip of the iceberg. Think of these resources as a menu of options to broaden your understanding. Choose the ones that best match your needs, relate to your circumstances, and pique your interest.

Resources and Information

American Mindfulness Research Association
https://goamra.org
This website is a terrific way to keep abreast of the latest research on mindfulness across a wide range of topics, including pediatric health. This organization also maintains a searchable database through which users can find local mindfulness training organizations.

Association for Mindfulness in Education
http://www.mindfuleducation.org
This is a collaborative association of organizations and individuals working together to provide support for mindfulness training as a component of K–12 education. It offers webinars on mindfulness topics, and users can sign up to join an online community via an email listserv.

Center for Mindful Awareness

https://centerformindfulawareness.org

This organization works to bring mindfulness to underserved populations, including homeless families, inner-city teens, formerly incarcerated women, and urban educators. The website includes stories from people the organization has served about how mindfulness has affected their lives.

Cultivating Awareness and Resilience in Education (CARE)

https://www.garrisoninstitute.org

This project of the Garrison Institute, a nonprofit organization seeking to expand the application of mindful practices to social issues, seeks to train teachers in mindful techniques so they are better equipped to interact with children from an emotionally present place and handle the stresses of the profession.

Greater Good Science Center (GGSC) at the University of California, Berkeley

https://greatergood.berkeley.edu

GGSC publishes a joyfully approachable online magazine that focuses on the science behind well-being, including mindfulness. Here you can find quizzes, videos, podcasts, books, and research studies.

Institute for Mindfulness South Africa

https://mindfulness.org.za

A provider of mindfulness trainings, this organization dedicates a section of its website to supporting individuals beginning their mindfulness practice, including motivations for mindfulness and a recommended reading list.

Mindful Education Institute

https://mindfuleducation.com

Daniel Rechtschaffen, author of *The Way of Mindful Education*, founded this website to provide trainings on how to incorporate mindfulness into the classroom. The site offers ideas and detailed instructions on developing a mindfulness practice.

Mindful Schools

https://www.mindfulschools.org/about-mindfulness/research

This is a clearinghouse for research and training related to mindfulness in education. The website offers five online training courses, plus easy-to-navigate explanations of topics related to mindfulness.

Mindfulness in Education Network

http://www.mindfuled.org

This organization was founded by educators who were also students of Thích Nhất Hạnh. The group offers an annual workshop about mindfulness in education and posts videos from previous workshops to their website.

Mindfulness Toolkit

http://www.mindfulness.tools

Managed by a health organization, this website is a resource for individuals looking to learn more about mindfulness. Check out the guided audio lessons on body awareness, mindful eating and breathing, plus the practical tip sheets on a range of mindfulness issues.

Openground Mindfulness Training Sydney, Australia

https://www.openground.com.au

Openground promotes the expansion of mindfulness practices through trainings and retreats for individuals and organizations in Australia. Be sure to check out the Mindfulness section of this organization's website. It has a wealth of information for anyone interested in the topic, including specialized information for children.

Sonima Foundation

https://www.sonima.com

This is a wellness website that provides an expanding series of resources on mindful issues, such as yoga, meditation, fitness, and nutrition. Users can access online courses and guided meditations.

The Still Quiet Place

http://www.stillquietplace.com

Amy Saltzman created this website to provide resources to help young people, families, educators, and coaches incorporate mindfulness into their daily lives. She includes advice on how families and educators can support children in learning mindfulness.

Stress Management and Relaxation Techniques in Education

http://www.passageworks.org

This nonprofit organization offers in-person trainings for a mindfulness-based approach to professional renewal. Focus points include meditation and mindful movement. It offers a sample Pause Practice guided exercise on its website.

Susan Kaiser Greenland

https://www.susankaisergreenland.com

Susan Kaiser Greenland is the author of *The Mindful Child* and is affiliated with the Mindful Awareness Research Center at the University of California at Los Angeles (UCLA). Her website contains resources for adults who live or work with children.

University of Massachusetts Medical School Center for Mindfulness

https://www.umassmed.edu/cfm

Jon Kabat-Zinn revolutionized the study of mindfulness in Western culture. His mindfulness-based stress reduction (MBSR) approach has become a best practice in the field. He founded this center, which offers MBSR courses, professional education, and online programs.

Mindfulness-Based Educational Curricula and Tools

Bent on Learning

http://bentonlearning.org

This nonprofit organization teaches yoga to more than two thousand students each week in New York City's public schools. The group visits primary, middle, and high schools. New York City public schools can apply to participate in the program.

Get Ready to Learn

http://home.getreadytolearn.net

Members can pay to join the Get Ready to Learn network and get access to a range of trainings and materials that help teachers bring yoga into their classrooms. The practitioners who developed the program designed it for students in general, inclusive, and self-contained classrooms.

Grounded Kids

https://groundedkids.com

The Grounded Kids Program and its teachers have been recognized by local, national, and international media for their work in yoga education for children and teens.

Headstand

http://www.headstand.org

This nonprofit organization works with urban K–12 schools to integrate mindfulness into the curriculum on an ongoing basis. The website offers case studies from its program.

Kindness Curriculum

https://centerhealthyminds.org/join-the-movement/sign-up-to-receive-the-kindness-curriculum

The Center for Healthy Minds at the University of Wisconsin–Madison developed this mindfulness-based curriculum for preschoolers and offers it as a free download on its website. The program considers multiple aspects of a young child's experience, including physical and emotional well-being, interpersonal relationships, and an individual's place on the planet.

Little Flower Yoga

https://www.littlefloweryoga.com

Little Flower Yoga offers a broad range of tools, resources, and events from teacher certification, professional development, and family engagement to The Yoga School Project, which brings yoga and mindfulness into the classroom.

MindBE Education Curriculum

https://mindbe.org/mindbeextra

This comprehensive mindfulness curriculum for two- to-six-year-olds is designed for a variety of practitioners, including early childhood educators, school counselors, social workers, and teachers in after-school programs. Created by Helen Maffini, an early childhood specialist, the curriculum includes mindful movement, play, and sensory work to help develop focus, attention, prosocial behavior, and mindfulness.

Mind Up Curriculum

http://teacher.scholastic.com/products/mindup

The Goldie Hawn Foundation developed a mindfulness-based curriculum for children. It offers books containing lessons that teachers can transfer to their classrooms. The series consists of three books, each focusing on a specific age: preschool–grade 2, grades 3–5, and grades 6–8.

Newark Yoga Movement

https://www.newarkyogamovement.org

This organization's model prioritizes teaching the school's teachers first, piloting with a small subset of the school, and then expanding throughout the school at a sustainable pace. It also offers free yoga classes to the Newark community.

Paws .b Curriculum

https://mindfulnessinschools.org

This curriculum for seven- to eleven-year-old children is a project of the UK-based nonprofit Mindfulness in Schools. It offers a three-day training programs for teachers who want to implement the curriculum in their classrooms. The website offers sample lessons available for download.

Set/Reset

https://setreset.org/

This nonprofit organization supports educational communities in implementing a dynamic curriculum that focuses on movement, breath, and mindfulness. Working closely with educators and others in the school community, the Set/Reset team creates responsive curricula, provides onsite and remote training and mentorship, and offers modular materials.

Stop, Breathe, Think

https://www.stopbreathethink.com/educators

This online portal offers meditation and mindfulness resources that teachers can bring into their classrooms. Downloadable toolkits provide a range of activities that teachers can share with their students. At the elementary level, there are activities for key school-day moments, such as entering the classroom and expressing gratitude. The website also offers an app with many guided meditations for both children and adults.

YogaKids Tools for Schools Program

http://yogakids.com/tools-for-schools

In addition to its online yoga-teacher certification training program, YogaKids designs yoga and mindfulness curricula for educators of all grade levels. Its online shop has books, DVDs, and games to support classroom implementation.

Apps for Guided Meditations

Each of these apps is available for download via Apple iTunes or Google Play. While breaking away from our electronic devices is a key component of a developing mindfulness practice, these resources can be helpful, are available 24/7, and can be accessed directly anywhere from a mobile device at no or little cost.

The Breathing App

https://eddiestern.com/the-breathing-app

This free app guides the user to breathe slowly and intentionally at a rate that is optimal for meditation and physically benefits the body. The app offers three different modes to support the user: visual, numeric, and auditory. The app was a collaboration of yoga instructor Eddie Stern, author and doctor Deepak Chopra, engineer Sergey Varichev, and musician Moby.

Calm

http://www.calm.com

Calm is a widely respected app offering guided meditations, relaxing sleep stories to help you wind down before sleep, original music and peaceful sounds, and mindful body exercises. It offers a seven-day free trial and then requires an annual paid membership.

Headspace

http://www.headspace.com

The Headspace experience begins with a series of questions to gauge how you plan to use the app for mindfulness: your goals, your experience, your preferred time of day. Headspace also offers meditations for children. This app offers a free seven-day trial and then requires a monthly or annual subscription.

Stop Breathe Think

http://www.stopbreathethink.com

Before you use the app to meditate, the app asks a series of questions related to your physical and emotional state. Using your answers, the app offers a selection of guided meditations meant to address your current needs. While the intended audience is adults, there is a companion app for children and a plethora of resources for educators. There are several free meditations, and additional meditations are available via a paid premium membership.

 ## Take It to the Classroom

Guided imagery can transport children (and adults!) to a different time and place. This mindfulness practice is a creative, playful, and fun one to add to your treasure chest of ideas. Children listen to guided meditations, either in person or via a recording, to get concrete guidance for quiet, relaxing contemplation. Below are two guided meditations that you can read aloud or record for later use and can be used one-on-one or in a group setting. These guided meditations were specifically created for young learners by Andrea Wesol, a graduate student in education, mother of two, and longtime student of meditation and mindfulness practices.

For each meditation session, take some time to prepare the environment for young children.

Make sure the space has fresh air, with low or no artificial lighting. You can do the meditation indoors or outside on a patch of grass or a smooth surface. Wherever you choose, the space should be quiet and private to prevent interruption, and, most importantly, safe and comfortable for everyone. The children should wear comfortable, loose-fitting clothing; their everyday playclothes are perfect—no need for a special wardrobe!

It helps to introduce and explain this exercise to children so they can anticipate what will happen and have a clear expectation that this is a quiet, peaceful activity that involves closing their eyes, taking calm breaths, and using their imaginations to have a relaxing experience. Consider asking children to lie down; they can choose the position they feel is most comfortable. For example, some might opt to go under a table in the classroom to get a cozy feeling. Anything goes, so long as they are safe. If available, you may want to offer small pillows for them to place under their heads or small beanbags to cover their eyes. This is optional, of course.

Read the meditations slowly, with enough time to allow for children to engage with the words. You can experiment, if you wish, with playing an audio recording softly in the background of waves rolling in on a beach. You might also invite children to identify where they would like to "go" for their meditation, perhaps with some ideas from you, such as a tropical rain forest, the African bush, or a majestic mountain. Feel free to work with children to find photographs, books, or other representations of some of these quiet, peaceful spaces.

To the Sea with Your Senses

Close your eyes.

Feel your eyelids touch.

Now take a deep breath through your nose.

Breathe it out through your mouth.

Take another deep breath in, and then breathe it out.

Keep breathing like this, slowly, naturally.

Keep your focus on your breath as you breathe in and out.

Let's breathe this way for ten seconds. (Count slowly to ten.)

Now keep breathing like that, and open your imagination.

Imagine you are lying on a quiet, beautiful beach. Warm, soft sand is under your body. Feel the warmth on your head, on your back, on your arms, on your legs.

Take a tiny amount of warm sand in your fingers and slowly rub them together. Feel the tiny grains of sand rubbing against your skin. (Pause for a length of time appropriate for the children. It might be ten seconds; it might be a minute. Provide enough time for them to engage in the meditation but not so much time that they stop participating.)

You can also feel the warmth from the sun shining brightly. Notice how it feels. (Pause for an appropriate time, as described above.)

Now breathe in salty sea air. Breathe deeply. Can you smell that salty air? It is such a strong, special smell that you can almost taste it. (Pause.)

You hear the sound of waves splashing on the shore. The waves splash, then fade back to the sea. Splash, then fade. Splash, then fade. Listen for the splash, then listen for the fade. (Pause.)

Imagine your body standing up and walking to the water. A tiny wave splashes and rolls over your feet. The water is warm and feels wonderful. (Pause.)

Slowly walk into the water. You feel the warm water cover your feet. You feel the warm water cover your ankles. You feel the water gently swirl around your ankles. Then the water fades back to the ocean like the tide coming to shore and going back out again. The water comes and covers your ankles and then goes back to the ocean again and again. It makes you feel calm inside. (Pause.)

Think about bringing this sense of calm into your whole body. Notice how you feel now. Notice your slow and peaceful breathing.

In a few seconds, we are going to open our eyes. But even though your eyes are open, you can still take this feeling of peace, calm, and warmth with you. And you can visit this beautiful place in your imagination anytime you would like to have more peace or calm inside.

Ready now? Start to wiggle your fingers and your toes. When you are feeling ready, slowly open your eyes. Welcome back!

Be Strong Tree, Tall and Still

Close your eyes.

Feel your eyelids touch.

Now take a deep breath through your nose.

Breathe it out through your mouth.

Take another deep breath in. And then breathe it out.

Keep breathing like this, slowly, naturally.

Keep your focus on your breath as you breathe in and out.

Let's breathe this way for ten seconds. (Count slowly to ten.)

Now keep breathing like that and open your imagination.

Picture your bare feet—no shoes on. You are standing on the ground, and your feet are firmly grounded in the earth. Your feet are so strong. Your feet feel so good as they are planted in the dirt.

Now imagine your feet becoming the roots of a tree. See yourself as a tree in a big, beautiful forest. There is green everywhere, and the air smells so fresh. Your roots burrow slowly and deeply into the earth. Your roots mix with the rich soil, and you are now completely connected to the earth. Imagine that your roots go very deep into the earth and you feel completely grounded. You feel very stable, safe, and secure. (Pause for a length of time appropriate for the children. It might be ten seconds; it might be a minute. Provide enough time so that they can engage in the meditation, but not so much time that they stop participating.)

Now focus on your legs. Your legs are together like the solid trunk of a tree. Your legs are strong. Your legs are still. Your stomach is strong and still. Your back is strong and still. Imagine your body as the thick, brown trunk of a really big tree. A big, brown trunk like this stands firm and still. Your body stands firm and still. You are strong and still. (Pause.)

Now focus on your shoulders. Imagine your shoulders slowly rising, lifting your arms and your hands up to the big, blue, sunny sky. Your arms are the big and small branches of your beautiful tree. Your imagination will be doing the movement here; your body is still. In your imagination, your arms reach high into the sky and gently wave back and forth like branches dancing in the cool breeze. Back and forth. Back and forth. Your branches are strong and solid, but they allow themselves to be moved by the breeze. Now imagine the leaves on your branches. What colors are they? The leaves on the branches blow softly in the cool breeze. Your leaves rustle together, making a gentle, relaxing sound. Listen to that rustling sound. Let it relax you. (Pause.)

Now see your whole body as a tree: your feet are your roots connecting you to the earth.

Your legs are strong and still. Your belly is strong and still. Your back is strong and still. Your trunk is strong and still.

Your arms are outstretched, waving branches.

Your hands are waving, and your leaves rustling.

Think about how your tree makes you feel. You are still. You are tall. You are strong. You are safe. (Pause.)

In a few seconds, we are going to open our eyes. But even though your eyes are open, you can still take this feeling of safety, stillness, and strength with you. And you can visit this place in your imagination anytime you would like to have more stillness or strength inside.

Ready now? Start to wiggle your fingers and your toes. When you are feeling ready, slowly open your eyes. Welcome back!

The Power of Presence

CHAPTER 3

Mindfulness and Social Justice: The Intersection of Dignity, Pride, and Respect

> **"Injustice anywhere is a threat to justice everywhere."**
> —Dr. Martin Luther King Jr.

When we practice mindfulness daily, there is a natural sense of connection to and compassion for all living beings. At the core of mindfulness is noticing and appreciating the inherent intersections of variation within each and every human being. In this chapter, we will explore how engaging in a discourse of dignity is at the very core of a mindfulness practice that leads us toward greater respect and understanding about ourselves as well as others.

When we are fully present, we can accept others and view them without judgment. When we view others without judgment, we become more aware of everyone's right to safety, peace, respect, and belonging. Being present starts with a simple choice to be fully aware in this moment and the next moment and the moment after that. All the choices we make count all of the time. This is why the quote by Dr. King is among my favorites. A quest for justice, a deliberate and conscious choice, has guided my teaching, research, and service in early childhood over the past thirty years. So, for me, this quote is about dignity, about humanity, about being present.

I am reminded of a sign I saw in a classroom that asked, "Did your words harm or heal a child today?" Consider how much power we each hold—by word or by deed—to either humiliate or help one another. When we are present, we can fully and honestly witness what is happening within and all around us.

Consider what messages we send to children when we hear name-calling on the playground and we stand by and do nothing or when a colleague speaks unfavorably about a child who is right in front of us, and we remain silent. This is exactly what Dr. King's quote is about. When we ignore injustice even once, then justice is threatened for anyone, anytime, anywhere. How can we pick and choose when, where, or for whom justice matters? When our minds are quiet and steady, we are more conscious of our connection to the world and to others.

Exploring Intersections of Identity

We live in a world where there are many different identities: race, social class, age, culture, gender expression, (dis)ability, religion, ethnicity, language, and more. Diversity is simply a natural part of the human experience. Each individual is part of a variety of identities. Whether the human diversity is consistently viewed as positive and worthy, however, in large part depends on how we talk about difference and diversity both inside the classroom and out.

In their article "Practicing Inclusion, Doing Justice: Disability, Identity, and Belonging in Early Childhood," Margaret Beneke and colleagues explain how multiple aspects and intersections of young children's identities will influence their sense of belonging in the early childhood classroom. They describe Leo, who is two years old. He is not only a child with a developmental delay but also a young boy of color whose parents are immigrants. Based on a combination of biological, environmental, geographic, historical, and political factors, Leo's sense of self and belonging as he grows may look very different from another child regardless of whether they share the same disability, gender, age, or other label. As educators, we must be conscious about the intersecting nature of identities that make up every human being and our power to nurture or damage children's sense of self and belonging.

Engaging with young children in critical examination across many aspects of diversity, such as race, gender identity, ability, religion, and language, and so on, reaffirms for them a world that is rich in difference. We each possess a unique compilation of diverse personal identity markers; these identities not only intersect but continually change and grow. We must step outside our individual comfort zones and engage in meaningful and sometimes difficult conversations, which invite a discourse of dignity in each moment with children. As we become more mindful of the multiple identity markers and the ways they interconnect, let us listen and learn from children about what they have to say.

As you read the following thoughtful narrative about a high-school student, written in her own words, ponder her intersecting identities and how they frame some of her ideas about the world:

> My name is Minal Rosenblum, and I am a seventeen-year-old female. I am Jewish American and half Indian. I have many friends at my high school. I take many classes with them, including dance, which I love! I started going to dance classes when I was a young girl. I have performed at dance recitals too. I began with modern dance and I also joined hip-hop. I enjoy acting and drama too.
>
> So now you know about me already, but here is something you may not know: I have a disability. It is called Down syndrome. One time, I went to the disability pride parade in New York City. The parade told me a message that everyone should be equal and they should have the same freedom. I connected with it because I have a disability too. Here is what I think: people who

have disabilities are basically normal. They should be included in what everyone else can do. They should not be separated. People should be together to make the world feel happy. If someone tells me that people should be separate, I would be upset. Everyone should love himself or herself just the way they are.

In her own voice, Minal articulates multiple aspects of her identity and what is important to her. By inviting students to identify and share the many diverse and interrelated aspects of who they are, we can learn about the world through their unique lens. It is important for young children to notice the intersecting nature of their own identities as well as the multiple, diverse identities of others. When young children learn that difference is a point of pride, they do not perceive difference as a source of deficit in themselves and in others. When we carefully listen to and seriously look at what children communicate, we cocreate with them a safe and just climate in the classroom and beyond.

There are many ways to maintain a natural and ongoing classroom conversation about diversity, which is firmly grounded in dignity, justice, joy, and pride. By taking personal accountability and collective responsibility for our words and actions, we teach young children to do the same. Here are teachers' voices discussing the intersection of some of their personal markers and the influence these identities have on their work in early childhood education. Ponder these educators' stories and the ways in which their unique and intersecting identities have shaped their narratives. As you read the following personal narrative of Bianca Fairley, a teacher of young children in a public school district, notice her intersecting identities and how they may have informed her teaching philosophy and practice:

> I am an African American female, middle-class early childhood educator who has resided in and dedicated most of my professional teaching years to students residing in urban towns. Most of my years as a lead prekindergarten teacher have been conducted in dual-language classrooms. English is my native language, and I speak Spanish as a second language . . . I was raised in a single-parent household, and my mother always described me as an inquisitive child who enjoyed reading to quench my zeal for knowledge . . . I am the niece of a woman (on my maternal side) who has autism and is nonverbal. Her disability has made me the voice of my students and of the families who are not knowledgeable of their legal rights when it comes to advocating for their child with a disability. My passion for inclusion has enlightened my teaching philosophy: "Education is not the filling of a pail, but the lighting of a fire." This quote written by William Butler Yeats holds me accountable as an educator.

In his article in *Contemporary Issues in Early Childhood*, Travis Wright describes his work over the past sixteen years as an urban early childhood educator, a licensed professional counselor, and a university-based researcher specializing in young children:

> As a man, particularly as one who identifies as gay, I am painfully aware of the stigma often placed on male early childhood educators. In navigating this treacherous terrain, I must confess that I have sometimes hidden or felt pressured to hide parts of myself to do this work that I love—a sentiment shared frequently with me by male colleagues.

We all have unique and various identity markers that intersect to make up who we are and how we might choose to identify ourselves. Think about the intersecting identity markers in your life and contemplate how these markers have shaped your journey as an educator. How do you define yourself in terms of race, ethnicity, age, ability, gender, culture, sexual orientation, socioeconomic class, religion, language, geographic location, and so on? How do society's perceptions about identity play a role in your life? in the lives of Leo, Minal, Bianca, and Travis? in the lives of the children you care for?

Exploring Diversity with Young Children

While it might seem that young children do not really notice differences and identities, research supports the idea that they do. When it comes to diversity, there is a growing body of research that demonstrates young learners are aware of and recognize differences such as race and ethnicity. For further reading about children's perceptions on identity and prejudice, consider the following resources:

Aboud, Frances. 1987. "The Development of Ethnic Self-Identification and Attitudes." In *Children's Ethnic Socialization: Pluralism and Development*. Newbury Park, CA: SAGE.

Aboud, Frances. 1988. *Children and Prejudice*. Oxford, UK: Basil Blackwell.

Aboud, Frances. 2003. "The Formation of In-Group Favoritism and Out-Group Prejudice in Young Children: Are They Distinct Attitudes?" *Developmental Psychology* 39(1): 48–60.

Aboud, Frances. 2008. "A Social-Cognitive Developmental Theory of Prejudice." In *Handbook of Race, Racism, and the Developing Child*. Hoboken, NJ: John Wiley and Sons.

Aboud, Frances, and Maria Amato. 2001. "Developmental and Socialization Influences on Intergroup Bias." In *Blackwell Handbook of Social Psychology: Intergroup Processes*. Malden, MA: Blackwell.

Aboud, Frances, et al. 2012. "Interventions to Reduce Prejudice and Enhance Inclusion and Respect for Ethnic Differences in Early Childhood: A Systematic Review." *Developmental Review* 32(4): 307–336.

Clark, Kenneth, and Mamie Clark. 1947. "Racial Identification and Preference in Negro Children." In *Readings in Social Psychology*. New York: Henry Holt and Co.

Morland, J. Kenneth. 1963. "Racial Self-Identification: A Study of Nursery School Children." *The American Catholic Sociological Review* 24(3): 231–242.

Stevenson, Harold, and Edward Stewart. 1958. "A Developmental Study of Racial Awareness in Young Children." *Child Development* 29(3): 399–409.

Swanson, Dena Phillips, et al. 2008. "Racial Identity Development during Childhood." In *Handbook of African American Psychology*. Thousand Oaks, CA: SAGE.

Van Ausdale, Debra, and Joe Feagin. 1996. "Using Racial and Ethnic Concepts: The Critical Case of Very Young Children." *American Sociological Review* 61(5): 779–793.

Van Ausdale, Debra, and Joe Feagin. 2001. *The First R: How Children Learn Race and Racism*. Lanham, MD: Rowman and Littlefield.

Young children are constantly receiving messages about themselves, others, and the world in which they live. These messages, whether they are blatant or unspoken, contribute to a child's awareness of and perceptions about diversity. This is where an on-going practice of mindfulness is key. The climate at home and school, therefore, can create positive, healthy messages about children's developing identities. And this can occur without even saying a word!

Andrea Wesol, parent of a second grader at a culturally and economically diverse public elementary school, describes how teachers, inspired by own their personal mindfulness practices, created a culture of mindfulness with young children. One of the ways they did this was through the Mindful Minute. The kindergarten teachers explained to their young students that a Mindful Minute is sixty seconds of silent, still sitting, with closed eyes and slow, peaceful breaths. The kindergarteners practiced Mindful Minutes in various ways for the first few weeks of school. They learned to be more aware of their breathing by putting small stuffed animals on their bellies as they lay down, breathing so the stuffed animal would not fall off. The teachers incorporated Mindful Minutes throughout the day, especially during transition times or if the classroom noise and activity levels bordered on disruptive rather than creative. In late September, the kindergarteners took center stage and led the entire school in a Mindful Minute during an assembly. Imagine the entire elementary-school gymnasium filled with about three hundred children, teachers, staff, and families quietly breathing together. It is possible and can happen anywhere!

Once mindfulness takes root, it can extend outward to touch circles of a community, from within the school and beyond. At the school of Wesol's daughter, it started with practicing mindfulness until that became an integral and systemic part of the structural foundation. Perhaps this one small step in a school could lead to a movement advancing presence worldwide, or perhaps practicing mindfulness is a very private commitment we make to simply be more present with young children.

The Mindful Minute, which offers a quick opportunity to practice mindfulness together every day, can elevate a greater sense of appreciation for difference, community, and connection. Creating a culture of mindfulness within and across schools, homes, and communities is one simple, sustainable way to promote a positive understanding of commonalities and differences in one another.

Young learners receive constant messages about the meaning of difference in the classroom through the presence or absence of rich and diverse classroom artifacts, such as wall displays, materials, books, technology, toys, rugs, fabric, furniture, and food. They also receive messages through the kinds of investigations, projects, music, art, and other influences that permeate the classroom space. Within naturally occurring routines, events, or discussions, the absence of conversation can also influence children's construction of meaning on diversity and difference. In their article "Rethinking 'We Are All Special': Anti-Ableism Curricula in Early Childhood Classrooms," Priya Lalvani and Jessica Bacon note how children learn that some aspects of difference may be negative, undesirable, or unworthy because of messages they do (or do not) receive from adults. For example, they describe how teachers may be informing or shaping young minds about a deficit-oriented perspective of disability. Many teachers may convey disability as bad or a tragedy, a pity, or a limitation instead of disability as an aspect of an individual that is worthy of respect, similar to other aspects of human difference such as culture, gender, race, or language. Young children may learn that experiencing a disability is undesirable if they frequently receive this kind of message from adults they know and trust.

In the highly regarded text *Reading Resistance: Discourses of Exclusion in Desegregation and Inclusion Debates* by Beth Ferri and David Connor, Ferri recounts her first day at a school where she had been hired to launch an in-district program for students with cognitive disabilities:

> When I arrived early in August to begin preparations, I was given a tour of the school and my new classroom. The principal was obviously proud of all the arrangements that had been made in preparation for admitting the new students [with disabilities] to the elementary school.
>
> I was shown how my classroom, which was the old art room, had its own door to the outside. This meant, I was told, that "my" students could come straight into the "self-contained" classroom from their own "special" bus. They would also be able to exit to the playground at their own "special" time. Then I was escorted to the lunchroom, where a "special" table had been set up in its own "special" room adjoining the cafeteria so "my" students would have their own place to each lunch. At this point I remember feeling a bit defensive for the students I had yet to meet! I told the principal that I didn't think all this "special" treatment was necessary or even desirable . . . I looked at the "special" table in the "special" lunchroom and quipped, "Well, since these students eat with 'normal' people at home, I am sure they'll be able to handle it here at school."

On pages 64–65, I offer some examples of classroom-ready ideas to critically examine specific identity markers and describe how to have conversations with children about difference. Talking with young children about the interconnectedness of personal identities can be a natural, integral part of every day. They are not meant to be implemented only one time or only during one unit but rather revisited again and again in many different ways. By transforming disapproving discourse into rich, positive conversations, we will be firmly planting lessons about dignity.

Who Decides What Is "Normal"?

Take a moment to read the following scenario from the article "'Doing Social Justice in Early Childhood: The Potential of Leadership," by Louise Hard, Frances Press, and Megan Gibson.

This scenario captures a snapshot of when his mother went to pick up four-year-old Jake at preschool. Notice his response and pay careful attention to the positioning of Humpty Dumpty's belt as you ponder the notion of a single set of standardized skills:

> My son was a four-year-old at preschool and he was eager to attend to play with friends. One day I arrived to collect him and noticed that the children had spent the day making Humpty Dumpty pastings with pre-cut pieces. The pastings were egg-shaped with two eyes, legs dangling freely, a hat, and a belt. I surveyed the walls of the room and could not see one with my boy's name attached. I asked Jake where his was and he pulled it out of his bag, somewhat crumpled, and I could see why it was not on the wall for public exhibition. [Jake's] Humpty had eyes and legs, but the belt was clearly vertical, not horizontal. I said, "Jake, tell me about your Humpty Dumpty," and he said, "Well, mum, those are the eyes and they are the legs and that [the belt] is the Band-Aid holding him all together."

If we view this scenario through a lens of creativity, intelligence, and kindness, we understand that Jake cleverly intended to repair a "broken" Humpty Dumpty. The teacher's apparent expectation for the children to produce an identical finished product reflects a focus on conformity. The teacher not only fails to acknowledge Jake's unique problem solving and originality but also misses the pivotal opportunity to encourage Jake's innovation and imagination. And perhaps most unsettling is that the crumpled project tucked away in his bag sheds light on Jake's feelings about his work that day.

Hard, Press, and Gibson assert, "Through such an unquestioning acceptance of normalcy, we silence the perspectives of those who have their own stories but are not afforded the opportunity to share them . . . such marginalisation of 'difference' stifles creativity, innovation, and critical reflection."

Our notions of *normal* shape who we are as human beings and how we perceive others. The concept of normality often goes unexamined or unchallenged in early childhood education; yet, our own perceptions of normality inform our teaching practices and extend well beyond the classroom walls. Collective beliefs influence actions and inevitably determine culture, structures, policies, and practices. When woven together, these core beliefs create a system of early childhood education and care. It is precisely these personal and collective perspectives that directly and dramatically shape the lives of children.

Cultural norms are a shared understanding about the standards, beliefs, behavior, and practices that generally guide how people live and what is deemed as acceptable. However, in her widely respected text *The Cultural Nature of Human Development*, Barbara Rogoff cautions against viewing culture as what "other people do" or common characteristics among a collection of people. Framing culture in this way can be limiting and can lead to deficit-oriented thinking about differences. Instead, Rogoff suggests that, just like individual people, cultural communities are dynamic and are in a constant state of growing.

Our schools are filled with rich and valuable cultural communities; however, when deficit-oriented thinking and actions are part of the school climate, many children are prevented from receiving an equitable education. Some education-reform initiatives are troubling because they aspire to use early childhood education as a vehicle to measure a single set of standardized skills for young children everywhere, without any consideration for rich and complex cultural, social, environmental, and individual diversity. Lisa Delpit, author of *Other People's Children: Cultural Conflict in the Classroom*, explains that "if we are to successfully educate all of our children we must work to remove the blinders built of stereotypes, monocultural instructional methodologies, ignorance, social distance, biased research, and racism." Delpit advises that these blinders must disappear so teachers can fully and genuinely know the children in their classrooms. We must be present in each moment to be aware of the blinders and to see each child completely and in all of her brilliance.

This is the path of mindfulness practice because we become even more tuned into our core beliefs and ways of thinking. When we engage in a steady mindfulness practice, the mind becomes quiet, and we become more aware and conscious. When we are present in the moment, we can see more clearly the deeper beliefs and perceptions that guide how we view the world.

Culturally driven and socially determined ideas about what is acceptable ultimately hold a mirror to reflect a society's core beliefs about normality. Our perceptions of what is normal are powerful indicators about what we deem acceptable in the classroom. Consider that practices, expectations, pedagogy, and climate in early childhood class-rooms are influenced by what educators deem as acceptable. Consequently, young children's emerging understanding of what is normal will be shaped by what they observe as acceptable in the classroom. Young learners may discover that the meaning of *normal* changes across different contexts—whether these messages are explicitly taught or learned through everyday and naturally occurring routines, conversations, and silences.

Examining the Discourse on Disability in Early Childhood

Over the thirty years of my career, I have noticed the same pervasive deficit-oriented conversations about children, learning, and schools as I did when I began my career in education. I am deeply aware of an unquestioning acceptance of exclusion, isolation, and stigma that still exists in many schools around disability. I want to spend a moment unpacking notions of normality and disability, specifically.

Patricia Cahill Paugh and Curt Dudley-Marling explain in their article "'Speaking' Deficit into (or out of) Existence: How Language Constrains Classroom Teachers' Knowledge about Instructing Diverse Learners" that the deficit discourse "focuses on what students cannot do, [which] dominates discussions of students who do not perform according to expectations in school." Paugh and Dudley-Marling note, for example, that terms such as *inclusive* and *differentiated instruction* that are commonly used in discussion around educational-reform efforts tend to recreate the boundaries of who is and is not normal, who is eligible to be included, and who is different. Too often, efforts to reform the language of schooling have had the effect of reinforcing rather than challenging inequitable practices. These underlying beliefs reinforce exclusion or stigma, thereby perpetuating educational and social injustice in the schools instead of confronting it.

Each day, young children learn about diversity from their personal experiences, observations, conversations, and silences in the classroom. Karen Watson, author of *Inside the "Inclusive" Early Childhood Classroom: The Power of the "Normal,"* notes that the perception of normal "contains a judgment about what is desirable and what should be achieved." Watson further suggests that young children are under endless examination, surveillance, and scrutiny, not only from their teachers but also from their peers, other adults, and from themselves. Reflecting on her own teaching practice, Watson candidly describes how notions of pity, empathy, and tragedy were so deeply embedded into her teaching beliefs about children labeled with a disability, it served to intensify the structures of bias, inequity, and a sense of "other."

In addition to pity, additional common perceptions of disability are deeply entrenched into our societal beliefs. In the compelling book *Freak Show: Presenting Human Oddities for Amusement and Profit*, Robert Bogdan points out how films often feature villains as defective, disfigured, or disabled, and how monsters tend to be depicted as scarred, deformed, or mentally ill. He argues that the term *monster* had been a routine term for infants with observable "defects." Bogdan's text was published in 1988, and yet it seems as if not much has changed since then about how disability and other diversity are depicted.

> Think about how discrimination and prejudice around disabilities is no different from thinking about other identity categories, such as age, race, gender, or social class. Exclusion and oppression occur when difference is viewed as inferior or abnormal.

In their article, "Rethinking 'We Are All Special,'" Lalvani and Bacon further explain that "not only is *ableism* [italics added] generally left unaddressed in schools, the otherness of individuals with disabilities is often manufactured or reproduced through [early childhood/early childhood special education] curricula." Teachers who may be transmitting negative beliefs—however unwittingly—about disability to young children contribute to beliefs that being able bodied is superior or preferable to a disability.

Children learn these negative beliefs about disability. Beneke and colleagues, in their article "Practicing Inclusion, Doing Justice: Disability, Identity, and Belonging in Early Childhood," suggest that, like other *-isms* such as racism and sexism, ableism is an oppressive ideology that permeates systems, policies, and practices. Ableism can be seen in children's literature, pedagogy, playgrounds, and classroom practices. Ableism is perpetuated when disability is positioned as deficit oriented, limiting, negative, and undesirable, especially in comparison to the notion of being able bodied.

Early childhood professionals can, and must, stand up both individually and collectively to confront the limiting ways that disability is positioned as "other" in classrooms, schools, and society. One way to begin to challenge ableism is to view disability as just one of the many aspects of human diversity. In *Reading Resistance* Ferri and Connor explain, "Viewing disability as primarily a social experience forces all individuals to examine and reflect upon their complicity in upholding or challenging perceptions of and interactions with people signified as abled and those signified as disabled." We must hold ourselves accountable.

Staying silent is not an option. In the *Journal of Early Intervention*, Ann and Rud Turnbull raise the fundamental issue about accountability and young children when they pose the question "Whose job is it?"

> This is a story about four people named Everybody, Somebody, Anybody, and Nobody. There was an important job to be done, and Everybody was asked to do it. Anybody could have done it, but Nobody did it. Somebody got angry about that, because it was Everyone's job. Everybody thought Anybody could do it, but Nobody realized that Somebody would not do it. It ended up that Everybody blamed Somebody when Nobody did what Anybody could have done.

Let us be impeccably accountable.

As a teacher educator on a journey for justice over the past three decades, I have learned that advancing equity in education boils down to presence, both individually and collectively. I believe that injustice anywhere is about a lack of presence. Where there is violence in word or deed, there is an absence of presence. Consider that when we engage in negative thoughts even about ourselves—I hate my life, my body, my job, my family—or turn that aggression outward toward another, we are no longer mindful.

When we quiet our minds, we can tune out the constant chatter. We can be deeply aware and grateful for being alive. We can live in harmony and with great respect for the world we share with all other beings. We can become more conscious and stand in awe of all things natural, such as rainbows, trees, sunsets, mountains, stars, thunderstorms, and the earth that is so beautiful and bountiful.

Young children can engage in conversations about respect, fairness, and justice. We must be prepared to notice and respond to young children's questions, narratives, and actions related to many forms of human diversity. This is difficult, if not impossible to accomplish, when we are not fully present in each moment. The steady practice of mindfulness helps us to quiet our minds so we can respond to any situation with a sense of calm, clarity, and kindness. Through identity-specific conversations about difference and dignity, we can construct with children what it means to be human. We can cultivate a widespread understanding of respect, pride, and self-esteem from the start. It's about time.

Thinking Critically about Pedagogy and Practice

In her book *Black Ants and Buddhists: Thinking Critically and Teaching Differently in the Primary Grades*, Mary Cowhey describes how changing the discourse of difference starts with a critical reflection. Cowhey explains, for example, how food drives may be well intentioned but can actually reinforce a disparaging discourse of difference, in this case on economic or social-class diversity. When thinking critically about a food drive, Cowhey asserts that unintentional and subtle messages are transmitted which oversimplify economic struggles, stigmatize people including peers at the school who are categorized as low income, and neglect to teach children about the fundamental causes of poverty and how some communities are working on solutions to improve economic circum-stances. Cowhey suggests thinking resourcefully with children so that a food drive could be an effective and powerful tool to transform teaching and learning. She suggests deepening inquiry and activism in the classroom by using a food drive to question beliefs about other; to understand the stigma, facets, and causes of poverty that can affect anyone; and to collaborate with local advocates on long-range economic improvements.

Similarly, Rudine Sims Bishop challenges us to think about whether literature for young children represents the mirror or the window in their lives. In her article "Mirrors, Windows, and Sliding Glass Doors," Bishop warns, "When children cannot find themselves reflected in the books they read, or when the images they see are distorted, negative, or laughable, they learn a powerful lesson about how they are devalued in the society of which they are a part." Bishop further admonishes that this absence of diversity in literature is also detrimental for children from dominant cultural or racial groups who are accustomed to seeing mostly mirror images of themselves. When we build a classroom or home library or introduce literature to young children, we should be conscious and mindful of the messages we are conveying.

Using a socially just and inclusive framework that explores disability and ableism, Lalvani and Bacon advise that teachers of young children should ensure "multiple entry points," so children with a range of learning, communication, preferences, and abilities can meaningfully engage with the curriculum. They offer teachers specific ideas to design anti-ableism activities and resources specific to young children. These tools are excellent ways to disrupt deficit-oriented thinking and embed a culture that values diverse human identities into the classroom community. Two of their lessons can be found in Take It to the Classroom on page 64.

Working in Partnership with Young Children to Question Ideas on Difference

In the early years, when children are forming ideas and beliefs about the world in which they live, we need to engage with them in ongoing conversations on difference and notions of normality. This is the time to spot and challenge deficit-oriented discourses. As human beings, we each play a vital role in creating a tightly woven tapestry that connects (or distances) us. The practice of being present, which offers us a powerful portal into our own beliefs, actions, and silences, ultimately leaves an imprint on our homes, schools, communities, and as well as the people in our lives. Our personal imprint may ultimately heal (or harm) the planet for generations to come.

We have complete power and control over our own thoughts. One of my favorite quotes by author Penney Peirce is, "I can't do anything about the thoughts that come into my head, but I can do something about the ones that stay there!" Our personal beliefs, therefore, matter. It is as if we draw to ourselves other similar ideas—whether we realize this or not. Consider what happens when one baby stars to cry in a day-care's nap room; in a matter of minutes, you have a room full of crying babies. Or think about when one person begins yawning in a meeting; pretty soon half the room is yawning. Similarly, there seems to be a magnetic force attracting similar beliefs and actions, which is continually evolving and transforming. Given the power of our thoughts and beliefs, I wonder how we can expand the mindfulness work that so many people practice on a regular basis. How can we elevate mindfulness in genuine partnership with young children? What might happen if we made a collective decision to use presence as a deliberate way of meeting injustice head on?

Change always begins with a thought. Let us be exceptionally conscious about the words we use in ordinary moments and reimagine and reclaim early childhood education. Darcey Dachyshyn's article "Being Mindful, Heartful, and Ecological in Early Years Care and Education" reminds us to think about approaching our work from these conscious, nonviolent spaces rather from a posture of aggression or harshness.

> I was keen to disrupt, interrogate, cut through, upset, disturb, overturn, interrupt, trouble, shift, dislocate, perturb, and dislodge all manner of normativity. I was a force to be reckoned with—and then it hit me. All these words we use to describe what we do, as reconceptualists, are hard words, strident, even violent words; words that cause discomfort and uneasiness. We say this is exactly what we need, that the field of early years care and education has for far too long been dominated by one right-way developmentally appropriate practice thinking, and it is imperative that we shift away from this complacency.

In light of more heartful approaches, let's be meticulously mindful about the words we use. Strength and power do not have to mean force, aggression, and hostility. There is power in presence, so let it begin with us.

••• Concluding Thoughts ·····································

Let us transform the unacceptable that has become acceptable in early childhood education and care. An unprecedented individual and collective opportunity exists to practice presence as one way to create sustainable and equitable early childhood education and care. We can consistently engage in critical conversations on human dignity, confront notions of normality, and explore intersections of identity with children. Together, with young children, we are creating a powerful mindfulness practice that simply strengthens our commitment to social justice and equity. It's about time that we elevate a discourse of dignity individually and together. This is the power of presence. In the next chapter, we will focus on mindfulness practices in and out of the classroom starting with stillness, silence, and the power of the pause.

· ·

A Menu of Options for Teaching Inclusively, Mindfully, and Equitably

 Children's Corner

Children's books hold the power to communicate diverse realities and authentic lived experiences to young minds. It's not only food that children digest; they also digest what they read, so let's be mindful to carefully select books that can nurture, inspire, and educate children. And, of course, young children's natural curiosity and unique interests will also play a part in the books they select for themselves.

The Council on Interracial Books for Children initially produced a valuable ten-item checklist that teachers and families can use to assess books for racism; Louise Derman-Sparks has expanded on this resource for selecting anti-bias children's books. Find it at https://socialjusticebooks.org/guide-for-selecting-anti-bias-childrens-books

Now is the time to take a careful and critical look at the books in your home or school library. Consider new book choices that you make on your own or together with young children. Remember that literature plays a vital role in nourishing or diminishing children's developing identities, positive beliefs about diversity, and compassionate ideas about justice in the world today.

de la Peña, Matt. 2018. *Carmela Full of Wishes*. New York: G. P. Putnam.

Hegarty, Patricia. 2017. *We Are Family*. Wilton, CT: Tiger Tales.

Kluth, Paula, Patrick Schwarz, and Justin Canha. 2010. *Pedro's Whale*. Baltimore: Brookes.

Levine, Ellen, and Kadir Nelson. 2007. *Henry's Freedom Box: A True Story from the Underground Railroad*. New York: Scholastic.

Love, Jessica. 2018. *Julián Is a Mermaid*. Somerville, MA: Candlewick.

Newman, Leslea, and Maria Mola. 2017. *Sparkle Boy*. New York: Lee and Low.

Phi, Bao. 2017. *A Different Pond*. North Mankato, MN: Capstone Young Readers.

Polacco, Patricia. 1994. *Mrs. Katz and Tush*. New York: Dragonfly.

Rabe, Berniece. 1988. *Where's Chimpy?* Park Ridge, IL: Albert Whitman and Company.

Richards, Beah. 2006. *Keep Climbing, Girls*. New York: Simon & Schuster.

Springman, I. C. 2012. *More*. New York: Houghton Mifflin.

Yum, Hyewon. 2011. *The Twin's Blanket*. New York: Farrah Straus Giroux.

 ## Caregivers' Corner

In the following list, I offer some noteworthy and indispensable resources to help you continue the conversation and turn that discourse into action.

Beneke, Margaret, and Caryn Park. 2019. "Introduction to the Special Issue: Antibias Curriculum and Critical Praxis to Advance Social Justice in Inclusive Elementary Education." *Young Exceptional Children* 22(2). https://journals.sagepub.com/doi/abs/10.1177/1096250619833337?journalCode=yeca

Block, Marianne, Beth Blue Swadener, and Gaile Cannella, eds. 2018. *Reconceptualizing Early Childhood Education and Care: A Reader*. 2nd ed. New York: Peter Lang.

Booth, Tony, et al. 2002. *Index for Inclusion: Developing Learning and Participation in Schools*. 2nd ed. Bristol, UK: Centre for Studies on Inclusive Education.

Booth, Tony, Mel Ainscow, and Denise Kingston. 2006. *Index for Inclusion: Developing Play, Learning and Participation in Early Years and Childcare*. Bristol, UK: Centre for Studies on Inclusive Education.

Cowhey, Mary. 2006. *Black Ants and Buddhists: Thinking Critically and Teaching Differently in the Primary Grades*. Portsmouth, NH: Stenhouse.

Delpit, Lisa. 2006. *Other People's Children: Cultural Conflict in the Classroom*. New York: The New Press.

Derman-Sparks, Louise, and Julie Olsen Edwards. 2010. *Anti-Bias Education for Young Children and Ourselves*. Washington, DC: National Association for the Education of Young Children.

Freire, Paulo. 1998. *Pedagogy of Freedom: Ethics, Democracy, and Civic Courage*. Translated by Patrick Clarke. Lanham, MD: Rowman and Littlefield.

Iruka, Iheoma U., Stephanie M. Curenton, Tonia R. Durden, and Kerry-Ann Escayg. 2020. *Don't Look Away: Embracing Anti-Bias Classrooms*. Lewisville, NC: Gryphon House.

Kissen, Rita M., ed. 2002. *Getting Ready for Benjamin: Preparing Teachers for Sexual Diversity in the Classroom*. Lanham, MD: Rowman and Littlefield.

Kuh, Lisa P., et al. 2016. "Moving Beyond Anti-Bias Activities: Supporting the Development of Anti-Bias Practices." *Young Children* 71(1): 58–65.

Lalvani, Priya, and Jessica Bacon. 2019. "Rethinking 'We Are All Special': Anti-Ableism Curricula in Early Childhood Classrooms." *Young Exceptional Children* 22(2): 87–100. doi:10.1177/1096250618810706

Nieto, Sonia. 2015. *The Light in Their Eyes: Creating Multicultural Learning Communities*. New York: Teachers College Press.

Shalaby, Carla. 2017. *Troublemakers: Lessons in Freedom from Young Children at School*. New York: The New Press.

Watson, Karen. 2017. *Inside the 'Inclusive' Early Education Classroom: The Power of the 'Normal.'* New York: Peter Lang.

Here are some highly regarded organizations worth knowing about because they share an agenda of equity, justice, and protection for the rights of all young children:

- **Reconceptualizing Early Childhood Education and Care (RECE)**
  http://www.receinternational.org
  RECE uses a powerful collective voice to reimagine education and care as spaces where young children's full citizenship is genuinely valued and recognized. RECE is a cross-disciplinary membership of teacher educators, scholars, researchers, policy makers, and practitioners from more than twenty-five countries. RECE continues to oppose and challenge the global agendas that push for privatization as well as economic- and market-driven education in early childhood and beyond

- **Campaign for a Commercial-Free Childhood**
  https://commercialfreechildhood.org/resources
  The Campaign for a Commercial-Free Childhood is a coalition of advocates for children who work to limit the influence that contemporary US culture's focus on consumerism has on the lives of children. Specifically, they work against marketing commercial activity to children. This organization's website is a clearinghouse for news and helpful resources on this topic for people who live and work with children. It sponsors an annual Screen Free Week for schools and families.

- **Children's Defense Fund**
  https://www.childrensdefense.org
  The Children's Defense Fund was founded by Marian Wright Edelman in 1973 to advocate for children's rights, with a particular call to serve children of color, children with disabilities, and children from low socioeconomic backgrounds. The Children's Defense Fund provides training for community members who want to learn how to best advocate for children at both the local and national levels.

Take It to the Classroom

Investigations on Exploring Identity

These sample investigations around disability, based on the work of Priya Lalvani and Jessica Bacon, can be used with young children at school or home to engage them in conversations and practices related to anti-ableism. It is recommended that these kinds of investigations are embedded into the culture of the classroom and take place over time, not necessarily over consecutive days or only within a distinctive unit. It is equally important to consider how these investigations can (and should!) be revisited often.

Goal: Each child will talk about fairness, begin to develop language to describe unfairness, and understand that unfairness hurts.

Essential Question

How can the words we use help or hurt ourselves or others?

Choose from among the following activities:

- Have a group conversation where you ask children for words that describe themselves and their families, and talk about how those words make them feel.

- Read *The Rainbow Tree* by Leon Shargel, and discuss how difference is described and how the characters in this book respond to difference.

- Expand the conversation to discuss words that hurt.

Goal: Each child will demonstrate empowerment and the skills to act against prejudice and/or discriminatory actions.

Essential Question 1

Can one person or a group of people working together make a difference?

Read a book about someone who worked to make a difference in the world. For example:

Bryant, Jen. 2016. *Six Dots: A Story of Young Louis Braille.* New York: Alfred A. Knopf.

Clements, Andrew. 1988. Big Al. New York: Simon and Schuster.

Green, Jen. 2005. *Why Should I Recycle?* Hauppauge, NY: BES.

Hood, Susan. 2016. Ada's Violin: The Story of the Recycled Orchestra of Paraguay. New York: Simon and Schuster.

McDonnell, Patrick. 2011. *Me . . . Jane.* New York: Little Brown.

Raschka, Chris. 2007. *Yo? Yes!* New York: Scholastic.

Thompson, Laurie Ann. 2015. Emmanuel's Dream: *The True Story of Emmanuel Ofosu Yeboah.* New York: Schwartz and Wade.

Willems, Mo. 2007. *My Friend Is Sad.* New York: Hyperion.

Talk with the children about what actions the main characters take to change something in the world for the better.

Talk with them about what they might want to change in the world. Discuss ways they could bring about change.

Essential Question 2

What issues can be addressed in our school community?

Build off of one of the books you read on day 1. Choose from among the following activities:

- Brainstorm ways to make a more inclusive environment, be a kind friend, help others, or help the Earth.

- Create posters, art, dance, and songs that promote ways to make a more inclusive environment, be a kind friend, help others, or help the Earth.

- Hold a schoolwide assembly to share art projects and plans to make a more inclusive environment, be a kind friend, help others, or help the Earth.

Adapted from Lalvani, Priya, and Jessica Bacon. 2019. "Rethinking 'We Are All Special': Anti-Ableism Curricula in Early Childhood Classrooms." *Young Exceptional Children* 22(2): 87–100.

The Power of Presence

PART II

To Be or Not to Be: Creating and Maintaining a Culture of Mindfulness in Early Childhood Education

In part II, we examine what a culture of mindfulness looks like in diverse early childhood classrooms. We delve into an exploration of mindfulness through a child's lens with a specific focus on inviting silence and stillness, reimagining time, and promoting a personal sense of safety.

The Power of Presence

CHAPTER 4

The Power of the Pause

Being present is about quieting the mind. As we discussed in chapter 1, mindfulness is silencing the incessant chatter or the constant stream of thoughts that prevent us from being in the moment. Being present is also about living in ease, harmony, and respect for the world around us. I tend to think about mindfulness as stillness. When there is stillness, it is much easier to be open to the here and now. We are better able to witness sensations, feelings, and thoughts without judgment, interpretation, or attachment. Being present can also occur when we are moving, such as in walking meditations or Tai Chi, an ancient Chinese practice that focuses on mindfulness. In stillness, however, there is a natural invitation for our bodies and minds to pause. Pausing is a powerful tool or pathway in any daily mindfulness practice. Yoga teacher, author, and lecturer Eddie Stern emphasizes the need for pauses in our lives. He cofounded the Brooklyn Yoga Club (now closed), and the logo for the yoga school was based on musical notation; above an image of five music notation lines was a comma, called the *breath mark*. When a musician comes to that mark, she pauses and takes a breath. Stern notes that this is one of the essential purposes behind a spiritual practice. A pause creates space, and in that space, we have the opportunity to experience who we are.

Ashtanga Yoga New York & Brooklyn Yoga Club

I appreciated learning that when musicians come to the breath mark, they literally pause and take a breath. What a wonderful metaphor for nonmusicians too! There is power in the pause because, as Eddie states, it creates space. Pausing is a simple way for anyone to return to the present moment—anytime and anywhere.

Staying Busy to Stay Connected

When I was considering the title for this chapter, I purposely wanted to focus on the significance of pausing because I've noticed how most Westerners and many others seem uncomfortable with silence and stillness. I became more aware of this in particular during the COVID-19 pandemic, as everyone was sheltering in place. I was struck at the ingenuity and resourcefulness of people who connected remotely with loved ones, locally and around the globe, even though many people were unable to leave their homes. At the same time, I noticed that solitude, silence, or stillness did not seem to be among the preferred or chosen activities, even though for many there was now much more time in the day.

It is rare to find anyone not texting, talking, playing, or surfing on an electronic device when alone (and you'll often find people on their electronic devices even when they are not alone). If our minds can be filled with incessant clutter, there is a good chance that our lives will mirror that very same busyness. In his book *Silence: The Power of Quiet in a World Full of Noise*, Thích Nhất Hạnh surmises one reason for this constant busyness: many people may be afraid of silence. He suggests that humans are constantly filling up space by taking in distractions, such as music, radio, television, and smart phones, and he adds that "we busy ourselves all day long in an effort to connect." This need for deep connection is something that all humans share.

The irony, however, is in how people are finding a sense of connection. These distractions prevent us from being in touch with deep-seated feelings, such as depression, anxiety, isolation, inadequacy, anger, or emptiness. Before we are able to courageously face and heal from feelings that diminish a sense of self, it would make sense that we must first be aware of them. Western society is often portrayed as wanting immediate relief from emotional or physical pain (hence the prevalent use of prescriptions drugs to eliminate discomfort). When we fill up our lives with a constant bombardment of sensory stim- ulation, we cannot be fully aware of our feelings. In his book Thích Nhất Hạnh advises, "But when there is silence, all these things present themselves clearly." Silence is one tool that can help us bring more focus and awareness into the present moment. The power is in the pause.

While many people, particularly in the West, are in a constant state of perpetual doing, others, particularly in some Asian and Nordic countries, place great value on listening. Silence during a conversation is welcomed and accepted. There are various cultural interpretations, nuances, and complexities associated with silence. In her book *The Cultural Nature of Human Development*, Barbara Rogoff explains how a silent response is suitable, particularly when one does not know the answer to a question, has no infor- mation to share, or wants to show respect. Even though the notion of silence may be deeply rooted within many cultures worldwide, the benefits and practice of silence have not been universally acknowledged.

Pausing is a deliberate and personal decision we make to invite a moment of silence into our lives. There is genuine power when we pause because when we intentionally invite silence and stillness in, we are not allowing our thoughts, feelings, or judgments to consume the moment. Jon Kabat-Zinn, in his groundbreaking book *Full Catastrophe Living: Using the Wisdom of Your Body and Mind to Face Stress, Pain, and Illness*, explains the risk of not being fully and consciously present over time:

> Much of the time you may get away with being only partially conscious . . . but what you are missing is more important than you realize. If you are only partially conscious over a period of years, if you habitually run through your moments without being fully in them, you may miss some of the most precious experiences of your life, such as connecting with people you love or with sunsets or with the crisp morning air.

Kabat-Zinn further suggests that when we are on autopilot, we neglect, disregard, and mistreat ourselves and ultimately lose touch with our own bodies. If we are not in sync with our bodies, how can we possibly be attentive and responsive to the young children in our care?

Exploring Silence and Stillness during the Early Years

I have found it curious that being still is not a value we automatically teach to young children in the same way that we teach them about being honest or kind. Here are some other questions that I have wondered about when it comes to silence:

- When and how do young children learn to pause?

- How do we inadvertently discourage children from welcoming silence?

- Given that time is allocated for movement and motion in early childhood education, why are silence and stillness not given the same attention?

Almost all early childhood environments have a physical outdoor and/or indoor space for children to run, jump, climb, swing, slide, and spin—whether using their feet, a walker, or wheels. Typically, there is a designated time and space for young children to be active. However, the same time and space are not always reserved for children to be quiet, to rest, and to contemplate. Why do we not place the same value on stillness and silence as we do for physical activity?

In early childhood education and care, particularly in Western cultures, there is an unspoken acceptance around doing but not the same emphasis placed on being. Consider, for example, most programs serving infants and toddlers, and some serving three- to five-year-olds, have a required nap time. But children are generally in a sleeping state during nap time, so there is actually little to no time for just stillness or silence. Although some early childhood programs may have a scheduled quiet time, children are typically engaged in doing something, such as reading a book or playing a quiet game. Without embedded moments of stillness throughout the school day, both planned and spontaneous, children are not receiving the message that silence is important. Young learners are missing out on the actual experience of stillness, not to mention the numerous benefits that go along with it.

Young children will naturally seek out quiet and stillness. However, over time the heavy emphasis on doing over being can undermine the desire for quiet. The sound of silence fills up quickly with activity, noise, and busyness. Infants, toddlers, and young children eventually learn the unspoken message that stillness and silence are not important. But when stillness and silence are embedded into the daily classroom routine, children learn to value these peaceful opportunities.

Lilly Bhaskaran, the director and founder of Sattva Montessori in Bangalore, India, describes silent sitting at her urban school that serves two- to five-year-olds. She explains that this special time occurs after outside play and before lunch is prepared. One child, assigned the role of leader that day, rings a bell alerting all the children that it is time to return to the classroom. Once inside, there is quiet as the older children help the younger ones wash their hands and then head to the silent sitting room. An article titled "Meditation, Rangoli, and Eating on the Floor: Practices from an Urban Preschool in Bangalore, India," which Bhaskaran wrote with Jennifer Keys Adair, describes this silent sitting routine:

> Sometimes silent sitting is a personal quiet time for open-ended thinking. Other times, silent sitting is a visualization session. As music plays, the children listen silently as a teacher takes them through a happy narrated journey. Lilly explains, "We may role-play being a bird flying high up in the sky, observing the earth and all its activities, and enjoying the cool air. It could also be a narration about the smells and sounds of nature."

There are many creative ways to promote silence and stillness. There is a distinction, however, between *silence* and *silencing*.

Silence versus Silencing

When adults ask children to be quiet in a space that encourages silence out of respect, such as at a religious ceremony, that is not what we are talking about here. The silencing I am referring to prevents young children from expressing themselves when they want to or attempt to. This type of silencing can have lasting and detrimental effects. Young impressionable minds may soon discover that what they have to say is not important or that their individual voices are not worthy or respected. They may eventually learn to silence their voices altogether. Adults' constant messages of "Shhh," "Hush," and "Not now. Be quiet," as well as unspoken communication through a turned back, a stare, or by simply ignoring children can silence their attempts to express themselves. I was riding a city bus not too long ago when I noticed a girl of about five years old excitedly asking questions and verbally commenting on what she was seeing out the window. She eventually stopped talking after a few minutes—it looked to me as if she simply gave up when she did not receive any response from her grandmother, who was sitting right beside her. Of course, this might have been an isolated incident in this child's life, but I think about this young girl every so often and wonder if she knows that her voice is important and that what she has to say matters. When we are fully present in the moment, we can more readily notice whether our words or actions encourage or silence the voices of young children around us. Silencing as a way of controlling another can happen when a child's voice is repeatedly ignored, minimized, or disrespected.

Besides frequent reprimands for children to be quiet, there are other missed opportunities in early childhood classrooms that could be easily transformed into teaching opportunities. Consider that children are repeatedly told to pay attention or to calm down, but often we fail to teach them how. It is the same when we tell children to simply relax, but we do not teach them the important skills to do so or why a sense of quiet and calm is helpful. This reminds me of a compelling story Jon Kabat-Zinn shares in *Full Catastrophe Living* about a Vietnam veteran who had intense back issues resulting from an injury sustained when he stepped on an explosive device during the war. When this veteran's doctor told him to relax, he responded, "Doc, telling me to relax is about as useful as telling me to be a surgeon." Kabat-Zinn explains that this man knew he needed to relax and even wanted to, but telling him to relax was not at all what he needed. It was only after this man was taught how to meditate and to be present in the moment that he was able to learn how to relax.

How Pausing in Adulthood Affects Young Children

Young children can experience ease and relaxation when the adults around them are relaxed. Consider how the notion of busyness anchors our day-to-day lives, and imagine the toll this takes on our bodies and minds. In his highly esteemed book *Clean: The Revolutionary Program to Restore the Body's Natural Ability to Heal Itself*, Alejandro Junger explains how and why this busyness causes our attention to be in a constant state of staying on:

> Today there is a constant assault on our attention that keeps the mind switched on at all times. There is more information circulating than at any other time in history. . . we are available for communication at all times (and in all time zones.) Cell phones, Bluetooth headsets, emails, text messages, faxes—it has become almost taboo to be disconnected. On top of this we are so busy all the time, striving for great careers, great relationships, great children, great homes—the pressure to achieve has never been higher and has us living in a constant state of planning, working, trying.

All this energy going on in the brain keeps it from being available where it is needed in the body.

The continuous stress to be "always on" highjacks our attention and limits the stillness and silence in our lives. No wonder so many people report feeling scattered, unfocused, and distracted. If this is the experience adults have on a regular basis, what could this mean for the young children around us day after day?

Whether we realize or admit it, when our attention is divided, we simply fail to show up for children we care most about. But it is never too late to remember the power of pausing. I humbly recall once when Alyssa was about four years old, sitting in the back seat of the car and being unusually cranky. I remember asking myself, "What happened to Alyssa? Where did she go? Why is she being so disconnected?" And then it dawned on me—we had had a very busy morning running errands, and it was me who had metaphorically left and was not present. It was almost as if I was on autopilot racing around to get errands done—and she, by default, became the coautopilot.

As soon as I realized this, I immediately looked into her eyes with lovingkindness and care and made the connection with her that I had lost when I was not being fully present. This is not to say that this snapshot of me not being present was one of only a handful of times during Alyssa's childhood. On the contrary, my mindfulness practice was (and still is) unfolding. Rather, when I realized that it was my behavior and my busyness that were causing my daughter to feel irritable, I paused. I simply paused as a way to step back into the present moment. And then I made the decision to reconnect with her. The power is in the pause. The pause is like a portal to help guide us back to presence. And then the speed bumps we encounter in life do not seem so high or enduring.

Early childhood educator Corrine Harney offers an insightful reflection about slowing down. In our article "'It's Like Breathing In Blue Skies and Breathing Out Stormy Clouds': Mindfulness Practices in Early Childhood," Harney talks about wanting to introduce the young children in her class to the contemplative mindfulness practice that she herself enjoys. Harney discovered how slowing down had a positive effect on the young learners in her class:

> As I evaluated my teaching practice and my self-awareness increased, I began to recognize that my students could benefit from learning skills often associated with contemplative practices, such as yoga, breathing, and meditation. I realized that my students always seemed to focus better when the environment, and I, moved slower.

Although this quote is not directly about silence, it speaks to moving more slowly, and I found it compelling for several reasons. First, it speaks to Harney taking the time to explore her teaching practice. When we have a steady mindfulness practice and take time to pause, these kinds of insights about our own presence (or absence) are more accessible and available to us. Second, Harney recognized how mindfulness practices would also be beneficial to the young learners in her class (not just helpful in her own life). Finally, Harney's thoughtful inquiry led her to understand that it was her own behavior that influenced the classroom climate—and that when she moved slowly, the children had better attention. This reflection is particularly interesting to me because when we begin to understand how being present in our own lives has an effect on others (especially young children), we are more fully aware of the stillness around us and within us. When I recently reached out to Corrine for permission to share her story in this book, she offered these insights about what she has more recently learned about mindfulness, teaching, and young children:

What I've come to understand since that time is that there is a true mirroring effect in the classroom between teacher and young students that goes beyond obvious examples like children repeating mindfulness phrases. When I acknowledged the world around us, brought to attention to our breathing, or used guided imagery during group time, that sense of mindfulness was mirrored by students—and not just in those moments but throughout the day. This kind of mirroring also continued between students as they could recognize emotional cues in one another because they were becoming so aware of their own emotional states. It was really incredible and powerful.

Just as teachers can unintentionally create a stressful classroom culture where speed, noise, busyness, and distractions prevail, we can deliberately cocreate environments with children where silence, stillness, and mindfulness serve as natural anchors.

Whether at home or at school, adults can consciously choose to design environments where harmony, ease, and comfort are felt from the moment we enter the space. When educators and family members regularly engage in their own contemplative or mindfulness practice, it becomes easier for them to recognize when to press their own pause buttons. And when we are too distracted to recognize the need for a pause, children are not shy about letting us know! Donna Bogart, a grandmother raising her grandson Jared, relayed the following story that underscores how perceptive children can be when it comes to needing a pause:

When Jared was a preschooler, we began noticing that he was having trouble dealing with frustration. The simplest challenge or disappointment would send him into a full-blown temper tantrum. He would end up on the floor, crying, thrashing, and hitting himself. He had little to no ability to cope with small (or big) stressors, and instead he acted out. We sought ways to help Jared manage his strong emotions and develop better self-regulation.

One technique we found to be very helpful was to create a cozy corner in Jared's room. A cozy corner is a quiet and safe place you can go to when you need to calm down. The most helpful sensory calming item we included in Jared's cozy corner was the peace pillow, a perfectly sized, round pillow with a beautiful peace sign on each side. We introduced Jared to the pillow and modeled how it helps someone calm down when they squeeze it, release, and squeeze it again.

For the first few weeks, we guided Jared to his cozy corner and the peace pillow when we observed early signs of distress. Gradually, Jared began asking for his peace pillow when he noticed he was getting frustrated or angry. We were amazed! And it didn't stop there. One day I was feeling particularly stressed and anxious. Frustration was mounting! Even though he was only four years old, Jared sensed I was having difficulty. He ran upstairs and got his peace pillow. "Here, Grandma. I think you need to squeeze my peace pillow really hard!" Out of the mouth of babes!

I so greatly appreciated Jared's wisdom for how he made such an intelligent connection in the moment about his grandmother's need for silence, stillness, and calm. This preschooler was starting to learn how to manage his own stress—in just a few weeks—when he observed that he was feeling upset. Consider all that Jared learned:

- To be self-aware of his anger or frustration, particularly when he was just beginning to feel upset

- To be aware of and notice his frustration or anxiety, as opposed to the typical full-blown outbursts he was used to

- To initiate a strategy to deal with his strong emotions

- To use the peace cushion and his cozy corner to find calm and stillness

The key here is that a loving adult did not resort to harsh punishment or consequences when Jared was having tantrums; rather, she understood that he was experiencing a high degree of stress and needed strategies to help him deal with his frustration and anxiety to feel safe again. All children and adults strive to feel safe. By taking moments to pause, especially when emotions feel intense, we can teach young learners the gifts of stillness and silence. And when we forget, we can always count on children to show us the way. There is power in the pause.

Silence and Stillness as Pedagogy in Early Childhood Education and Care

Jeromi was a precocious four-year-old when her mother, Yajaira, recounted this story to me. At school one day Jeromi did not get to the bathroom in time. She immediately called out, "I had an accident. Quick—someone get me my change of clothes!" Then Jeromi paused for a second before saying, "Wait—God gave me two hands. I can get my own clothes!" And she did.

A pause can help us to stop what we are doing or saying and take a moment to reflect, as Jeromi did. Inviting stillness and silence into our lives is also a way to allow creativity to blossom, contemplation to intensify, and concentration to deepen. And pausing for no reason at all is actually what being present in the moment is all about.

Welcoming silence and stillness into our daily lives is an unfolding, lifelong journey. By engaging in this mindfulness practice, we can more easily quiet our minds and stay present. In his book *The Courage to Teach: Exploring the Inner Landscape of a Teacher's Life*, Parker Palmer reminds us, "Words are not the sole medium of exchange in teaching and learning—we educate with silence as well." When we model for young children how to welcome stillness or silence into their lives, they learn valuable, practical tools that they can apply for the rest of their lives.

Given that we designate spaces and times for young children to be active in early childhood education, let us also intentionally cultivate spaces for stillness, calm, and quiet.

This first step is to create a classroom culture where stillness and silence are perceived as significant and necessary parts in each day. Instead of just adding a couple of mindfulness moments throughout the week, infuse the importance of pausing and stillness into the routines, expectations, and philosophy of home, classroom, and school. When we think of and embed silence and stillness as pedagogy, we transform our teaching. This happens by our beliefs, thoughts, words, and deeds. In essence, when we pause, children will too.

Spaces that Invite Stillness, Silence, or Solitude

Creating a quiet, safe space for stillness and silence starts with a simple choice. A space for pausing can happen at anytime and anywhere when we take the time to make it so. Amy Saltzman, a physician and author of the celebrated mindfulness program for children, *A Still Quiet Place*, recalls:

> . . . when my son, Jason, was almost three, he asked if he could meditate (practice mindfulness) with me. At the time, my daughter, Nicole, was six months old, and we were all adjusting to life with a new baby. My sense is that Jason knew he would have my full and calm attention when we practiced together. His sweet request prompted me to begin sharing mindfulness with him.

I appreciate how young children will often seek fulfillment of their need for us to be fully present with them. When we sit in quiet contemplation with our very little ones, everyone benefits. Like Amy and Jason, I used to do the same thing with Alyssa when she was a toddler—and it was all her idea. One day Alyssa literally plopped herself in my lap as I was sitting quietly meditating, and that evolved into irreplaceable, magical moments for us both. We would sit together for a few precious minutes like this in the early morning. No doubt she could feel my breath as I peacefully inhaled and exhaled, and I could feel hers. Creating a space for stillness and silence can happen for children of any age, including infants. It is never too early to begin, which is why many expectant parents enjoy making the time and space together to regularly engage in quiet contemplation with their unborn child.

In addition to finding spaces for stillness or silence within, teachers can easily establish physical spaces, as Cathleen Haskins, a Montessori early childhood teacher, did in her small Wisconsin town. In her 2011 article "The Gift of Silence," Haskins shares how she created a simple, quiet place just outside her classroom door that included a homemade rock garden and one healthy plant. She describes how this simple, peaceful space made a world of difference for one child, James, who is described as a "tense, hesitant, distrusting child":

> [James] was clearly drawn to it; he used it often, along with the other children. I saw how raking the paths around the pebbles in the rock garden calmed him. Sometimes he just sat and looked out the window. At the end of the year he gave me a hand-drawn picture of himself in the classroom, and across the top he had written, "I love this class. I wish I could be in it next year." From then on, I always found a way to incorporate a quiet/peace area in my classroom.

Establishing welcoming spaces where children can explore stillness and solitude could not be easier or more affordable. Working in partnership with young children is the key to planning, designing, constructing, and maintaining these spaces. I have observed how a cozy secondhand couch, soft pillows in a peaceful corner of the room, or a colorful sheet draped like an inviting canopy or tent can encourage children to seek stillness when they want some quiet time. These kinds of spaces can be especially beneficial for young children who feel overstimulated by sensory information or who require extra time to follow classroom routines. Young children do not always have the words to tell an adult that they need a break or would like some alone time, but just observing their behavior will tell an observant adult exactly what a child needs to feel safe and supported.

Another idea young children (and adults) can enjoy is having a silence table at home or at school. Put up a big sign reading "Silence Table," and read it to the children to let them know the space is reserved for quiet. Some ideas for this quiet space include magnifying glasses and interesting objects for investigations, small blocks or other manipulatives for quiet constructions, or open-ended art supplies for creative expression. There are countless ways to ensure stillness and silence maintain a prominent place in early childhood education and care. We need to ensure that silence is securely and continuously embedded into the lives of young children. In the next sections, we will explore some innovative and simple ideas to use within and outside silent spaces.

The Basics of Breathing

It is the first thing we do when we come into this world and the last thing we do when we leave. Taking a breath is perhaps the single most important function of our bodies, yet most people tend to take this precious gift for granted. How does breathing affect us in our day-to-day lives? Sat Bir Singh Khalsa, an assistant professor at Harvard Medical School and editor-in-chief of the *International Journal of Yoga Theory*, answered this question at a conference on yoga and science. Khalsa described how our breath regulation is directly connected to emotional regulation and stress reduction. He explained that how we breathe affects our cognitive and emotional regulation, an observation that is firmly grounded in research. If how we breathe directly influences our internal states such as stress, cognitive functioning, and emotional well-being, then it follows that we should acknowledge and practice intentional breathing in early childhood education and care.

Thích Nhất Hạnh offers one simple solution to how we can pay more respect to and have a greater awareness of our breathing. In his book *Peace Is Every Step: The Path of Mindfulness in Everyday Life*, Thích Nhất Hạnh reminds us how we have a distinct room for almost everything in our homes—sleeping, bathing, eating, entertaining—yet what we really need is a small room for breathing. He describes this little room as a special, cherished place where both adults and children can practice "just breathing and smiling at least in difficult moments." This breathing room, Thích Nhất Hạnh suggests, can be a small, simple space in our homes that can might include a small bell with a beautiful chime, a few seats or cushions, and perhaps lovely living flowers to reflect in us our own authentic nature. Having a separate space is a simple yet powerful way to invite stillness and silence into our everyday lives. If limited space is an issue, then select a small, private place, such as a corner of the room, where you can create a distinctive, beautiful breathing space. This presents a perfect opportunity to cocreate a very special place with young children.

Although having a designated breathing space is excellent for cultivating mindfulness, it is also relatively easy and beneficial to become aware of breathing anytime and anywhere. There are countless ways to tune into our breath and to guide children to do the same. For example, we can encourage young children to notice how their breathing changes. Point out to them, for example, how their breathing is faster and even sounds different when they are moving actively outside. And point out that their breathing is slower when they are inside quietly reading a book.

In addition to focusing on when and where mindful breathing can occur, Eddie Stern describes on his website, https://eddiestern.com/the-breathing-app, why breathing in a particular way helps to bring a sense of calm and stillness, especially living today in our technologically driven societies. He says that in our fast-paced, information-heavy world, we often lean toward acceleration. Spending just a few minutes consciously breathing sends signals of balance to our brain, telling us that we are okay and bringing us out from the part of our brains that makes us feel overwhelmed, into a state of calm. With resonant breathing, we learn how to apply our "brakes" at will, rather than being sidelined by anxiety, distractedness, or excess stress.

Resonant breathing, Stern describes, offers a natural yet powerful way to stay present in the moment:

> *Resonance*, the scientific name that describes what happens when our heart rate, heart rate variability, blood pressure, and brainwave function come into a coherent frequency occurs spontaneously when we breathe at a rate of six breaths per minute (instead of our usual fifteen to eighteen) and is the rate of breathing that Buddhist monks and yogis naturally enter into while meditating.

By simply slowing down our breathing to a rate of six breaths each minute, we can quiet the mind and naturally support the important work our bodies perform. Resonant breathing is particularly helpful for the autonomic nervous system, which controls many automatic functions of our bodies, such as heart rate, digestion, and respiration. In his highly esteemed book, *One Simple Thing: A New Look at the Science of Yoga and How It Can Transform Your Life*, Stern notes that the solid research base on resonant breathing dating back to the early 1960s shows improvements in stress, resiliency, pulmonary function, heart-rate variability, among many other benefits. Resonant breathing is a simple tool anyone can use anywhere, because it is natural for our bodies, easy to access, and does not require a huge time commitment. In addition, resonant breathing is highly effective and produces immediate results. According to Stern, "Resonant breathing is like a stress reset button."

As a longtime student of Eddie's, I have practiced this type of breathing for years, so I was delighted when he created a simple tool that can be used regardless of age, language, country, or experience. In collaboration with internationally known experts such as Deepak Chopra and others, he developed the The Breathing App, which can be downloaded at no cost.

Since its creation a few years ago, I have used this app with my graduate students in early childhood inclusive-education courses with great success. One of my students, Dana, shared with me her experience when she turned to the app to bring her a sense of calm—not only in her classroom but also in the delivery room! She was comforted with the help of the breathing app (and the aroma of some lavender essential oil), contributing to what she described as a fairly easy delivery. She also relayed to me how she relied on The Breathing App throughout the transition of bringing her newborn daughter home.

Dana's story is a great reminder that we can turn to mindfulness in moments of difficulty, tension, or pain. Resonant breathing is not a tool to use only for challenging moments; it is also an important lifestyle choice. Dana shared with me recently that she continues her mindfulness practice, including resonant breathing. Her practice has been a source of comfort and peace now that she has returned to teaching after a brief maternity leave. By practicing mindfulness regularly, Dana has found a sense of calm in balancing her teaching career with a new baby and all the responsibilities that go along with taking care of a family.

The Sounds of Solitude

It is not surprising how the idea of silence or being alone can be terrifying for many people. That is precisely what a 2017 article by Neel Burton published in *Psychology Today* revealed: "According to a recent study, many people prefer to give themselves a mild electric shock than to sit in a room alone with their own thoughts." In his book, *Silence: The Power of Quiet in a World Full of Noise*, Thích Nhất Hạnh notes how humans maintain a constant state of busyness in an ironic attempt to find connection. Perhaps, people fear being alone and, therefore, avoid making a connection with themselves. On the other hand, others find spending time in solitude as a way to experience deep contemplation and reflection, rest and renewal, and even amusement and fun. The connection we have to ourselves can be the most exhilarating, complicated, and joy-filled one we encounter in our lifetimes.

People who do choose to spend time alone are often misunderstood or falsely labeled as lonely. On the contrary, people are not necessarily lonely simply because they are alone. In early childhood education and care, this confusion is reflected in the research base. Specifically, there is a dearth of research on solitude and young children, and the studies on being alone that do exist tend to examine issues related to social isolation, shyness, anxiety, exclusion, or avoidance. I wonder about changing the negative narrative about intentional solitude, particularly in childhood, so it is understood not only as important but also as a necessary part of everyday living. Yes, there are young children who are excluded, ostracized, stigmatized, and misunderstood by their peers, teachers, and a larger institutional school system. This type of being alone, however, is different from intentional solitude.

It is difficult to determine at what point adults should intervene when noticing a child alone, but I suggest using common sense. If a child is alone most of the time with little to no interest in exchanges with peers, this might raise a red flag. If a child prefers to play alone at times and also engages with peers at other times, that would seem to be a healthy balance. Instead of pushing a child to engage in social interactions, friendships, or play, step back and take a closer look at the underlying reasons children may be alone.

By closely observing classroom or home dynamics, adults can critically reflect on possible reasons why and how a child is frequently alone. In addition, promoting a deliberate sense of belonging as well as a discourse of dignity across settings—classroom, home, community—can shift the climate so that isolation and/or exclusion are no longer acceptable.

Take the time to listen carefully and observe children's behavior to learn how they prefer to engage with the others and the world. This is particularly useful with young children who appear shy or who struggle with peers, especially since they may choose solitude as a way to feel safe and protected. In his candid book *The Reason I Jump*, a wise and perceptive thirteen-year-old boy named Naoki Higashida answers the question, "Do people with autism, like himself, prefer to be alone?" Here is what Higashida has to say:

> "Ah, don't worry about him—he'd rather be on his own." How many times have you heard this? I can't believe that anyone born as a human being really wants to be left all on their own, not really. No, for people with autism, what we're anxious about is that we're causing trouble to the rest of you or even getting on your nerves. This is why we often end up being left on our own. The truth is, we'd love to be with other people. But because things never, ever go right, we end up getting used to being alone...

Naoki shares how painful it is when people inaccurately presume that he prefers or chooses to be alone; it makes him feel "desperately lonely." All human beings, especially children, need the connection of other human beings. For Naoki Hagashida and countless others, there is a high risk of the resignation to being alone. It is up to teachers, therefore, to be highly observant and responsive to the social dynamics in a classroom community, particularly if there are signs of exclusion or isolation. There is a difference between forced solitude and intentional solitude.

There are many hidden treasures when we welcome stillness and solitude into the present moment. There is power is pausing, even briefly. In his book *The Book of Awakening*, distinguished poet and author Mark Nepo describes the precious gifts found in solitude:

> Often, in our solitude, we can discover the miracles of life, if we take the time and risk to be alone until the glow of life presents itself. This is the reward of all meditation. It's like taking the path of our aloneness deep enough through the woods so we can reach that unspoiled clearing.

The Simplicity of Silent Walking

We generally think about sitting silently to invite a sense of stillness inside. But silent walking or a walking meditation is another very simple yet effective tool for cultivating stillness. I observed silent walking with young children when my colleague Christer Ohlin took me on tours of preschools in Sweden. In one of the schools, Trollungarna at Trolleholm, very young children, one to five years of age, spend most if not the whole day outside. Trollungarna is based on nature education, also known as forest schools, a concept that will be further examined in chapter 8.

One of the highlights for me at Trollungarna was a silent walk. Children formed a line in single file behind the preschool director, Janne Ollson, and we walked quietly and slowly through the woods. At certain points, Janne would gently tap the child at the front of the line, which prompted the child to immediately and quietly sit down on the ground at that very spot in the woods. The group would continue walking in silence, then the director would tap another child. Eventually, all the children (and the adults) were sitting on the ground in the woods, far enough away from each other to have some privacy but close enough to see the others. There were no words spoken or directions given, and none seemed necessary. We simply sat silently in the woods. There was no talking or moving—it was very quiet, still, and peaceful.

Although I lost track of time, after approximately ten minutes, Janne walked by where each child or adult was sitting, and without speaking or gesturing, he looked at each child and the child immediately got up and went to the end of the line as it passed by. After all the children had joined the line, we walked to a clearing and sat on beautiful handcrafted wooden benches (that children had designed and built) to discuss our sitting experiences. Given their animated expressions, wide smiles, and lively discussion, it was clear that the children immensely enjoyed this silent walking.

Silent walking can deepen our connection with nature and promote inner peace and a sense of calm. Listening walks, in particular, are beneficial any time of day and any time of year with children at any age. In addition to a listening walk, there are other ways to walk in silence by using other senses. In the picture book *The Listening Walk*, author Paul Showers explains to young children how easy and delightful this quiet walk can be. Embark with an individual child, small group, or the whole school community on many various kinds of silent walking:

- A nose or a smelling walk, noticing the different scents in the air

- A feeling walk to tune in to feelings and moods as well to physical bodies, noticing a cool breeze against the skin, little beads of sweat forming in sticky and hot weather, and so on

- A breathing walk to simply notice the gentleness of inhales and exhales

- A nothing to do except walk walk

Walking in silence can be a beautiful and simple way to quiet the mind. Sitting in silence is another way to welcome stillness, silence, and solitude.

Peace Cushions: Another Pathway to Silence, Stillness, and Solitude

At age five, my daughter Alyssa was enamored by a beautiful meditation cushion I received as a birthday gift from a dear friend. I told her that it was very special and named it my peace cushion. Then I explained that she can use it, like I do, anytime she feels happy, sad, mad, or just wants to feel more peaceful. A few weeks later Alyssa was visibly upset, crying uncontrollably about something. Suddenly, it got very quiet in the house. When I went to see where she had run off to, I found her lying facedown on the peace cushion.

That was a profound awakening for me on many levels. First, I discovered how my young daughter not only remembered that the peace cushion was a safe space and where it was stored but also took the initiative to retrieve and use it. I was intrigued with how Alyssa found great comfort in the peace cushion and realized it can be a terrific tool for other young children who are learning to manage their emotions.

Peace cushions can be used at home, at school, and anywhere in between. The best part is that any pillow will do, so there is no need to purchase anything. I have suggested using an old, clean pillowcase that a young child can decorate and stuff with a pillow, old clothing, fabric, newspaper, or anything that is malleable, environmentally sustainable, and safe. Peace blankets or carpet remnants, which can be playfully called magic peace carpets, are other affordable options for designing with children and teaching them how to create a private and personalized peaceful space.

There are many ways to introduce young children to the idea of a peace cushion. Here is my original peace cushion poem:

> When I feel mad or all alone
>
> When I don't want to play or talk on the phone
>
> I can sit on my peace [cushion] and breathe deeply in.
>
> I know how to feel peace and this is how I begin.
>
> I close my eyes and sit very still.
>
> I breathe in and out—I do this until
>
> I start to be quiet and feel calm inside.
>
> I know I can feel peace—I am so glad I tried!

The benefits of a peace cushion are endless, given that young children can independently use them anytime they choose, with minimal to no adult supervision or support. The peace cushion can be stored and used in a designated private and safe space where children can come when they want to find quiet, stillness, or solitude, or for any reason at all.

Many adults over the years have expressed interest in peace cushions as an alternative to time-out. I have never endorsed time-outs because I believe they reinforce shame, isolation, humiliation, and exclusion. They do not teach children meaningful or positive lessons, promote independence and agency, or enhance self-esteem. Peace cushions, on the contrary, teach children how to be present in the moment and to find comfort and safety within.

Concluding Thoughts

In this chapter, we took an in-depth look at pausing and why it is an important and useful tool for quieting the mind and maintaining presence in the moment. We also explored why stillness, silence, and solitude are beneficial and how inviting silence into everyday living is not simply a tool to use with young children when feeling anxious or upset but a necessary part of a classroom culture. In the last part of the chapter, we identified creative and simple ways of embedding silence and stillness into early childhood teaching practice. By viewing silence and stillness as pedagogy in early childhood education, we can find countless ways to teach and learn with young children how, when, and why there is power in the pause.

In the next chapter, we investigate the construction and perception of time through different lenses, and how our understanding of time affects classroom routines and practices as well our interactions with young children.

A Menu of Options for Teaching Inclusively, Mindfully, and Equitably

 Children's Corner

Goennel, Heidi. 1989. *Sometimes I Like to Be Alone*. New York: Little Brown and Co.

Goldsaito, Katrina. 2016. *The Sound of Silence*. New York: Hachette.

Portis, Antoinette. 2017. *Now*. New York: Roaring Book Press.

Showers, Paul. 1991. *The Listening Walk*. New ed. New York: HarperCollins.

Sosin, Deborah. 2015. *Charlotte and the Quiet Place*. Berkeley, CA: Plum Blossom.

 **Caregivers' Corner**

In his *New York Times* best seller, *The Book of Awakening*, Mark Nepo shares this simple yet powerful walking meditation that can be done anywhere and anytime:

- This is a walking meditation. Take fifteen minutes during your day, and silently walk wherever you are—in the city, in the country, in the parking lot, down the long hall to the one window of light.

- Breathe evenly as you step, feeling your breath in your feet.

- Feel the air that others unknown to you have already breathed.

- Stop in a patch of light, no matter how small. Close your eyes, feel the light on your face, and say to yourself, "This is my home."

 Take It to the Classroom

Breathing Activities

Susan Lederer, a professor of communication sciences and disorders at Adelphi University in New York, recommends eight breathing activities for children to help foster focus and calm. These exercises use props, movement, and imagination to keep children engaged. Try them first on yourself, and then share them with children.

- **Belly breathing:** Begin with hands on bellies. Instruct the children to slowly breathe in through the nose for a count of five (1, 2, 3, 4, 5) and out through the nose to a count of five (1, 2, 3, 4, 5). After a few rounds, have the children close their eyes. Guide them to notice how the belly fills with the fresh oxygen we need to grow and empties the carbon dioxide that trees need to grow.

- **Take five with a Hoberman's sphere:** Use this prop (available online or in toy stores) as a breathing ball to help children visualize and regulate their breathing. As you expand the breathing ball, have children inhale to the count of five (1, 2, 3, 4, 5); as you contract the ball, have them exhale to the count of five (5, 4, 3, 2, 1).

- **Triangle breath:** Teach children how to draw a large triangle on a sheet of paper. Trace each side with a finger, inhaling for a count of five, holding for five, and exhaling for five. You can shorten the counts for younger children, but keep them equal on all sides of the triangle.

- **Sun breath:** Begin in a seated or standing position, palms together and touching the heart. On the inhale, sweep the arms out and up until palms touch overhead. Have children look up at the hands and say, "Thank you, sun." On the exhale, reverse the path of the arms and return palms together, touching the heart.

- **Bumblebee breath:** Have the children press their forefingers against the tragus in their ears (the bump outside the ear canal) to close it off (no fingers in the ear!). Instruct them to inhale slowly and on the exhale, buzz quietly like a bumblebee.

- **Lion breath:** Begin with heads down. On the inhale, instruct children to raise their heads. Once they are looking forward, instruct them to open their eyes and mouths wide, stick out their tongues, and exhale forcefully through their mouths.

- **Octopus breath:** Encourage children to make an octopus, using a paper plate for the head and crepe-paper ribbons for the tentacles. They can decorate their octopi any way they like. Ask them to inhale through the nose and exhale slowly through the mouth as they hold their octopus, making the tentacles move so the octopus can swim.

- **I am feeling calm:** Practice first with eyes open, then offer the opportunity to close them. Instruct children to inhale, then on the exhale say, "I," while touching forefinger to thumb. As they inhale again then exhale, say, "Am," while touching middle finger to thumb. Inhale again and, as they exhale, say, "Feeling," while touching the ring finger to thumb. Inhale again and, as they exhale, say, "Calm" while touching the pinky to thumb. Children can choose their own four-word phrases.

A Silence Place

In her article "The Gift of Silence," Montessori teacher Cathleen Haskins shares how she creates a welcoming, calm, and beautiful Silence Place in her classroom. She advises: "Making space for a Silence Place in the classroom can be as simple as a small table in a corner, a comfortable chair near a low window, or a cushion on a rug in an out-of-the-way area. . . Students should have free access to this place with a reasonable time frame agreed upon for a visit. An exact amount of time need not be stipulated, but sometimes it is helpful to give students a general idea of how much time they may spend in the space. Consider a small clock for older children or a sand timer for younger children." She offers ideas for peaceful contemplation in your classroom Silence Place, such as a Zen rock garden, Japanese brush painting, a mandala peace ring, a pendulum, or a sand timer.

CHAPTER 5

The Gift of Time: Unwrapping Presence in Early Childhood

> **"We turn not older with years, but newer every day."**
> —Emily Dickinson, poet

"Mommy, I don't like when we go speedy." My daughter was two years old when she shared this with me as I took her hand and told her we needed to go speedy across a busy parking lot. Her words have stayed with me ever since. Twenty years later, I continue to ponder how the concept of time is dramatically different for adults and young children. In the spirit of full transparency, I am deeply humbled to admit that I unknowingly taught Alyssa certain beliefs about time that added unnecessary stress to her life.

As adults, our own perception of time informs how we live and how we teach. For young children, an understanding about time will likely be shaped by the adults and environments that surround them. When a child's life is regulated by a steady stream of tension around time—"We have to hurry or we'll be late" or "It's not time to play"—children may learn to navigate the world through a lens of worry and pressure. On the other hand, as children discover how time plays an indispensable role in maintaining a sense of order, predictability, and harmony, they are likely to develop a sense of safety and trust.

Despite being recognized as a universally accepted concept around the world, time remains abstract and represents various meanings depending on the context in which it is viewed. The quote at the beginning of this chapter by Emily Dickinson is a beautiful reminder that the meaning of time lies in how we perceive it, and that with each passing day, we can always start fresh and renewed. In this chapter, we will unpack the concepts of time and being present and how these ideas influence early education and care. Let's start by reflecting upon cultural, institutional, societal, and personal beliefs about time and how they influence decisions we make inside and outside the classroom.

Differing Concepts of Time

The notion of time is culturally constructed depending on where and how time is perceived. With the following proverb, Lesley Rameka of the University of Waikato in New Zealand explains a Māori understanding of time in her article in *Contemporary Issues in Early Childhood*:

> Kia *whakatōmuri te haere whakamua*. "I walk backwards into the future with my eyes fixed on my past." This *whakataukī* or proverb speaks to Māori perspectives of time, in which the past, the present, and the future are viewed as intertwined and life is seen as a continuous cosmic process.

Through a Māori lens, time can be understood as a continuation where no limitations or boundaries exist. Rameka further explains, "This conceptualisation of time does not leave the past behind; rather one carries one's past into the future." As educators, our familiar cultural understandings about time will influence our belief systems and play a strong role in determining how we make sense of time in our personal lives and in the classroom.

Similarly, institutional expectations can shape our perception of time. Some educators experience a sense of ease, wonder, and peacefulness as they move through a school day; whereas, others may feel an urgency to "get through" the day. If teachers must adhere to a district's rigid prescribed curriculum or a school's predetermined classroom schedule, additional pressure can mount, particularly when instruction must be completed within a certain time frame. Additional tensions may come from an administration that requires regular standardized assessments, from family members who continually ask, "When will my child learn to read?" and from supervisors who ask for excessive documentation on particular outcomes. These and other kinds of external tensions can contribute to early childhood teachers' sense of not having adequate time during the school day.

The issue of rushing during the school day presents a challenge for educators and young learners. Children are generally aware of institutional expectations about time and may feel the need to hurry as adults do. In her article published in the *Journal of Early Childhood Research*, Marianne Knaus writes about seven-year-old Kristy, who talks about needing to be on time for school and her younger sister, Mia, age four, for whom lateness is not an issue:

> Today I slept in and was late for school . . . I felt really rushed, but I felt excited to go to school . . . she [referring to Mia] doesn't have to hurry, not much. It doesn't matter if she is late or not. But for me it does matter. I have to go to places like school. I need a note if I am away from school.

Kristy's comments demonstrate her sense of responsibility about being on time but also reveal an understanding that she must hurry to comply with school expectations while her younger sister is not held to the same standard.

Given the growing institutional demands facing many early childhood practitioners in the West, it is no surprise that many teachers express difficulty in finding time for mindfulness practices during the school day. In a 2015 article in *Young Exceptional Children* about mindfulness in early childhood education that I coauthored, one teacher commented, "There is so much to get done in classrooms that it is difficult to fit in yoga or meditation." This teacher echoes a familiar sentiment that I hear frequently. Despite a curiosity or an interest in infusing mindfulness practices, many teachers feel challenged to do so given time constraints at school. This may be one reason many teachers are finding that a personal mindfulness practice can produce unexpected benefits and positive outcomes in their teaching practice. As discussed in previous chapters, mindfulness practices are not to be crammed in between activities but rather viewed as valued parts of the classroom and school culture. Ultimately, the notion of being present as a societal value is naturally rooted in all aspects of life, including early childhood education and care.

David Elkind warns in his landmark book *The Hurried Child* that tremendous stress and expectations are being placed on young children to do more. Nearly four decades after his book was published, not much has changed in the lives of young children except they may be feeling more hurried than ever. Although children today may be experiencing a constant state of hurrying, Andrew Gibbons challenges us to consider what we mean when we refer to a "rapidly changing world." In his 2016 article, Gibbons suggests that, from an early childhood lens, when we view time as a modern issue that affects our society today, we mistakenly assume that time has not been an issue during other periods throughout history. Gibbons proposes that early childhood educators could start "doing something differently with time," which may include challenging our own notions of time, questioning dominant discourses related to time, and considering new ways of thinking about time in education. Toward this end, we might start reframing our personal beliefs about what we think we know about time.

Young children do not perceive time in the way adults do. Teachers and families can expose young children to time concepts, even though they would not expect mastery of these concepts until children are older. During her infant and toddler years, words such as *now*, *soon*, *later*, and "We are going to leave in one minute" were part of the naturally occurring conversations I had with my daughter, Alyssa. Even though I did not expect that she would fully grasp these concepts at such an early age, these and other concepts about time conveyed a general sense about time, trust, and order in the world.

Yale University researcher Louise Bates Ames was one of the first psychologists to study the development of time concepts in young children. In 1946 she explained in an article in *The Journal of Genetic Psychology* how time may be perceived in very young children: "The 18-month-old child lives in the immediate present and has little if any sense of the past and future. He cannot wait. No time words are used by him, but he responds to the word now . . . there is a slight sense of timing as he may roll a ball and wait for it to stop before he pursues it." She also examined how young children use time-related words as a stand-in for their conceptualization of time. In both observed conversations and test scenarios, she investigated children's divisions of time, such as time period of day, clock time, days of the week, month, year, personal age, past/present/future, duration, and succession. She discovered the following:

- Half of four-year-olds can correctly verbalize time-of-day concepts, such as *morning* versus *afternoon*.

- Half of five-year-olds can correctly report the day of the week.

- Half of seven-year-olds can correctly report the month and season as well as the number of minutes in one hour.

- Eight-year-olds can correctly report the year and the day of the month and can give a working definition of *time*.

Ames's findings support a theory that children develop time concepts in stages. In her 2013 article, "Time Perception in Children: A Neurodevelopmental Approach," researcher Sylvie Droit-Volet reports that infants have a basic sense of time and that a sensitivity to time increases throughout childhood. She writes, "Children appear to be more variable in their timing than adults," suggesting that children are not concerned with time in the way adults are and that young children generally tend to live in the present moment.

In 2009, Marianne Knaus explored perceptions of time through a lens of childhood. In her article, "Childhood Today Explored through Notions of Being and Time," she describes that when it comes to the future, young children are not as preoccupied as adults are because they are living in the here and now. Their perceptions of time are not the same as adults' sense of time. She explains, "How a child views of [sic] time is different to that of an adult. Being absorbed in the now or present moment, children enter a state of being, that of the inner world, an intermediate area of total involvement and satisfaction." She warns that a child's use of time can be restricted and controlled through the power relations that are embedded in our culture. Particularly in Western society, children are expected to achieve and are, consequently, overscheduled and required to have supervised experiences that limit their opportunities to explore and play freely. She suggests, instead, that we consider time from a child's point of view and respond respectfully.

Given the many demands and expectations families, caregivers, and teachers face on a daily basis, it can be challenging for some adults to fully tune in and be responsive to a child's sense of time. Like adults, institutions that hold authority in a child's life can restrict and regulate how young children spend their time. When we position children in a very limited way and think of them only as future adults, we place stress upon these young learners to accomplish and achieve more. This can impede unplanned play and other valuable childhood experiences. Therefore, we must take the time to perceive time through a child's lens. By gaining an understanding about young learners' use and perception of time from their own perspective, adults can learn indispensable information about what it means to be present. What does this mean for the early childhood practitioner?

It's Always Time to Dance in the Rain

There will always be puddles to splash in and rain to dance in throughout the early years (and hopefully beyond). Young children do not need to learn how to dance in the rain; it comes naturally to them. Given that children's sense of time is generally focused in the present moment, what are the implications for the early childhood classroom? Sandy Farquhar, in her 2016 article "Time in Early Childhood: Creative Possibilities with Different Conceptions of Time," suggests, "To speak of childhood and curriculum in light of multiple and varied understandings of time is to invite more inclusive formulations of education than that which currently prevails." If we consider how young children's sense of time differs from that of adults, we might invite different ways of being in the classroom. For example, daily routines tend to focus on adults' needs to follow a predetermined schedule or expectations.

> "Life isn't about waiting for the storm to pass. It's about learning to dance in the rain."
>
> —Vivian Greene, author and motivational speaker

A few years ago, when I spent five weeks of my sabbatical in Australia to study early childhood policies and practices, I became aware of significant differences related to time and space. In a 2017 article in *Global Education Review*, I wrote about these observations. Here is one example that demonstrates the teacher's response when one child voiced that he did not want to follow the class outside during their morning routine:

> I noticed that in classrooms, time and space were not constrained in Australia, as they often can be in the West, so children had unlimited opportunities to investigate, create, discover, and to simply be in the present moment. In one children's center, the children were getting on their shoes, sun block, and sun hats to go outside, and one child spoke up.
>
> CHILD: I don't want to go outside.
>
> TEACHER: That's fine. The other children want to go, so we can leave the door open in the other room and you can stay with them. And I can keep this [outside] door open to still see you.

This brief scenario underscores, among other things, a respect for the child's sense of time because the adults did not insist that he join the class even though it was part of their daily morning routine. An understanding of time and space in early childhood educational environments will generally be constructed differently, depending on contextual influences such as social, cultural, or historical perspectives. Specific school-based philosophies and policies may or may not reflect the broader cultural values within the community. As early childhood educators and families start to consider notions of time from young children's perspectives, keep in mind societal or cultural influences about time. Here are some ideas to start you thinking about time during the early years from multiple, diverse perspectives:

- Examine a day in the life of a child from the child's point of view. Pay very close attention to how one specific child uses time, including what factors limit or challenge his time. Consider also doing this exercise from the perspective of the whole classroom community. Where do children seem to be the most engaged? least engaged?

- Review the daily schedule, as well as the monthly and yearly routines, to identify when imbalances of power in the classroom might exist. Consider how to create a more equitable balance of power with children about perceptions and uses of time.

- Trust and respect a child's sense of time to determine when to start an experience, project, or investigation and when and how to decide it is completed.

- Frequently make shared decisions about time with young children across different configurations—individually, in small groups, and with the whole class, so children have a meaningful voice in deciding the sequence or flow of activities during the day or the need for extended time for favored activities.

- Take careful notice across each week of how young children prefer to spend their time. For example, do they seem to like science investigations, imaginative play, or music? Adjust routines, spaces, and expectations so what children deem as important, engaging, or fun is respected.

- Engage with children in investigations about time that emerge from their questions and interests. Some ideas to ignite a spark about time might include documenting the stages of a seed growing, exploring what the seasons tell us about time, or observing the sun and moon and their relationship to time. At the end of this chapter, in the Take It to the Classroom section, I offer a sequence on sun salutations that can be easily integrated into a class inquiry or investigation about time or used as a daily mindfulness practice.

In many traditional early childhood classrooms, the daily practices, routines, and expectations determine where, when, and how long children should be in a particular space and what is expected of them in these spaces. Karen Watson, author of *Inside the "Inclusive" Classroom: The Power of the "Normal,"* provides an excellent and compelling look at how timetables in the classroom dictate to young children what they need to be doing and where they should be doing it, thus teaching them to defer a sense of enjoyment or satisfaction because they cannot do what they want. Although many might consider this skill is important for children to learn during the early years, Watson suggested that these timetables establish a sense of what is normal, meaning *acceptable*, in the classroom. She explains how young children's bodies are not all regulated in the same way or at the same time: some need to use the bathroom, others feel hungry, some want more time for movement, and so on. Watson's research findings reveal that young children who are not labeled with a disability or diagnosis are often taught that there is a "right" time to things. They learn the "right" time to play, to pack away, to hear a story, to listen, to wash hands, to use the toilet, to eat, and so on. Children who deviate from these timetables are often perceived, especially by adults, as outside the normal and therefore, "are often under surveillance of teachers, who aim to remediate and normalize them." This deficit-oriented or disapproving view of children gets deeply entrenched into the culture of the classroom or care setting, reinforcing limiting beliefs about what is acceptable and what is not. We can begin to make sense of how the construction of normal gets produced in the early childhood classroom around the notion of time, and how this can set into motion a cycle of "fixing" children to conform to classroom rules and expectations.

As children enter school, teachers often have expectations about staying seated or still, especially in Western countries. These required periods of sitting gradually increase as children get older. What does this mean for young children who thrive in outdoor spaces? Or for children who learn best when they are active and moving? What about all children who need to move about in playful, unbridled, and unconventional ways? How about children who need alone time in stillness and quiet? Reimagining early childhood places and practices requires us to think about how young children use time and space. It is a common understanding that young children need to be active and engaged participants when it comes to learning. Toward that end, educators and families alike will want to be highly responsive to children's use of time and space, especially their expressions of needing to move or to be still.

At the end of this chapter, I have included an excellent resource called "Ninja Run," written by a teacher to describe how he integrated more mindfulness and movement into his busy classroom routine with first graders. As we become more aware of our perceptions of time, let us remember there is no time like the present moment.

•••• Concluding Thoughts ···

In this chapter, we examined time and being present and the effects these notions have on early education and care. As we took some time to reflect on time and what this means for young children, it seems as if adults and young children perceive and use time quite differently. We explored the multilayered meanings and constructions of time that are often reflective of cultural, societal, and personal beliefs. We also looked at how young children know that it's always time to dance in the rain because they are living in the present moment and do not have the constraints that adults put on expectations, routines, and timetables.

Understanding and reimagining ways to think about time and space in early childhood classrooms and other settings will help children live in the present moment, as they already know how to do. The next chapter focuses on how to create and maintain safe spaces and how to support young children in comforting themselves. We also examine stress and trauma.

· ·

A Menu of Options for Teaching Inclusively, Mindfully, and Equitably

 Children's Corner

Gibson, Amy. 2014. *By Day, by Night*. Westminster, MD: Boyds Mills.

Liu, Sylvia. 2016. *A Morning with Grandpa*. New York: Lee and Low.

Portis, Antoinette. 2017. *Now*. New York: Roaring Book Press.

Willems, Mo. 2014. *Waiting Is Not Easy!* New York: Hyperion.

 Caregivers' Corner

The following resources on the intersection of time and mindfulness are useful for early childhood teachers and caregivers as well as for parents of young children.

Greenland, Susan Kaiser. 2010. *The Mindful Child: How to Help Your Kid Manage Stress and Become Happier, Kinder, and More Compassionate*. New York: Simon and Schuster.

Kabat-Zinn, Jon, and Myla Kabat-Zinn. 2009. *Everyday Blessings: The Inner Work of Mindful Parenting*. London, UK: Hachette UK.

Koster, Alex. 2019. *Roots and Wings: Childhood Needs a Revolution: A Handbook for Parents and Educators to Promote Positive Change Based on the Principles of Mindfulness*. Dublin, IRL: Kazoo Independent Publishing.

Naumburg, Carla. 2015. *Ready, Set, Breathe: Practicing Mindfulness with Your Children for Fewer Meltdowns and a More Peaceful Family*. Oakland, CA: New Harbinger.

Siegel, Daniel J., and Mary Hartzell. 2013. *Parenting from the Inside Out: How a Deeper Self-Understanding Can Help You Raise Children Who Thrive*. New York: Penguin.

Siegel, Daniel J., and Tina Payne Bryson. 2016. *No-Drama Discipline: The Whole-Brain Way to Calm the Chaos and Nurture Your Child's Developing Mind*. New York: Bantam.

Von Lob, Genevieve. 2017. *Five Deep Breaths: The Power of Mindful Parenting*. New York: Random House.

Willard, Christopher. 2016. *Growing Up Mindful: Essential Practices to Help Children, Teens, and Families Find Balance, Calm, and Resilience*. Louisville, CO: Sounds True.

 ## Take It to the Classroom

Sun Salutation

Surya Namaskara, also known as the sun salutation, is a classic yoga sequence. As the rising sun warms a brand-new day, the sun salutation warms up our bodies for the practice of *asanas* (postures) and *pranayama* (breath control). The power of sun salutations is in linking the breath with the movements. Notice that the inhales are linked to upward movements and the exhales to downward movements. After a little bit of practice, the breath will flow naturally with the movement. Be patient and don't worry about making it perfect. Eventually your body will remember the movements and breathing cues on its own, allowing the mind to relax a bit. Here is a simple and traditional version of a sun salutation:

> Stand tall with the feet close together.
>
> **Inhale**: Reach the arms up, press palms together and look up.

Exhale: Jump or step into a plank position (top of a push-up), and slowly lower the whole body toward the floor.

Exhale: Fold forward placing hands on the floor next to the feet (bending the knees if necessary).

Inhale: Look up, lifting and opening the chest.

Inhale: Press into the palms, straighten the arms, and arch the back (lifting only as high as is comfortable).

Exhale: Lift the hips up and back into a downward dog position (arms and legs stretched out, hands and feet touching the floor, the buttocks in the air).

Take five full breaths here.

Inhale: Step or jump the feet between the hands and look up, lifting and opening the chest.

Exhale: Fold forward (bending the knees if necessary).

Inhale: Come all the way up, reach the arms up, press the palms together, and look up.

Exhale: Return to standing tall with the feet close together and arms by your sides.

Repeat the whole sequence five times.

Scripted by Lindsay Hilscher, yoga teacher and integrative nutrition health coach. She works with individuals to create balanced and healthy lives through movement and nutritional support. To learn about how to work with her, visit her website: https://www.lindsayhilscher.com

The Ninja Run

Greg McGrath is a first-grade teacher at a public elementary school near New York City. He loves to be active outdoors because he knows that his energy, focus, inner peace, and reflection improve. Greg created engaging classroom practices that will support his young students' emotional well-being and physical fitness. One of the practices he has used is the Ninja Run, which capitalizes on his students' interest in ninjas. Because ninjas are supposed to be silent and in control of their bodies, Greg used the name Ninja Run to describe these silent large-movement activities that help his students transition between academic tasks and release pent-up energy. Soon after introducing the Ninja Run, Greg observed that his students

- exhibited increased self-regulation, self-determination skills, and concentration.

- were calmer, which changed the general classroom climate.

- demonstrated a deeper understanding of their own bodies, moods, and feelings.

To do a Ninja Run, Greg asks his students to stand up and spread out in the classroom so that no one is touching another person or object. They begin by stretching; Greg's class uses the sun salutation as a first stretch (see page 95 for a description). Greg chooses a Ninja Run leader, who will begin by standing in place and then leading the class in a series of silent movements, such as the following, for two minutes total:

- Tiptoe running in place

- Climb the rope (one hand on top of the other above your head, as if climbing a rope)

- Move to a crouching pose and hold

- Climb the ladder (left hand up, then right hand up, as if climbing a ladder)

- Stay on your feet and drop to the crouching position, then quickly pop back up.

They finish with a calming exercise to bring the students' excitement levels and heart rates back to a resting point. Greg's students use the child's pose:

- Children kneel on the floor with their big toes touching and their knees slightly out at an angle.

- They lower their upper bodies so that their tummies rest on their thighs and their faces are at or near the floor.

- Their either rest their arms at their sides or extend them above their heads in front of them on the floor.

- They take five to ten slow breaths in this resting pose.

You can easily modify this practice to respond to students' range of physical, emotional, cognitive, and learning preferences.

Adapted from Erwin, Elizabeth, et al. 2015. "'It's Like Breathing in Blue Skies and Breathing out Stormy Clouds': Mindfulness Practices in Early Childhood." Young Exceptional Children 20(2): 69–85.

CHAPTER 6

Space Exploration: The Pursuit of Safety in the Inner and Outer Spaces in Young Children's Lives

> **"There are two ways of spreading light: to be the candle or the mirror that reflects it."**
>
> —Edith Wharton, author, humanitarian, first woman to win the Pulitzer Prize for Fiction

This chapter focuses on space exploration but not the kind that is associated with space travel. We will begin to investigate the inner (emotional) and outer (physical) spaces that we inhabit as human beings. We will also focus on a personal sense of safety and what this looks and feels like for young children. The examination of feeling safe in this chapter will go a little further than basic notions of keeping children safe and away from harm, for example, or helping frightened children feel safe during a thunderstorm. Through a deeper understanding of the powerful link between body and mind, we will explore the connections between being present and the inner and outer spaces of early childhood.

In a spirit of transparency, it was not my original plan to devote an entire chapter to safety. However, as I began researching this topic, I recognized multiple layers related to inner and outer spaces and children's well-being, so it seemed impossible to discuss safety without addressing the everyday reality that many young children and families face. As a teacher educator, I have become aware of a steady increase in anxiety, anger, depression as well as physical issues in the lives of teachers and students. On a side note, this book was written before COVID-19 changed our lives forever. As I read through final edits before this book goes to press, I am struck how this topic of personal safety is more relevant now than ever before—for children as well as adults.

The Edith Wharton quote above is not necessarily about body and mind, or the inner and outer spaces we inhabit, but it reflects, to me, what is possible when we choose to be a lighthouse for someone else. We cannot fully provide safety for young children if we are not tuned into the safety net that exists within us. Wharton's insight about spreading light can be a powerful reminder about how being present can give us awareness to be the candle or the mirror.

Although this chapter examines issues around safety, stress, and trauma, among other topics, the emphasis is not on how mindfulness can reduce or eliminate stress. Instead, the focus is on ways to embed mindfulness into the fabric of everyday living. When our bodies and minds are in healthy states, we are better able to manage the stress in our daily lives. In this chapter we also explore the science behind the powerful connection between the body and brain and how we can support young children's well-being.

The Human Body as a Navigational System

You may recall Jared, the spirited and wise child from chapter 4 who used a peace cushion to help manage his strong emotions. He had this to say about how his body and brain work together, as recounted by his grandmother:

> During pre-K and the early elementary years, Jared really struggled with impulsive behavior. He described it vividly: "Sometimes my body goes before my brain tells it what to do!" We spent a lot of time talking about how to help his brain and body work together. Jared found that pausing to take a few deep breaths really helped him get centered.

Young children can quickly learn that there is great power in pausing. During the early years, it is useful to teach children the strong connection between body and mind and how they work together to support a sense of harmony in both the outer and inner lives. Naturally, teaching is a two-way street with young children, because they often have much to teach us about these important connections. Jared's grandmother shared that one morning it became evident that Jared really understood the purpose of this mindfulness technique:

> It was 7:00 on a school morning and I was already into full swing! I had showered and eaten breakfast, my makeup was on, beds were made, a load of laundry was in the washing machine. Next things on the list: give Jared breakfast, prepare his morning snack, fill his water bottle, and help him load his backpack. I was dizzy! Jared noticed that I was getting a bit wound up. In a kind and caring tone, Jared said, "Grandma, I think you need to stop and take a few deep breaths. Your body is just moving too fast."

As adults become more proficient at reading signals from our own bodies, we are better equipped to teach children to do the same. And when we forget to pause or to be present, children are very willing to remind us. Our bodies are talking to us all the time through feelings, sensations, and thoughts, but we sometimes choose not to listen, cannot hear, or do not even recognize these valuable signs. If the physical body is expressing discomfort, tension, annoyance, or anxiety, for example, these are not random symptoms. Any symptom or signal, such as anxiety, is not to be ignored; it is an indicator that something in our outer or inner space needs our immediate attention. It is like when a warning light flashes on the dashboard of our car, which is another kind of indicator that alerts us that something needs our immediate attention. If we do not attend to what the dashboard indicator light is communicating, such as low air in our tires, the situation often gets worse, and then we experience a flat tire. It is very similar to how our body responds when we miss or ignore the signals it sends to us.

We can think of our bodies as wonderful, unique, and complex navigational systems. Like the navigational systems in planes and cars, we can know exactly where we are and where we are headed just by tuning in to the signals. When we feel depleted, angry, anxious, impatient, or distracted, for example, we are not able to be fully present in the moment. Conversely, our bodies and minds feel more ease, focus, and awareness when we practice mindfulness on a regular basis.

Gut feelings, recurrent pain, or feelings of bliss let us know how well we feel in our inner and outer spaces. Our levels of energy, comfort, flexibility, joy, strength, resilience, and so on serve as signals to let us know if, and to what extent, we are out of balance. For example, Jared's grandmother described feeling "dizzy" with all that she had to accomplish that morning. Her feelings of being "wound up" reflected her inner world or emotional state, which was not grounded in the present moment. Jared was not only aware of this but also provided support to his grandmother.

Think about the messages you are receiving in your own inner and outer spaces. What signals have you received lately? What do you think these signals or messages might mean? How have you responded to these signals, and are there any changes you would make in the future?

Given that the practice of mindfulness has been an unfolding journey for me, my understanding of the connection between mind and body has strengthened over the years. Although I am a researcher and have had a fascination with mind-body connection most of my life, I admit I had been less interested in the research on the brain-body relationship until now. Perhaps this was because I do not feel that ancient mindfulness practices needed to be scientifically measured, evaluated, or scrutinized. At the same time, I also recognize that scientific evidence is often required before new ideas are widely accepted. More recently, I have become intrigued by the science behind a personal sense of safety in the body and mind. In this next section I want to offer a meaningful context to better understand the following questions:

- What does the latest science reveal about what humans need to achieve well-being?

- How and why do our bodies and minds communicate to us?

- How can we become more aware of and responsive to the brain and body connection?

- What does children's feeling of safety have to do with their learning?

- What are some of the best tools to support and enhance emotional and physical health?

What Every Human Being Needs: The Science behind Our Pursuit of Safety

"When the body feels safe, it can regulate itself." It was one of those light-bulb moments when I heard these words spoken at a conference by Stephen Porges, distinguished scientist at the Kinsey Institute at Indiana University and professor of psychiatry at the University of North Carolina at Chapel Hill. In his groundbreaking text, *The Polyvagal Theory: Neurophysiological Foundations of Emotions, Attachment, Communication, and Self-Regulation*, Porges describes this revolutionary theory and emphasizes how our focus today must be to live in a nondefensive state.

The constant pursuit of safety is our greatest priority. We are, therefore, continually detecting and determining threats to our personal sense of safety: "By processing information from the environment through the senses, the nervous system continually evaluates risk," Porges states. He notes that humans make a myriad of decisions about conditions, events, and people as either safe, dangerous, or life-threatening, decisions that happen through a subconscious system called *neuroception*. For example, when two toddlers approach one another at a sandbox in the playground, "they may decide that the situation and each other are safe if the sandbox is familiar territory, if their pails and shovels have roughly similar appeal, and if they (the toddlers) are about the same size." Through this lens, we can be aware of how toddlers observe, distinguish, and adapt to the demands and information in their immediate environment. The process of neuro-ception occurs throughout the day as we are constantly in pursuit of feeling safe. If we understand that feeling safe is our highest priority as humans, our thinking about behavior in infants, toddlers, and young children that may appear puzzling can be completely transformed.

In his Polyvagal Theory, Porges discusses the primary role of the vagus nerve, which runs from the brain to the face and through the trunk to the abdomen and can be thought of as a superhighway. It is responsible for carrying important signals between the brain and the rest of the body. Porges acknowledges:

- Our body is on a continuous quest for safety, and yet our body is perceiving a chronic threat by living in our modern environment. Therefore, we are living in a constant and very defensive, reactive state.

- The vagus is not just one central nerve but rather a collection of neural pathways. It is the portal between the brain and body.

- When we engage and exercise specific vagal pathways, they provide portals to compassion and enhanced well-being.

In her book *Five Deep Breaths: The Power of Mindful Parenting*, clinical psychologist Genevieve Von Lob explains why the vagus nerve plays a crucial role in maintaining a sense of well-being in our lives:

Picture a car speeding down a motorway at 100 mph; that's the build-up of stress. Taking slow, deep breaths engages something called the vagus nerve, which acts like a brake. This huge nerve connects our brain with our heart and other major organs before meandering all the way down into the depths of our gut. (The word *vagus* in Latin means "wandering"—the word *vagabond* has the same root.)

Consider that if young children are not receiving or perceiving important messages about feeling safe in their environment, it is highly likely that they will be unable to actively or joyfully engage in learning. By looking through the lens of Porges's Polyvagal Theory, we can shed light on our mindfulness practice as well as our teaching practice.

Connectedness is our ability to mutually regulate (synchronically and reciprocally) physiological states. Face-to-face interactions (with people and pets) can literally coregulate our state of being, Porges notes, which naturally supports our health and growth. Consider that face-to-face interactions between parent and child can coregulate behavior and physiological states. This is significant—we can coregulate one another! So when a father smiles and looks lovingly into his infant daughter's eyes, they are both getting signals during this tender interaction that coregulates their states of being. Quite simply, human beings need each other.

Porges warns, however, that in our modern society people are not getting the important signals needed to connect or to feel safe. Given the unrelenting bombardment of data and information, for example, coupled with an increasing overreliance on technology and decreasing emphasis on in-person interactions, humans are missing out on the irreplaceable signals they need to feel safe and protected. In short, because they are not receiving these essential signals, humans are perceiving a constant threat to their personal sense of safety and living in an extremely defensive state.

What does all of this mean in early childhood education and care? Barbara Sorrels, executive director of The Institute for Childhood Education and author of *Reaching and Teaching Children Exposed to Trauma*, describes what happens when the brain detects a threat and how this affects young children. She explains how the brain and body perceive danger and address it in the following three ways:

- **Fight mode:** a child becomes verbally or physically aggressive (swears, hits, bites, spits) as if she is fighting for her life

- **Flight mode:** a child does everything to flee or to get away from the perceived danger (hiding under a blanket, refusing to look or talk, running away, and so on)

- **Freeze mode:** a child reacts initially to danger or a traumatic event (spaces out, seems lethargic or unresponsive, daydreams) as the brain evaluates what is happening and prepares for an impending attack, assault, or harm to the body

Sorrels suggests that there is a wide range of potential triggers that can intensify a child's perceived threat, including the following:

- A new child or adult entering familiar surroundings

- Noise level

- Quick movements

- Changes in the routine

- A new room arrangement

- Disorganized materials or equipment

- The absence of a caregiver

- Unwanted tickling

- Something being taken away

In addition, many triggers are sensory based, such as certain smells, textures, sounds, noises, lighting, and unexpected or harsh touch and/or voice, especially if these sensations are new to the child. The key is to understand what infants, toddlers, and young children are telling us about feeling safe or unsafe through their words, moods, and behavior so we can better support them, protect them, and be present with them.

The following poem was written from the perspective of a preschooler by Sarah Veniero, a highly skilled and knowledgeable early childhood inclusive-education teacher. Think about this young child's perspective related to her personal quest for safety:

Tell Me

Tell me what you want to hear

So I can get it right

Tell me what you want to hear

To be worthy in your sight

Tell me how I need to sound

So I can get a pass

Tell me how I need to sound

To be included in my class

Tell me what I need to say

To express what I feel

Tell me what I need to say

To make my feelings real

Tell me what you really heard

When I made my own choice

Tell me what you really heard

When I used my own voice

I'll tell you what I really heard

When you told me how to speak

I'll tell you what I really heard

That my voice is much too weak

There are many layers and complexities of this poem, although the theme of safety seems to be at the core. Take a moment to identify what you observe as the threats to this child's personal sense of safety. Why might this child experience danger in the classroom?

As interest continues to grow in the science of the relationship between the brain and body, a variety of disciplines are studying this powerful connection, including early childhood education, mental health, psychology, psychotherapy, and medicine. Mindfulness and contemplative practices have and will continue to play a significant role in expanding our understanding of mind and body connections. Refer to the resources in Caregivers' Corner on page 122 to explore a deeper and broader explanation of these innovative ideas.

Implications, Ideas, and Insights about Safety and Mindfulness

Given this snapshot about our common, primary pursuit for personal safety, early childhood professionals are rethinking how to understand behavior in young children. In his talk at the 2019 Yoga and Science Conference at the Tandon School of Engineering at New York University, Porges explained how the Polyvagal Theory "transforms the human narrative from a documentary to a pragmatic quest for safety." When we acknowledge that infants', toddlers', or young children's behavior may actually be in response to a situation or surroundings in which they perceive a threat, we are better able to genuinely understand and support their quest for safety.

When we are present, we are better able to bear witness to our surroundings. Being present also reminds us that all human beings, including those we feel uncomfortable around, share a common need to feel safe and protected. Before beginning to contemplate how to genuinely help young children feel safe, adults must feel a sense of personal safety in their own lives. I believe the answer lies within, with our inner spaces and engaging in an individual practice. When we practice mindfulness regularly, we are rooted in the present moment more often and have greater resilience to notice when we feel unsafe or distracted. The steady and ongoing practice helps us to return more easily to a state of mindfulness. When we experience a true sense of inner safety and calm, it is because the mind is quiet and we are present in the moment, regardless of what is happening around us.

Being present is an excellent way to feel safe from within. In his book *Protecting the Gift: Keeping Children and Teenagers Safe (and Parents Sane),* Gavin de Becker, a security expert well-known for teaching people worldwide how to manage fear and risk over the past twenty-five years, suggests that worry actually increases the risk of danger. He explains:

> That's because as you worry about some imagined danger, you are distracted from what is actually happening. Staying present in the moment keeps our focus on what is right in front of us. Projecting ahead, which is basically what worrying is, keeps us from being in the here and now and subsequently compromises our own inner sense of safety. When we are consumed with anger, worry, fear, or anxiety, it is not possible to feel a personal sense of safety. If we are not feeling safe from within, it is likely we will not be able to help others, especially young children, feel safe and secure.

In other words, being present helps us to be more aware and to detect risk, which ultimately decreases the threat of danger. This deeper understanding of safety and being present in our own lives is worthy of further examination. Mindfulness practices can enhance a personal sense of safety. In his talk at the 2019 Yoga and Science Conference, Porges noted how ancient contemplative practices are neural exercises of the vagal pathways. When we modulate certain movements or frequencies in a particular way, they make us feel better and support our emotional and physical well-being. Porges explained that these neural exercises include the following:

- **Chants, prayer, and meditation:** these sacred sounds, particularly indigenous chants, represent a physiology of compassion

- **Vocalizations:** certain types, such as a mother talking to an infant or a child talking to a dog in a melodic voice, make us feel good

- **Breath:** we shift our physiological state by breathing; when we shift between inhaling and exhaling, we calm the body through the vagus nerve

- **Posture:** posture shifts, such as bowing or sitting taller, trigger vagal activity allowing us to feel safer and connected to ourselves and to others; yoga postures or asanas are a family of neural exercises regulating physiological state

- **Listening:** compassionate listening, such as listening without judgment or the intention to fix, integrates the neural regulation of the heart and other organs

As we engage in contemplative or mindfulness practices, an enhanced sense of emotional and physical well-being is not only possible but probable. Contemplative traditions such as yoga and other practices have existed for centuries, but modern science is just beginning to understand why and how they are so effective.

When we practice mindfulness on a regular basis, we are in a more solid and credible position to help young children feel safe in both their inner and outer worlds. For infants, toddlers, and young children who may have difficulty detecting, analyzing, or interpreting sensory information, their perception of feeling safe depends on each of their unique ways of being in the world. In other words, we already know that no two children are alike regardless of any common attributes. What makes one child feel safe, therefore, will likely be completely different for another child. Adults can literally change an environment so that young children *perceive* and ultimately *feel* safe. Ensuring that young children feel safe and protected so that they can begin to gradually take care of themselves has long been a primary responsibility for teachers. Let's look at ways to take proactive measures to design environments, spaces, and routines that are highly responsive to nurturing individual children's inner and outer spaces.

Designing for Safety in Early Childhood Environments

Educators and others in the field of early childhood acknowledge the need for all children to feel safe. Yet the contradiction is unavoidable given the growing concerns about the increasing pressures to focus on academics, standardization, and uniformity in early childhood education and care. Children cannot be calm and relaxed if they do not feel safe. And if children are not feeling calm and relaxed, it is not realistic to expect they are able to maintain focus, engagement, or joy in their learning. Take, for example, the growing and serious concern about the rise in preschool suspension rates. In a 2017 article titled "New Data Reveal 250 Preschoolers Are Suspended or Expelled Every Day," Rasheed Malik of the Center for American Progress suggests that, on a daily basis across public and private preschools in the United States, more than two hundred young children are reported as either being expelled or suspended. This does not even seem possible. *Preschool* and *suspension* are two words that simply do not belong together. How can the youngest students be suspended from school—the very place they are sent by trusting families to learn and grow? Why is it that young children are so misunderstood that they are not welcomed at school?

Protecting a young child and ensuring that she feels safe requires two interrelated actions. First, adults must recognize as well as emphasize that safety is one of the most important considerations in a human being's life. Second, adults must learn what feeling safe means for each child.

Remember Naoki Higashida, the thirteen-year-old author of *The Reason I Jump?* He does not specifically mention safety, but consider the implications for his personal safety as you read his insights about what happens when he and others are not understood: ". . . for a person with autism, being touched by someone else means that the toucher is exercising control over the person's body, which not even its owner can control properly. It's as if we lose who we are. Think about it—that's terrifying!"

Naoki's reflection is profound. Adults may have no idea that their uninvited action toward a child can leave lasting, devastating imprints. Behavior is communication. Let us pay attention in each moment to what children are communicating through their behavior. Children are expressing themselves about how safe they feel in every moment. It is our responsibility to invest the time and care to observe and decipher what messages are being transmitted from each child about how safe they feel. When we meet a child where she is, we take the time to pause and to thoughtfully respond instead of reacting to a situation we may not fully understand.

In his talk at the 2019 Yoga and Science Conference, Porges offered some basic principles and implications for adults to translate into practical applications related to safety and schooling:

- Without safety there is no social engagement, which is the precursor for healthy social bonding. When people feel safe, reciprocal social connection can occur.

- Safety is closely linked to predictability. If the environment (geographically and relationally) is safe, people are more likely to be in state of calm and connection; unpredictability triggers fear and fight, flight, or freeze responses.

- Children who do not feel safe in the classroom are not able to be calm and relaxed because they are focused on surviving perceived dangers.

- Current societal perceptions often position human beings as learning machines, which disregards that they are in survival mode, always on a constant pursuit of safety.

This notion of how humans are frequently viewed these days as "learning machines" as opposed to the living, breathing beings we are resonated with me. It is as if the incessant quest to accumulate—information, skills, materials, achievements, time—becomes the only narrative when children are expected to perform as learning machines. That is not a space in which any human can feel valued or safe.

Creating a Sense of Safety in the Outer Spaces Young Children Inhabit

When schedules, routines, and physical environments are organized and highly predictable, infants and young children know what to expect. They can anticipate what is about to occur and feel safe because what they expect to happen actually does. When children live with constant uncertainty, ambiguity, or chaos, being in the world might seem like one big surprise after another because they never know what they are going to face around the next corner. When children do not feel safe, they maintain a defensive state and are operating in constant survival mode. This would be exhausting to any human being, but especially to a young child. Establishing and maintaining a climate that is highly predictable throughout the entire day, every day, is essential. Here are a few ideas to translate this into classroom practice:

- Ensure that the children understand and have easy access to a visual daily schedule, which they can consult throughout the day. A weekly and/or a monthly schedule can be very helpful for older children.

- Develop and organize the daily activities around highly predictable routines, some of which young children can develop or cocreate with adults.

- Use consistent anticipatory cues, such as a wind chime, soft music, or a sand hourglass, to alert children about upcoming transitions to a new activity, routine, or space. Encourage children to teach and share these anticipatory cues with classmates so they can prepare for an upcoming transition.

- Be worthy of children's trust. Teachers and staff must prove to children their compassion and a capacity to provide a sense of personal safety and protection.

These suggestions are just a few of the ways to build a predictable environment that can support infants, toddlers, and young children in feeling safe and protected. It is this last bullet that deserves a deeper exploration, because not all practitioners possess the knowledge, skills, or capacity to enhance children's personal safety during these critical early years. The following observation, shared with permission, was part of an inquiry project in one of my advanced teacher education courses. The graduate student who completed this project focused her observations on Beau, a four-year-old student with a diagnosis of autism spectrum disorder. As you read, think about the role that trust plays.

> The students were playing in the kitchen, and Beau attempted to leave the area. He was stopped by his aide and asked, "What do you want?" Beau responded, "That," and pointed to a toy fire truck. Understanding his request, Beau's aide responded, "Tell me, 'I want the fire truck.'" In turn, Beau repeated, "Fire truck." Again, his aide prompted to him to repeat, "I want the fire truck." This time Beau dropped to the ground and began to cry. His aide grabbed the truck, held it close to Beau, and for a third time said, "Tell me, I want the fire truck." Finally, Beau imitated the phrase, and his aide verbally praised him, "Good boy," and handed him the fire truck. This type of exchange occurred countless times during this week-long observation.

Although this is just one snapshot, it provides a brief insight into this child's sense of safety. This graduate student provided the following thoughtful analysis about several observations and interpretations. Take a moment to think critically about these reflections and additional impressions about Beau's sense of safety and trust:

- Take a look at the sentence prompted by the aide, "I want the fire truck." It was established that Beau could have the fire truck if he imitated this verbal phrase. This exchange told Beau a lot. It informed him that his membership and belonging in the classroom community depended on how he communicated. To be considered a member, the desirable form of elaborate verbal language was required. Beau needed to not only use verbal language but also reproduce specified language for his decision to have any meaning to his aide.

- In contrast, his peers who were capable of verbally requesting a different toy by using a complex sentence were not asked to demonstrate this skill. To explain further, when Beau was prompted to repeat the fire truck sentence, there were several students who also decided to leave the kitchen area and pick a new activity. Beau was the only student who was given a condition, which provided Beau with a clear understanding of who is in power and made it quite clear to his peers as well.

- Beau understands that he does not have the control to make any decisions in his classroom without abiding by established rules. If he does not repeat precisely, "I want the fire truck," then he will not obtain it. Beau made it clear that he wanted to play with the fire truck, and his decision making was intercepted by applying power over his choices. This power dynamic discouraged Beau's motivation and ability to make choices independently.

- In the book *Disrupting Early Childhood Education Research: Imagining New Possibilities*, toddler teacher Emmanuelle Fincham's "Words and Bodies" chapter says that by placing so much emphasis on children's language, we are encouraging a distancing from the body; this limits the possibilities of engagement with one another or understanding what children are communicating. Fincham further explains how the voice of children includes gestures, movements, and/or sounds. In our example, Beau instinctively exhibited all three of those things to display how he felt. But by perpetuating the "use your words" approach, the aide restricted the relationship with Beau in terms that may not make sense to him. It is more important for a child to know he is being heard.

- The use of the phrase "good boy" to praise Beau once he repeated the sentence can be quite problematic. While this simple phrase may seem harmless, it is important to take a deeper look. If Beau hears that he is a "good boy" for repeating a phrase, what would he be considered if he did not use his words on command? One could discern that Beau would be a "bad boy" if he did not repeat after his teacher. Beau's peers see that he is included only when he is being a "good boy" and copying the aide's phrases.

By examining carefully how this exchange between a classroom aide and child unfolded, several factors emerge that threaten Beau's personal sense of safety and comfort. Beau kept responding correctly to the adult's question, so by the third time, he resorted to throwing himself on the ground out of sheer frustration. (I likely would have done the same.) Some may have interpreted Beau's outburst as noncompliant or manipulative behavior to get his way, but we can understand this scenario within the context of a child's quest for safety. When Beau detected danger (complying with the adult's requests but to no avail), we can see the flight response as he quickly removes his body from the perceived threat by dropping to the ground and crying. Beau felt threatened, given that he answered repeated questions correctly (when other classmates did not have to) and was still asked to do more. Sometimes a familiar adult can be the threat.

Educators have a serious responsibility to establish and maintain a sense of safety for all children in their care. To ensure a personal sense of safety for young children, whether at home or in the classroom, adult expectations, organization, schedules, spaces, time, and the adults themselves must be highly predictable as well as trustworthy. When adults are calm, mindful, and perceived as safe, children feel safe.

Inner and Outer Space: Creating and Maintaining Well-Being in the Safe Spaces

Creating healthy, predictable environments in which infants, toddlers, and young children feel safe is one of the best ways to support the precious inner and outer spaces during the early years. In essence, being present enhances our understanding about how to protect children's well-being emotionally and physically. However, situations, such as surprise fire drills, are going to arise that are beyond our control or occur because of changes in routine, such as holidays or field trips. While many young children easily adapt to changes in routines, environments, materials, people, expectations, and so forth, others find that these changes create stress. Like adults, children have their individual triggers, tolerance levels, and preferences. A very noisy environment might feel highly distracting and tense for one child, and another child might be able to tolerate and adapt easily to the loud intensity. It is neither realistic nor possible to eliminate all the stress in our lives. Instead, let our attention be on creating and maintaining physical and emotional well-being.

The words we choose carry important meaning and intention. Consider how words that are sometimes used in early childhood education might evoke a sense of aggression, violence, and tension: *reduce frustration, eliminate aggression, no biting*. Also consider expectations that are passive, such as *tolerate touching* or to *sit quietly*. Now consider more mindful, dynamic, and supportive words that focus on an intention in a positive way and position children to preserve their inner and outer spaces communicate safety:

- *Restore health*

- *Maintain inner calm*

- *Focus on the breath*

- *Strengthen focus*

- *Enhance flexibility*

- *Increase energy*

- *Improve resilience*

- *Choose wisely*

- *Elevate joy*

These intentions represent choices that align with a more positive, child-focused perspective rather than with a perspective that diminishes a child's autonomy or participation and focuses on what is not wanted. When it comes to health in body and mind, our words can make all the difference. This is part of any mindfulness practice.

As suggested previously, mindfulness practices should not be thought of as a quick fix to a problem but rather as choices to live in the moment. When stress does show up, we can choose from a menu of mindfulness tools that we have practiced and teach children to do the same. A daily mindfulness practice can serve as an anchor in your life, to (re)mind and (re)turn us to the present moment, especially during challenging times.

Supporting Young Children to Comfort Themselves

Like adults, children find their own ways to self-soothe when they feel upset, angry, stressed, and challenged. However, as adults, we already have tools and life experience from which to draw on in our pursuit of safety, security, and comfort. During the early years, children are just beginning to experiment with and learn these strategies and to determine the ones that feel best. If aligned with a family's cultural beliefs, teaching children to take care of themselves is an excellent investment to make.

Taking care is one of the most fundamental ways humans demonstrate kindness and gratitude. By taking care of ourselves, we turn the kindness and appreciation inward. It is a sign of respect to ourselves. Taking care of ourselves also means we hold deep respect for others, because when we are well rested, focused, nourished, and present in the moment, we are better equipped to take good care of others, especially young children.

We can provide meaningful support to young children by being present in the moment with them as we identify each child's preferred way of self-calming or self-soothing. There are countless ways young children find comfort or seek safety during a difficult situation. I recall when Alyssa was very young, she exclaimed, "I am so mad. . . . I think I will go read a book!" She instinctively knew that a book could provide her with the comfort she needed in that moment. "Our ability to regulate ourselves in the face of stress is rooted in how well we were regulated in the first three years of life," notes Barbara Sorrels, executive director of The Institute for Childhood Education in Oklahoma, in her book *Reaching and Teaching Children Exposed to Trauma*. What happens during those early years can largely determine the future landscape in the inner and outer spaces in children's lives.

At the end of this chapter, I offer a simple script to use with children to help them find their own stillness and safety. The popular and widely respected "Still Quiet Place," developed by Amy Saltzman, introduces children to a special, safe place deep inside of them. Children can find this place anytime just by breathing. I also list valuable online sources to help adults gain a deeper understanding of the theory, research, practice, and implications about how the brain functions in early childhood. These resources offer guidance about how to support young children's emotional regulation and other important foundations on their quest for safety during the first few years of life. Every child is designed as a one-of-a-kind human being with a distinctive set of interests, dispositions, temperaments, and preferred learning modalities that ultimately influence their perceptions about safety.

Young children may find comfort and safety in a wide variety of sensory modalities:

- Auditory: familiar melodies, soothing voices

- Tactile: soft blanket, cuddly toy

- Olfactory: lavender scent, parent's shirt

- Kinesthetic: swinging, swaddling

Every human has a unique individual imprint, and each infant, toddler, and young child knows what makes her feel safe and unsafe, although she will likely not have the language to communicate this. It is up to adults to be attentive to the messages and signals young children are communicating about what they need to feel anchored and protected.

Early in my teaching career, an enchanting three-year-old girl, Janine, would sit on my lap at quiet time and suck her thumb while her other hand extended straight over her head and was planted directly under my nose. It didn't matter that Janine was socially engaging and could light up a room with her sunny disposition, that she had Down syndrome, or that she was Caucasian—none of these attributes would have told me about who Janine was or what gave her comfort and stability. What did matter was the solid partnership between her home and school. With open and consistent communication, Janine's mother, who knew Janine better than anyone, was able to share with me that her daughter liked to feel the rhythmic inhale and exhale of a familiar adult's breath. This is why Janine kept her hand placed right under my nose. The information I received from her mother helped me know Janine even better, so I could provide her with precisely what she needed to feel safe and calm. Partnering with families not only provides invaluable knowledge for everyone involved but also strengthens the critical bond and respect between home and school.

Alice Sterling Honig, early childhood expert and author of *Little Kids, Big Worries: Stress-Busting Tips for Early Childhood Classrooms*, notes that some children will have a large and expanding repertoire of self-soothing strategies. Other children may choose one specific toy or activity over and over again to find comfort. Honig shares a story about a child who sought repetition as a way to self-soothe. Robbie, five years old, lived in a home where screaming fights between his parents were common. To calm his feelings of helplessness, Robbie would sit quietly and turn the pages of Maurice Sendak's book *Where the Wild Things Are*. Honig relates: "Choosing this book over and over, Robbie gained reassurance to face his own inner monsters without fear that he would be swept away by their anger and frenzied antics."

Although some teachers might unwisely characterize Robbie's behavior as a fixation with the book, labeling his behavior would not have been helpful, necessary, or even accurate. The key here is that his teachers not only acknowledged that Robbie had found a solution to help him deal with a stressful situation over which he had no control but also respected and supported his choice because it worked for him. Trust that young children have the capacity to find comfort. In addition, when educators prove again and again their unwavering trustworthiness to young children, a personal sense of safety is fostered during the early years.

When considering the needs of the whole class, educators can cocreate with children safe spaces for silence, stillness, and solitude, so young children have multiple opportunities to pause in a busy classroom community. There is a myriad of ways adults can elevate the inner emotional spaces in young children's lives, which naturally support their quest for safety. Understanding the unique and sometimes complex inner worlds within each child is essentially about being present and fully aware—before, during, and after moments of stress—so we can learn precisely what it is they need from us.

We do not always have control over what happens to us, but we can have a degree of control about the environment we inhabit. When our environments feel safe, we feel calm inside. When we feel calm inside, we feel calm in our bodies, and when our bodies are calm, we can more easily feel a sense of peace and well-being from within. The inner (emotional) and outer (physical) spaces that we inhabit are interconnected. The teacher or caregiver naturally assumes this most important responsibility for developing responsive, trusting, and nurturing environments where young children feel safe and cared about.

Fundamental Differences between Daily Stress and Trauma

The human body has an extraordinary capacity to restore, repair, recover, and recharge in an effort to find balance, harmony, and safety. Barbara Sorrels's influential text *Reaching and Teaching Children Exposed to Trauma* eloquently describes how the human body is beautifully designed to protect itself: " . . . the body is a remarkably well-orchestrated symphony of neuro chemicals and electrical impulses exquisitely designed for self-protection." In other words, our human bodies have an incredible capacity for self-preservation and protection. Sorrels describes this process of self-protection as analogous to accelerating and braking when driving a car. As a threat is perceived, it is as if the gas pedal is completely accelerated to deal with this stressful event. When the situation is over, the brake is applied, which slows down the body. However, for young children experiencing trauma and other serious threats to personal safety, such as chronic neglect or violence, Sorrels explains that their gas pedal is always in the accelerating position. It is like driving a car with one foot pressing the accelerator and the other foot on the brake—both at the same time. Their bodies are not able to detect a sense of safety, and therefore they simply cannot return to an inner state of balance, stability, or harmony.

When it comes to stress, there is a difference between serious, traumatic, and life-altering struggles and the customary pressures of living in the world today. Sorrels further explains that as human beings we are naturally built for survival and have the capacity to deal with threats to our emotional or physical security and health. She notes, however, that there is a big difference between toxic stress and manageable stress because " . . . when children live with chronic neglect, abuse, or violence, the stress-response system remains stuck in the 'on' position, and the brain and body are never able to return to a state of equilibrium or calm. The implications are profound and lifelong."

Trauma literally affects how a young child's brain and body function; therefore, care of such children requires both immediate and long-term solutions. Awareness about who is affected by trauma, violence, neglect, and abuse is a first step in acknowledging not only the lifelong implications of traumatic events but the widespread prevalence as well. The sheer number of young children experiencing traumatic circumstances is vast and overwhelming. In a 2017 report, *The State of America's Children*, the Children Defense Fund documents the daily and harsh realities of trauma for children and families. In the United States, every single day:

- 2 mothers die from complications of childbirth

- 4 children are killed by abuse or neglect

- 8 children or teens are killed with a gun

- 22 children or teens die from accidents

- 45 children or teens are injured or killed with a gun

- 64 babies die before their first birthday

- 879 babies are born with low birthweight

- 912 babies are born into extreme poverty

- 1,414 babies are born without health insurance

- 1,759 babies are born into poverty

- 1,854 children are confirmed as abused or neglected

When calculated over months and across years, the collective impact of trauma on humanity is staggering. The numbers reported do not capture even a fraction of the lasting implications of what this means in just one child's life. Consider there are countless wounded young children dealing with trauma and its devastating effects right now. No doubt some of these children have crossed our paths.

As educators, we must be vigilant to notice children who live with chronic worry and tension. For example, *The State of America's Children* report reveals that in the United States nearly one out of five children—well more than 13 million—are poor, and approximately 70 percent of those are children of color. More than 1.2 million homeless children are enrolled in public schools. About 14.8 million children struggle against hunger in food-insecure households. The number of young children who do not have their basic survival needs met, in a country that has every available resource, is not only astonishing, but inexcusable. Take a moment to pause and digest this. These are young children struggling in our classrooms and in our schools right now to make it through the day.

So where does mindfulness fit in? Teaching a kindergartener to breathe deeply when her stomach is aching from hunger is not the solution. When we are present in the moment, we can take careful note of what might have been unseen or too difficult for us to fully grasp before. We can concentrate more fully, for example, on who does not have the essentials—enough food, water, shelter, clothing, sleep, and tenderness. How can we expect children to learn and to focus when their basic needs for survival are barely met?

The power is in the pause. We have a human responsibility to take the time to notice. By seeking out and partnering with others who are knowledgeable and qualified, we are in a more strategic position to troubleshoot and provide critical support and resources. Addressing trauma can involve layers of complexity, which is why knowing where to turn for help is crucial. The following list will provide some assistance to you about where to go to for guidance in reaching, teaching, and supporting young children exposed to trauma.

Resources to Support Young Children in Crisis

Child Trauma Academy (CTA)
http://childtrauma.org
Service, research, and education: these are the three venues that CTA works in to serve children affected by trauma. They work with a neurosequential model of therapy that is based on children's development.

National Child Traumatic Stress Network (NCTSN)
https://www.nctsn.org/what-is-child-trauma/trauma-types/early-childhood-trauma
NCTSN is a nonprofit organization that educates about issues related to trauma, provides expert advice on how to support children who have experienced or are experiencing trauma, and implements service programs to aid children and their families. Its website is a thorough resource on childhood trauma.

Child Mind Institute
https://childmind.org/article/how-trauma-affects-kids-school
The Child Mind Institute recognizes that any acute or chronic trauma that children experience accompanies them into the classroom. They offer information to help teachers be aware of the effects that trauma has on their students.

Center for Child Trauma Assessment, Services, and Interventions
http://cctasi.northwestern.edu/family/child-trauma
Researchers at Northwestern University have developed a comprehensive system for addressing the needs of children affected by trauma. Their work with early educators is particularly informative. They offer free resources for children, families, and educators.

Some simple ideas might provide additional comfort and security in the classroom for children who may be dealing with trauma and will do so in ways that don't require them to ask for anything. Consider having the following:

- Fresh water available in a small pitcher or dispenser with cups, so children can get a drink whenever they are thirsty. Offer fresh water—for hydrating the body and energizing the mind—rather than juices. According to a 2016 article by James DiNicolantonio and Amy Berger in *Open Heart*, the official journal of the British Cardiovascular Society, the more added sugar that is consumed (like that in sugary drinks and juices), the more depleted the body can become of valuable nutrients.

- A bowl of fresh fruit out on a small table, so children can choose to stop by and have a snack when they are hungry. I saw how this worked beautifully at a Montessori preschool as children learned to regulate how often they visit. Rotate a variety of healthy choices, such as bananas, berries, oranges, apples, raisins, mango slices, and apricots. Or offer cut-up fresh fruit or vegetables in a bowl or platter. Some seeds, such as pumpkin and sunflower, can work well too.

- Safe, inviting quiet spaces, so any child at any time can recharge her batteries or take a quick nap if she is exhausted and drained.

- Various displays of things that are alive and growing to represent a sense of thriving and blossoming, such as plants of different sizes and shapes, fresh flowers, or seedlings that are watered and cared for by children. I frequently place plant clippings in a glass or clear container filled with water, because I love to watch as the roots sprout and grow.

Remember that not all children experience the same kind of trauma in the same way. The presence of a loving, trusted adult can relieve or soften challenges, even under dire circumstances. In her book *Little Kids, Big Worries*, Alice Honig describes this phenomenon from firsthand accounts of children who experienced the devastating effects of the London Blitz during the Second World War, when German V-2 rockets obliterated parts of London.

> Many families sent their children to live with strangers in the countryside so that the children would be safe from the bombs. Families whose children remained with them hurried down to the deep underground train platforms as soon as the sirens screamed their warnings of an imminent bombing attack. The children sent away were found to suffer more bedwetting and nightmares. Stresses were less and mental health better for those children who had to go to sleep lying on the cold subway station floor but close to a loved parent or neighbor.

It is almost impossible to predict how a person, especially an infant, toddler, or young child, will deal with traumatic situations. Whether the deeply disturbing ordeal occurred as a single event, such as a major accident, natural disaster, or fire, or is recurring trauma, such as abuse, neglect, or abandonment, the impact on a young child's sense of safety across a lifetime is dramatically altered. In her chapter, "Growing Up in a Violent World: The Impact of Family and Community Violence on Young Children and Their Families," in *Putting Children First: Visions for a Brighter Future for Young Children and Their Families*, Betsy McAlister Groves, a highly regarded expert on the impact of community and family violence, offers key recommendations to support young children and their families dealing with violence in their lives:

- Communicate a willingness to talk about the violence and to be a nonjudgmental listener, which provides a safe and open context to let children and families know it is acceptable to talk about violence.

- Support families by helping them stabilize the environments for their children. This is particularly important for women trapped in domestic-violence situations who need resources to seek safe options or to create safety plans.

- Remind families that they are the most important emotional protectors for their children, which acknowledges that families are capable of providing better emotional support and reassurance to their children than professionals can.

Experiencing as well as witnessing violence can have a devastating effect on the human psyche, even if children (or adults) do not show any signs of this trauma. An essential part of supporting young children and their families impacted by violence is to not only show up but also be fully present with and for them.

A full examination of the topic of trauma is well beyond the scope of this chapter. Let us all learn more about how young children are affected by violence and what can be done about it. Refer to the end of this chapter for excellent resources. You also will find a set of key recommendations for communicating with very young children about tragedy and violence developed by Gerry Costa, a nationally recognized expert on infant mental health. In the Caregivers' Corner on page 122, there are resources about living in a violent world and how to address this in early childhood.

Another Kind of Trauma: Is All Unkindness the Same?

Today young children do not have to leave their homes to be exposed to hostile and contentious behavior, because we welcome it into our homes and communities on a regular basis. Aggression is deeply embedded into the cultural fabric of our society. "Violence has become a hallmark of American culture and society," writes Betsy McAlister Groves. Young children are witnessing an excessive amount of aggression on screens and on a variety of platforms, such as books, print advertisements, media commercials, and toys, all intentionally designed for young audiences. Advertisers, marketers, tech companies, and other large corporations are in the business to make profits, not to elevate the well-being of children.

In a provocative essay titled "Our Children Are Getting the Wrong Message," concerned father and early childhood educator Ralph Beach warns about the inherent messages young children constantly receive about violence:

> I believe the most damaging violence to children is the subliminal violence they are bombarded with daily. At home, I closely monitor the commercials specifically targeted at my children (I have a son, age nine, and a daughter, age three). Of the toys specifically marketed primarily for boys, a considerable majority are violent toys, reinforcing the concept that the bigger the gun, the more powerful the individual.

The acceptance of hostility has found its unwanted place and stayed firmly planted in the lives of young children in ways that are both conspicuous and subtle. Being unkind to another or to oneself is a form of aggression, and any act of aggression reflects hostility and a state of mindlessness. Bret Turner, a first-grade teacher in Oklahoma, describes that, as young children learn to negotiate the world they live in, they begin to experiment with unkind behavior or language. Turner, in his 2019 article titled "Teaching First-Graders about Microaggressions: The Small Moments Add Up," explains how unkindness can cross the line:

> . . . not all unkindness is the same. It can be particularly detrimental when the hurtful language relates to race, gender, religion, or other aspects of a child's identity. These are microaggressions: small, subtle, sometimes-unintended acts of discrimination.

These microaggressions, as negligible as they may appear at times, carry the weight of a hostile or violent act. As we examined in earlier chapters, deficit-oriented thinking about human diversity perpetuates discrimination, oppression, exclusion, and humiliation inside and outside classroom environments. Turner explains why:

> It can be hard enough for adults—particularly adults with privileged identities—to recognize microaggressions. But it's crucial we address them. At their core, these are coded messages of disapproval that are based in identity: comments and actions that echo larger, structural bigotry, telling marginalized people they don't belong, that they are less than. Children start internalizing these messages while they are still developing their identities.

When we dismiss, ignore, or take lightly any form of microaggression, we are essentially teaching young children that prejudice, bias, and injustice are acceptable. We must begin to notice—alongside young children—when microaggressions occur. Let's return to the wise words of Ralph Beach, who demonstrates where microaggressions are rooted deeply in the world around us. I share his profound concern about how Black men are portrayed in American society. Given the intersecting identities in Ralph's life—African American, male, father raising a son—he feels as if he has an obligation not only to serve as a role model but to actively challenge the disparaging and inaccurate myths about men, especially men of color:

Television suggests that men are either beer-drinking sportsmen, boring intellectuals, or brutes who use violence to solve conflicts. They are rarely seen as caring, sensitive, responsible people. The media stereotype African American men even further: They are portrayed as super athletes, individuals who are addicted to alcohol and/or drugs, or criminals. I constantly remind children that I am big, and I am gentle, that when I am angry I do not hit, and that I have feelings and I respect other people's feelings.

Beach teaches children about microaggressions and provides a positive alternative narrative. The destructive, intersecting narratives about race and gender, which are profoundly and painfully embedded into the cultural fabric of society, will prevail until they are challenged and disrupted.

The impact of these hostile narratives on the human spirit is incalculable. Psychologist and certified yoga therapist Gail Parker describes race-based traumatic-stress injury as a deep, painful emotional injury that is unpredictable, uncontrollable, recurrent, and cumulative. Although not life-threatening, it is the context and not the physiology that makes ethnic- and race-based wounding so devastating and unique. She explains that there is a growing field in race-based trauma and stress injury. A targeted individual or group reexperience past racial trauma while also experiencing current stress related to racism.

Racism, sexism, ableism, ageism, and other forms of deficit-oriented thinking exist because a widespread public discourse of dignity is absent. The unacceptable becomes acceptable when injustice is tolerated. At the core of our teaching, we must critically examine and challenge narratives based on deficit thinking. In early childhood education, we can replace discourses based on oppression, prejudice, and bias with discourses of dignity for all living beings. Our diligent focus on dignity can naturally promote a climate of respect across all forms of human variation. When children feel respected and understood, they feel safe. When children feel they matter, they feel safe. Therefore, we must create individual and collective safe spaces with young children that encourage their active involvement in conversations that challenge microaggressions. We must elevate the inner and outer spaces for young children by remembering the profound connection between mind and body. We do this by recognizing what connects every human being: the highest priority is for each of us is to feel safe. As Edith Wharton put it, "There are two ways of spreading light: to be the candle or the mirror that reflects it." This is the path of mindfulness and the ongoing practice of being present.

●●●● Concluding Thoughts ·······························

The focus on this chapter was on space exploration—specifically the pursuit of safety in the inner (emotional) and outer (physical and environmental) spaces of young children. We initially examined the human body as a navigational system and took an in-depth look at the science behind our human need and pursuit of safety. We considered various implications, ideas, and insights about mindfulness related to safety. We also explored enhancing safety through creating and maintaining safe early childhood environments and supporting young children in comforting themselves. We looked at differences between stress and trauma, with an emphasis on race-based traumatic-stress injury, microaggressions, and young children's engagement in recognizing whether all unkindness is the same. In the next section, we will investigate mindfulness pedagogy and practices during the early years.

· ·

A Menu of Options for Teaching Inclusively, Mindfully, and Equitably

 ### Children's Corner

Angelou, Maya. 2018. *Life Doesn't Frighten Me*. 25th anniversary ed. New York: Harry N. Abrams.

Bang, Molly. 2004. *When Sofie Gets Angry—Really, Really Angry*. New York: Scholastic.

Kluth, Paula, and Patrick Schwarz. 2010. *Pedro's Whale*. Baltimore: Paul H. Brookes.

Liu, Sylvia. 2016. *A Morning with Grandpa*. New York: Lee and Low.

Verde, Susan. 2019. *I Am Love: A Book of Compassion*. New York: Abrams.

Willard, Christopher, and Wendy O'Leary. 2019. *Breathing Makes It Better: A Book for Sad Days, Mad Days, Glad Days, and All the Feelings in Between*. Boulder, CO: Bala Kids.

Witek, Jo. 2014. *In My Heart: A Book of Feelings*. New York: Harry N. Abrams.

Wood, Douglas. 2011. *No One but You*. Somerville, MA: Candlewick.

Caregivers' Corner

Understanding the Science behind the Brain-Body Connection

Chopra, Deepak. 2001. *Perfect Health: The Complete Mind/Body Guide*. New York: Random House.

Hanson, Rick. 2016. *Hardwiring Happiness: The New Brain Science of Contentment, Calm, and Confidence*. New York: Harmony.

Hanson, Rick. 2020. *Neurodharma: New Science, Ancient Wisdom, and Seven Practices of the Highest Happiness*. New York: Random House.

Kabat-Zinn, Jon. 2013. *Full Catastrophe Living: Using the Wisdom of Your Body and Mind to Face Stress, Pain, and Illness*. Rev. ed. New York: Bantam.

Khalsa, Sat Bir Singh. 2007. "Yoga as a Therapeutic Intervention." In *Principles and Practice of Stress Management*. 3rd ed. New York: The Guilford Press.

Khalsa, Sat Bir Singh, and Jodie Gould. 2012. *Your Brain on Yoga*. New York: RosettaBooks.

Porges, Stephen W. 2011. *The Polyvagal Theory: Neurophysiological Foundations of Emotions, Attachment, Communication, and Self-Regulation*. New York: W. W. Norton and Company.

Porges, Stephen W. 2017. *The Pocket Guide to the Polyvagal Theory: The Transformative Power of Feeling Safe*. New York: W. W. Norton and Company.

Siegel, Daniel J. 2010. *Mindsight: The New Science of Personal Transformation*. New York: Bantam.

Stern, Eddie. 2019. *One Simple Thing: A New Look at the Science of Yoga and How It Can Transform Your Life*. New York: North Point.

Taylor, Jill Bolte. 2009. *My Stroke of Insight: A Brain Scientist's Personal Journey*. New York: Plume.

Resources on Childhood Trauma

American Academy of Pediatrics Council on Communications and Media. 2016. "Childhood Exposure to Violence." https://www.healthychildren.org/English/safety-prevention/at-home/Pages/Crime-Violence-and-Your-Child.aspx

Campaign for a Commercial Free Childhood. https://commercialfreechildhood.org

Erwin, Elizabeth J., and Naomi Morton. 2008. "Exposure to Media Violence and Young Children with and without Disabilities: Powerful Opportunities for Family-Professional Partnerships." *Early Childhood Education* 36(2): 105–112.

Groves, Betsy McAlister. 2003. *Children Who See Too Much: Lessons from the Child Witness to Violence Projec*t. Boston: Beacon Press.

Sorrels, Barbara. 2015. *Reaching and Teaching Children Exposed to Trauma*. Lewisville, NC: Gryphon House.

Turner, Bret. 2019. "Teaching First-Graders about Microaggressions: The Small Moments Add Up." *Teaching Tolerance*. https://www.tolerance.org/magazine/teaching-firstgraders-about-microaggressions-the-small-moments-add-up

Resources on the Developing Brain and How to Support Self-Regulation

Alert Program

https://www.alertprogram.com
Occupational therapists Mary Sue Williams and Sherry Shellenberger developed this program to teach self-regulation skills. Their framing metaphor of a car's engine provides children with a concrete image with which they can assess their state of readiness: Am I revved up? Am I slow-moving? Or am I ready to learn and interact with others? The website offers products such as books and games for sale, plus in-person and online training sessions. There are also free resources available.

Child Mind Institute

https://childmind.org
The Child Mind Institute is a research organization focused on advancing knowledge on young people's mental wellness. This website provides online resources for both families and educators, including guides for developmental milestones, how to access quality care, and how to support students with attention challenges in the classroom. These resources are also available in Spanish. Look for *mindfulness* in the "Topics A–Z" section of the website.

Harvard University's Center on the Developing Child

https://developingchild.harvard.edu/science/key-concepts/brain-architecture
Scientists at Harvard have developed this excellent online resource that provides both basic overviews and the latest, in-depth research into key aspects of children's brain development including self-regulation, executive function, resilience, toxic stress, and the vital role of interactions with caregivers. They situate their work in the real world, advocating for social policies that support a child's essential developmental needs.

Zero to Three

https://www.zerotothree.org
Zero to Three is a nonprofit organization committed to educating families, caregivers, educators, and policy makers about the research and best practices related to babies' and toddlers' brain development. It publishes a research journal, hosts annual conferences, and also offers a wide range of ready-to-use resources, including materials in Spanish and state-specific information. Be sure to check out the free downloadable curriculum for early childhood educators relating to young children's brain development, *The Growing Brain: From Birth to 5 Years Old*.

A Message from the Center for Autism and Early Childhood Mental Health College of Education and Human Services Montclair State University

During the past two years, we have witnessed multimedia messages with hurtful and divisive interpersonal behavior and discourse about how our nation will be led and how we speak of, and regard, each other. The behavior and language about those from other nations and creeds, and about those with differences and disabilities, have resulted in a level of fear and anger rarely witnessed in our lifetimes. Despite efforts made by many parents and educators to insulate and protect young children from these experiences, children are always watching, always listening, always feeling what is being said and done. . . .

Young children see the images and actions directly on TV and other electronic media, and witness these events indirectly through the words, affect, gestures, intonation, and actions of adults, and in how it changes those who love and spend time with them. Children form understandings based on their level of development, and, much more than adults, they begin to make interpretations about what this all means to them, their families, and their friends. This is not an abstract "ideological" debate for them. It is personal. It is about their safety, their family, their community. It is local, not global. These worries lay atop the "new normal" fear of terrorist acts from outside of our nation, and threats from within about intolerance, nationalism, deportation, and violence.

Here are some guidelines about how to speak with your children when they show worry and fear about these events and about their future:

- **Be there and be calm.** Children need to feel safe. This is a human biological requirement, that children (and adults) scan the faces, voices, and movements of others to discern safety. This occurs at the level of deeply embedded brain systems. Your presence, voice, words, and soft and loving touches provide each child with the best ways of feeling safe.

- **Ask children what they know and what they have heard.** Listen to the child's story and follow the child's lead. Ask children what they know and have heard. Correct the accounts and give permission for many different feelings: scared, angry, worried, and so on. Use simple language and correct any misunderstood accounts. Tell a child what they need to know, not all that you know.

- **Tell children what happened avoiding graphic accounts or unnecessary details.** For example, don't say, "A bad person had a rifle and went into a building and started shooting people and many people were hurt and died." Instead, say something like, "Someone did some bad things and people were hurt. But you are safe here and we will protect you."

- **Practice conversations with other adults.** Use simple language. Avoid imposing meanings or interpretations. Often children will experience and express their feelings through their body states. Ask them "what" and "where" they feel (head, tummy, chest, neck, and so on) as well as "how" they feel.

- **Share your feelings.** It is okay and important for children to know that the adults in their lives have the same feelings when bad things happen that they do. Let children know you feel these feelings and that you are there for them.

- **Remain in control.** Monitor your own emotion and tone of voice. Pay attention to your gestures, affect, and voice because children pay special attention to these ways of communicating. You can help children feel safer and calmer when your behaviors convey these feelings. If your own reaction is difficult to manage, enlist another adult to help you with the children. When there is uncertainty, say something like: "We don't know everything that happened but police and firefighters are helping people who were hurt." Let the child's responses guide what you say next.

- **Limit repeated exposure to images and reports of the events.** When children do see images or reports of tragedies, Fred Rogers of *Mister Rogers' Neighborhood* suggested that we help them "look for all the people who are helping." Couple the sad tragedy with the comforting presence of others who are helping and taking care of others.

- **Remember the 3R's of security: relationships, routines, and restoration.** Highlight relationships with familiar and consistent caregivers, family, and friends. Protect and increase routines that are familiar and normalizing, such as playtime, going to school, reading books, and other patterned activities.

- **Intervene with the particular learning style and temperament of the child in mind.** Children with autism and other disabilities may process information, such as gestures, pictures, and language, in different ways. Often a 4Ls strategy may help: less language and longer latency. This means that you can use fewer words and wait longer for a reply. Ask the child what he was thinking and feeling and even draw pictures or tell stories. Use your own facial expressions, voice, and words to reflect and tune in to the child's emotions. If helpful, use pictures or drawings to identify and label different feelings. Be prepared for misunderstandings and misinterpretations, and keep clarifying and reassuring the child that you will be sure he is safe.

- **Provide structure and communicate safety.** Uncertainty is the province of adulthood. While we as adults may feel unsure of the possibility of future tragedies, we must always let children know that we will take care of them and protect them. Children thrive when provided structure and safety.

- **Remember to take care of yourself.** If the adults in a child's life are overwhelmed, overstressed, and overtired, it will be more difficult to be safe, secure, and stable for the child. Pay attention to the ABCs of self-care—awareness, balance, and connection—in your own life.

- **Engage your child in communal and social gatherings of care and support.** Immerse children in a network of social relationships that reflect messaging that countermands the threatening, divisive themes that have become so common in the social discourse. There is no greater antidote to fear than social engagement and experiences of security. Encourage children to get involved in a community or service program, such as collecting items for a food bank, involvement in an event or gathering where they experience a culture outside of their own, visiting the sick or those who are alone.

- **Kindle in children a belief and expectation that you and they will be okay.** Building on the notion of repair and survival after loss and disappointment, children understand through everyday human experiences and participating in sports that sometimes you win and sometimes you lose. Many children have encountered more personal losses, such as changing teachers or going to a new school, moving to a new neighborhood, the loss of a pet, or the death of a grandparent. Allow for disappointment, but couple that with the conviction that good things will still happen and new opportunities will arise.

- **Recognize that there are some feelings that we can only share and cannot fix.** Children need us to be there with and for them at such times. It is appropriate to both not have an answer and be with the children in their sadness and confusion.

Source: Center for Autism and Early Childhood Mental Health at Montclair State University, 2018.

 **Take It to the Classroom**

Still Quiet Place

Amy Saltzman is widely known and respected for conceptualizing and creating the Still Quiet Place. She invites children to discover their own personalized Still Quiet Place, a space deep within, to deal with difficult emotions or to feel ease or for no reason at all. She describes this place as one that is inside the individual, a place where each child can go anytime they want just by breathing. She invites the children to take slow, deep breaths and feel the warmth within. She encourages the children to go to the Still Quiet Place whenever they want, but particularly when they feel angry, sad, or afraid. Feelings, she says, are not as big and powerful as they seem. In their Still Quiet Place, children can feel their feelings but not be overwhelmed by them.

Saltzman, Amy. 2014. A Still Quiet Place: A Mindfulness Program for Teaching Children and Adolescents to Ease Stress and Difficult Emotions. Oakland, CA: New Harbinger.

Calming Corner

My name is Alyssa Kovach, and I am a kindergarten teacher in a public elementary school located in an urban neighborhood in New Jersey. My class consists of twenty students who come from diverse backgrounds, ethnicities, and abilities, and often school provides a place of comfort and stability for them. In kindergarten, I believe that it is essential to teach young minds how to understand their emotions and navigate adversity and conflicts in life, as well as provide them with the tools to be positive and productive citizens. Throughout the year, I teach these ideas through read-alouds, videos, explicit modeling, and role-playing techniques. One particular concept that I incorporate into my classroom environment is the Calming Corner. I dedicate an area in my classroom as a safe, private place where my students can take a break periodically throughout the day, based on how they are feeling. The Calming Corner offers beanbag chairs, pillows, stuffed animals, playdough, squeeze toys, sensory bottles, coloring books, and cards with photos of yoga stretches.

Before introducing the Calming Corner to my students, I explain to them the importance of mindfulness, teaching them how to understand and recognize their emotions. As a class, we discuss and role-play how and when to use the space when we are feeling upset, frustrated, angry, or just needing a break. We discuss positive ways of calming down by modeling each tool in the corner.

For the Calming Corner to run effectively without interruptions, it is important to teach students how to be independent when using this strategy. I teach my students to use a timer to help regulate their time in the space and know when to return to their work. Ultimately, I have witnessed once-frustrated students self-soothe, resulting in increased productivity, patience, and motivation. I believe students leave my classroom with greater emotional autonomy, hopefully leading them to become more successful and capable students now and in the future!

The Power of Presence

PART III

Informing Our Teaching Practice: Mindfulness with Young Children

This final section expands upon the first two foundational sections by providing a deeper inquiry into being present and illustrating how this informs and broadens our teaching practice. By reflecting on our pedagogy and engaging in social action with young children, we offer new ways of thinking and teaching to create new paradigms in early childhood education and care.

The Power of Presence

CHAPTER 7

Teaching Inclusively, Mindfully, Equitably

> **"Everybody is a genius. But if you judge a fish by its ability to climb a tree, it will live its whole life believing that it is stupid."**
> —Author unknown

Anyone can practice mindfulness anytime and anywhere. Inviting the notion of being present into early childhood education, however, is more than a handful of mindfulness exercises, yoga, or belly breathing three times a day. When a climate of mindfulness exists in the classroom, there is a noticeable commitment to well-being in body and mind. The focus of this chapter is to examine how mindfulness practices can be integrated into classroom culture and how early childhood pedagogy and practice can elevate well-being for children as well as teachers. Essentially, it's about time that we become present in our teaching and learning, both locally and globally.

Keeping this in mind, I want to introduce you to Christina, a dear friend who recently shared with me her compelling early school experiences. Christina is a twenty-eight-year-old woman and a first-generation American whose family is from Mexico. Christina explains how as a young child she had to put on two very different and conflicting masks—one for home and one for school:

> My home will always be the US, and going home will always mean I can count on frijoles and tortillas being served. But growing up in America, I felt like I had to wear two different masks and at any given moment I would need to exchange one for the other. I would get up and put on my American clothes to go to my American school where I would speak and learn in English, and I would get scolded by teachers for speaking in Spanish—my native language. Only when I went home could I be Mexican and speak in Spanish, eat my Mexican food, watch my Mexican telenovelas, and sing mariachi songs with my grandpa.

I was not able to make sense of everything that was happening in my world at that time because when I first started going to school, I did not know any English and yet I was expected to speak it. I honestly didn't like the language because it felt harsh and cold on my tongue compared to the sweet melody of my native language. In kindergarten, I felt scared and confused because I couldn't understand my teachers or classmates at all. I felt like my teachers were frustrated with me because I couldn't follow directions. I felt ostracized because I was taken out of class to go to Mrs. Lopez and other "special" classes.

I remember on the bus one time, a boy was yelling and screaming at me, and though I didn't have a clue as to what he was saying, I was terrified and refused to go back to school for a whole month. When my mom finally made me return to school, I made a ritual of putting on my American school clothes and used them as a shield to protect the child I was at home, and a mask to be the person my teachers wanted me to be at school.

Christina's story would be a troubling and traumatic experience for any person, but especially for a child, to bear. It is as if Christina had to not only hide but also deny important aspects of her intersecting identities by wearing invisible masks. This is confusing and painful for any young child. Teachers are expected to provide safety, protection, and an understanding about how each child learns best. As you read through the rest of this chapter, think about the title—teaching inclusively, mindfully, and equitably—as you consider how a child's early education experiences might be.

When Well-Being Is the Highest Priority in Early Childhood

Many insights and inspirations for this book were harvested in 2016 during my sabbatical in Australia. Although seeds had been planted over the course of my academic and teaching career, they blossomed in bounty and abundance during my sabbatical. This is where I witnessed how early childhood narratives and practices in Australia reflect a core belief about well-being within a holistic perspective. Here is what I wrote about these impressions in a 2017 article published in *Global Education Review*:

I observed that well-being was not only uniformly considered significant in the lives of young children, but was actively encouraged and supported across environments and with people responsible for care and education during the early years. Well-being was simply a natural part of the cultural fabric and embraced as a core value, particularly at the policy level.

When well-being is the priority in early childhood education and care, as reflected across policy, teacher education, pedagogy, curriculum, and practices, a systemic culture of mindfulness is naturally created and sustained.

When a culture of mindfulness is present, educators can question and even challenge the pressures to emphasize academics and uniformity and can integrate mindfulness in their early childhood environments in different ways. Here is one snapshot to illustrate how kindergarten teacher Carissa Olivi began incorporating mindfulness practices into the culture of her classroom:

I introduce different techniques to help the children pay attention to their breath. We learn about and watch our thoughts. Then we notice when different thoughts pop up when we are paying attention to our breath. We bring our attention back to our breathing by counting or using chosen anchor words or anchor spots, which are used to bring the attention back to the breath when you get distracted with thoughts. There are three anchor spots: belly, chest, and the tip of the nose. As far as anchor words, I make suggestions for the children and we work with the suggestions for a few days. Then I tell students to find words that work for them. One of the children is using "breath in, breath out," which was her own idea.

The young ones love to count their breaths. Sometimes they sit for one minute and tell me they counted seventy-nine breaths or something! Then I ask them how many they would have counted if they slowed their breath down. We put our hands on our stomachs to find a natural rhythm. Then I remind them the next time they can put their hands on their stomachs to keep count of their breaths. It is very important for children to have time to share after the practice so I may ask some questions such as:

- Are you feeling any different from before practice?

- What happened today?

- Did your mind wander?

- What did you do to pay attention to your breath?

- How many breaths did you take?

- If you counted your breaths, how did you count?

- What are you feeling in your body?

- Can you feel your nervous system?

- Would anyone like to share their experience?

Recently I have been having children listen inward to themselves. I ask them what they need in any given moment. Instead of simply reacting to behaviors, I reassure them that they have everything they need and encourage them to get still enough to choose something they need to support them in the moment. Maybe it's a sip of water or a visit to the calm center we have in the classroom or a hug or a walk. This is all about self-regulation. We also practice gratitude and kindness: sending kindness, feeling the room around them, mindful listening, and calming the body.

This thoughtful narrative demonstrates how simple it can be to engage young children in deepening an awareness of their bodies, breath, and the immediate environment. And when children feel safe, relaxed, and focused, they can learn and flourish.

When well-being is the foundation from which all educational decisions are made, the focus is always about children's health in body and mind. Since yoga is the practice many people first associate with mindfulness and being present, let's begin by taking a closer look at how yoga might be fully realized in early childhood education and care.

Introducing or practicing yoga in the classroom does not have to be complicated, but educators need a basic understanding of fundamental principles before they decide to teach. First, have a mindfulness practice of your own. Perhaps take yoga classes or commit to a self-practice at home. This will then give you a foundation from which to teach.

Contemplating the Practice of Yoga in Early Childhood

Although many people associate *asana* or postures as the primary or exclusive form of yoga, practicing asana is actually only one part. There are eight limbs of yoga, including asana, which serve as a powerful and practical guide to help us make conscious decisions about how to engage with our personal growth, the people in our lives, and the world all around us. These eight limbs of yoga can help us to consciously make personal choices about practices and experiences related to who we are and what we are doing on Earth:

- **Yama:** There are five ethical considerations that guide our thoughts, words, or actions in interpersonal interactions: non-harming, truthfulness, non-stealing, sexual responsibility and fidelity, and non-coveting.

- **Niyama:** There are five rules of personal behavior: cleanliness in body and mind, contentment, self-discipline, spiritual study of sacred texts, and devotion or surrender to the divine.

- **Asana:** This is the practice of physical postures.

- **Pranayama:** This is the conscious practice of breath control.

- **Pratyahara:** This is the practice of withdrawing attention from sense organs and external sensations and enhancing attention on inner awareness.

- **Dharana:** This is focused and sustained concentration.

- **Dhyana:** This is effortless, uninterrupted meditation.

- **Samadhi:** This is the experience of a harmonious union of the individual self with pure consciousness.

In his book *One Simple Thing*, Eddie Stern discusses that yoga has various meanings, including knowledge, union, and a path. He offers the following concrete suggestions about how to apply the eight limbs of yoga in ways that help us assume personal responsibility on a spiritual path, and how to translate them into conscious, practical applications: choosing to be thoughtful, loving, and respectful with oneself and others, devoting to a personal spiritual practice, practicing asanas to maintain a healthy body and mind, and using conscious breathing to balance the nervous system.

The eight limbs are a powerful and practical guide that can serve as a roadmap over one's entire life. As we engage in a practice of mindfulness on an ongoing basis, the mind becomes quieter and steadier, thus making us better equipped and experienced to teach. Because young children typically live in the present moment, adults may need to be (re) minded how the youngest citizens of the world can be among the wisest teachers.

In addition to providing clarity and direction in adults' personal lives, these classic eight aspects of yoga can serve as a valuable guide in the early childhood classroom. For example, some of the eight limbs of yoga might influence decisions about how to maintain a classroom culture of mindfulness, how to establish discourses of dignity with young children, or how to engage collectively in daily contemplative practices. In the following illustrative examples, you will see the first four limbs of yoga with corresponding ideas as ways to consider how these aspects of yoga might inform an early childhood teaching practice.

Yama: Ethical Codes of Nonviolence and Truth

- **Looking out for others:** Engage children in thinking and talking about ways to keep one another safe. Invite them to illustrate or document in some other way why taking care of each other is a good idea and what it could look like within and beyond classroom walls.

- **Ensuring safety in inner and outer spaces:** Help children to gradually help themselves so that all children feel safe in their emotional as well as physical spaces. I offer some specific suggestions at the end of the chapter.

- **Noticing acts of kindness:** Engage the children in natural conversations with questions such as the following:

  o Who was kind to you today?

  o What kind thing happened to you today?

  o How did you feel in that situation?

  o What else did you notice?

- **Using children's literature to think critically about peace:** After children are familiar with a book, consider expanding concepts by inviting them to write or draw a prequel to the story, "read" the book to a partner or in a small group, or support self-reflection by posing questions such as:

  o What would you do in that situation?

  o What does this story remind you of?

o How would you feel in that situation?

o What questions do you have about this book?

o What character is most like you and why?

- **Creating a Solutions Station:** Establish a designated space in the classroom (or home) where young children can go to solve an issue or problem. Teach children to go over and find out how they can help their peer if a child goes to the station alone. Provide paper and pencils, pens, markers, crayons, or tablets for children to map out or brainstorm various solutions.

Niyama: Personal Observances of Cleanliness, Contentment, Persistence, Austerity, and Repetition

- **Making commitments to ourselves about how to live:** Creating a sense of harmony and respect for the classroom and school community. Start with individual spaces, such as cubbies, or shared spaces, such as the playground or hallways. Work with children to identify ways to keep personal and collective spaces clean, beautiful, and organized. Engage in ongoing conversations about what children are most proud of in their surroundings and how to maintain a sense of pride and joy about the environment they inhabit.

- **Planting and cultivating seeds of peace:** Design with the children a "peace place" in the classroom that might include a minicouch, a large pillow, beanbag chairs, or larger carpet squares so more than one child can contemplate peace together. Consider recording and having available guided meditations (several are offered throughout this book) so young children can visit their peaceful places on their own. Review chapter 4 for the peace cushion and other ideas to foster peaceful contemplation, silence, and stillness.

- **Engaging children in conversations about accumulation:** Brainstorm ways to consume less in the classroom, such as using less paper, replacing plastic with more sustainable objects, or conserving power by turning lights off or dimming them when possible.

- **Building confidence and competence in young children:** Invite children to send love notes, repeat positive affirmations, or affix daily reminders that deliver healthy messages to themselves and to others. Encourage children to return often to messages such as the following:

o I am a great problem solver.

o I can breathe deeply to calm my body.

○ When I am mad, I find healthy ways to share my feelings.

○ I am becoming a strong reader.

Asana: The Practice of Postures

- **Committing to an asana practice:** Practice postures daily. Consider beginning by teaching children sun salutations. Embed this classic yoga sequence, which stretches the body and calms the mind, into the daily classroom routine. Refer to Take It to the Classroom in chapter 5 for teaching this sequence.

- **Facilitating a formal class inquiry that emerges from children's questions:** Ask children if they have any questions about breathing, asanas, or related ideas. For example, design an investigation with the class on sun salutations and study the sun and moon.

- **Engaging in stories, games, poems, songs, and books:** Encourage children to create original games, sequences, raps, or poems. See the Children's Corner at the end of this chapter for book recommendations on yoga-related literature for young learners.

- **Connecting yoga and the curriculum:** Thoughtfully integrate postures into the current class theme, unit, or investigation. When teaching patterns during math, for example, you might encourage children to move with their bodies to create patterns of different shapes such as a triangle pose (Trikonsana) or a wheel pose (Urdvha Dhanurasana).

- **Cocreate with children fun yoga sequences that can be revisited throughout the year:** Nature-based themes work particularly well. Here are a few suggestions:

  ○ Rainforest: tree pose (Vrksasana) and mountain pose (Tadasana)

  ○ Water and ecology: boat pose (Navasana) and turtle pose (Kurmasana)

  ○ Four-legged friends: downward dog pose (Adho Mukha Svanasana) and camel pose (Ustrasana)

- Other themes can be about personal qualities such as strength—warrior poses (Virabhadrasana I and II)—or gentleness—child's pose (Balasana) and butterfly pose (Baddha Konasana).

Pranayama: The Practice of Breath Control

- **Breathing deeply and mindfully:** Teach children about the importance of breathing by reviewing key ideas about the breath and how to engage young children in noticing and exploring their own breathing. Consider using The Breathing App, which is available for free in iOS and Android systems. Cocreator of the app Eddie Stern says that through breathing, a sense of balance is evident in increased alertness; a healthier immune function; and reduced symptoms associated with stress, insomnia, depression, and post-traumatic stress.

These ideas are just scratching the surface when it comes to embedding mindfulness practices into the early childhood classroom. As we deepen our own practices, we will be able to reflect upon our own learning and transmit this energy to the young children in our lives. Keep in mind that we are not designing hour-long yoga classes but rather embedding meaningful and engaging mindfulness practices into the classroom and school culture.

One of the most essential features to remember about yoga, especially during the early years, is that it is a practice about being present. Therefore, reaching and teaching all children and being present with them is what counts most. Yoga is about an individual expression as opposed to feeling pressured to "perform an asana correctly" or "look like everybody else." Joyful learning is perhaps the most important lesson we can convey to young children, and this is essentially transmitted from us by simply being present in the moment. As we continue to explore how mindfulness practices can be incorporated into the rhythm and culture of the classroom, let us notice how well-being can be elevated through our pedagogy in early childhood education and care.

Teaching Well: It's Just a Matter of Time

As you read the following quote from author Timothy Gallwey in *The Inner Game of Tennis: The Classic Guide to the Mental Side of Peak Performance*, which I often share in class, think about all the connections you notice between a rose and a child:

> When we plant a rose seed in the earth, we notice that it is small, but we do not criticize it as "rootless and stemless." We treat it as a seed, giving it the water and nourishment required of a seed. When it first shoots up out of the earth, we don't condemn it as immature and underdeveloped; nor do we criticize the buds not being open when they appear. We stand in wonder at the process taking place and give the plant the care it needs at each stage of its development.

Keep in mind this compelling image of children as roses as we continue exploring mindfulness practices and the classroom culture, with an eye to teaching (and learning with) young children about being present. We will address three main aspects: teaching inclusively, teaching mindfully, and teaching equitably.

Teaching Inclusively

When we teach inclusively, the core belief is that every child matters and belongs in the classroom and school community. This teaching commitment is firmly etched into policy, pedagogy, and practice. Further, we are also teaching young learners that everyone matters in the shared community called *humanity*. If this is a fundamental belief, then children will be educated together in the same classrooms, not in separate spaces or schools. Markers such as English language learner or autistic would not be used to separate children to educate them, just as other markers such as a child's ethnicity, religion, or gender would not be used to isolate children and teach them separately.

There are many, however, who still associate the term *inclusive* as solely a disability issue. Teaching inclusively is about reaching and teaching every child in the classroom. In their classic text *Teaching Everyone: An Introduction to Inclusive Education*, Whitney Rapp and Katrina Arndt clarify how special education has been perpetuated: "Special education evolved as a separate system because educators, legislators, and administrators believed that children with disabilities are so different from their peers that they must need specially trained teachers."

A belief about difference that is based on deficit or disapproval in any form does not have a place in any early childhood environment. When diversity or difference is perceived from a deficit-oriented perspective, disapproval is manifested in thought, word, and action. Therefore, any discourse about difference—in and out of the classroom—which is not anchored in dignity is rooted in injustice.

There are several early childhood guidelines and curricula that directly inform and shape inclusive teaching practices for young children. Even more interesting is that they have elements of mindfulness threaded throughout. Although it is beyond the scope of this chapter to critically analyze them now, here are a few highlights:

- ***Belonging, Being and Becoming: The Early Years Learning Framework for Australia***: Developed in 2009 and updated in 2019, this is a progressive set of national guidelines "designed to inspire conversations, improve communication, and provide a common language about young children's learning among children themselves, their families, the broader community, early childhood educators and other professionals." This framework is respected globally for its focus on inclusivity, well-being, nature, and play-based learning, among other features. Specifically, young children are prominently positioned as full and competent partners with educators and families in their own learning, and families are acknowledged as the first and most influential educators in young children's lives. What makes these guidelines most distinctive is the central focus on mindfulness practices: belonging (connection and interdependence), being (presence here and now), and becoming (changing identities and knowledge).

- ***Te Whāriki: He whāriki mātauranga mō ngā mokopuna o Aotearoa Early Childhood Curriculum*** (**Te Whāriki**): First published in 1996 and updated in 2017 by New Zealand's Ministry of Education, Te Whāriki is rooted in rich Māori tradition. It is an inclusive curriculum for all children across various aspects of diversity, such as gender, ethnicity, ability, learning needs, family structure and values, socio-economic status, and religion. The vision recognizes young children as "competent and confident learners and communicators, healthy in mind, body and spirit, secure in their sense of belonging and in the knowledge that they make a valued contribution to society."

The whāriki, or woven mat, is used as symbol for this curriculum to represent the interwoven, multilayered understanding of the curriculum principles and strands proudly rooted in Māori culture.

- **Reggio Emilia pedagogy:** This pedagogy from Italy recognizes an inclusive, emergent, and play-based approach to learning and teaching. Loris Malaguzzi, founder of the Reggio Emilia approach, metaphorically describes a crucial conceptual understanding of this educational philosophy in the poem "The Hundred Languages of Children." Malaguzzi celebrates the multitude of ways in which children express themselves and the rich uniqueness of their ability to wonder, ponder, discover, and question.

These frameworks are noteworthy because they present a set of guidelines and philosophical underpinnings that situate young learners at the epicenter of their own learning, in active partnership with adults, peers, and the land. The focus on teaching inclusively emphasizes the notion of belonging, connection, and interdependence with people, places, things, and living beings, including nature. Further, a holistic perspective places well-being and learning in the here and now, acknowledging a steadfast commitment to mindfulness and being present.

There are many other notable early childhood pedagogical approaches that promote inclusive teaching from a holistic lens, even if the word *inclusive* is not present. Inclusive teaching not only recognizes each child as a magnificent, unique human being filled with endless potential but also acknowledges the profound connections within and outside children. These underpinnings are in stark contrast to instruction in many Western countries, where discourses of accumulation, conformity, and standardization exist. Although an acknowledgment of inclusive teaching is growing in the West, there is still much work to be done to ensure that the unacceptable is transformed to being acceptable and even celebrated. Being present is one way to begin to reimagine our own teaching. When early childhood educators teach inclusively, they find the genius inside each child.

Teaching Mindfully

Given that teaching and learning are intricately intertwined, when we are teaching mindfully, we are also learning mindfully. When we are teaching mindfully, we are also deeply aware of the inner journey we take as learners.

In *Pedagogy of Freedom*, educator and activist Paulo Freire articulates how self-inquiry in teaching is an ongoing process, journey, or search. When we teach, we are also learning as we continue to search and re-search as Freire writes:

> Teaching, which is really inseparable from learning, is of its very nature a joyful experience. It is also fake to consider seriousness and joy to be contradictory, as if joy were the enemy of methodological rigor. On the contrary, the more methodologically rigorous I become in my questionings

and in my teaching practice, the more joyful and hopeful I become as well. Joy does not come to us only at the moment of finding what we sought. It comes also in the search itself. And teaching and learning are not possible without the search, without beauty, and without joy.

Freire points out so eloquently that we do not find joy only when we discover what we are looking for; joy is also found in the search itself. Joy is already in the fabric threaded throughout our teaching and learning, especially when we practice mindfulness. Read what Bianca, whom you met in chapter 3, discovered about herself and her students when they engaged in mindfulness practices:

> As an early childhood educator, I believe mindfulness practices are imperative in the classroom. My personal definition of mindfulness is taking a respite from the busy tasks that sometimes consume my day. In my prekindergarten classroom, I've introduced a concept called "brain breaks" in which my students engage with their peers by doing a silly dance and/or finding a quiet space in the classroom to read, do yoga, and/or sit quietly before returning to the group table to continue working. I have noticed that my students who have engaged in these mindfulness practices have shown an improvement in self-regulation. I have also noticed an improvement in my health with these mindfulness practices. A recent visit to the doctor has shown that I have lost eight pounds and that my blood-pressure reading was significantly lower than the times prior when I was so consumed with work that I didn't fully take care of myself physically, mentally, and/or spiritually.

There are many ways to cultivate being present. How then can we remain conscious about inviting mindfulness into our teaching and learning? The practice of listening, which is an essential feature in any mindfulness practice, might be the place to start. When awareness increases as we engage in our yoga practice, for example, we are able to tune in and listen to what the poses and our breathing have to teach us. Every person has a unique way of adapting to or dealing with life's challenges. Our human pursuit of safety will shape our behavior, especially when we are feeling vulnerable or challenged in some way. By becoming more consistently aware of the present moment through ongoing practice, we are able to be more responsive to and authentic with young children. Teacher Corrine Harney learned a valuable lesson from a young student about yoga practice:

> While teaching in an inclusive preschool class of four- and five-year-olds, I began instituting daily yoga and meditation practices. At the end of several months, I concluded there were numerous benefits to including these mindfulness practices. Both students and staff, including myself, appeared more aware of ourselves both physically within our classroom space as well as emotionally, especially being in tune with others.
>
> On one occasion, we were doing the volcano pose. The emphasis is on releasing energy. We were all standing with our palms touching and thumbs resting on our chests, then raising our arms way up from the chest, hands

together and opening them up as they reach high above our heads, as if we are powerful volcanos exploding. One student, however, was doing the motion in the opposite direction, starting with her extended arms over her head and bringing them, palms together, down to her chest. When I went to "correct" her, she explained how that was the way she needed to do it. It was in that moment that I realized my error. The student was truly in a mindful state, understanding she needed to feel more grounded and stable. She was following her instincts, knowing what she needed in that moment.

When we are engaged in a mindfulness practice, we are more aware of the present moment, like Corrine was, and we can not only listen but also truly hear. Most noteworthy to me is how this child not only tuned into and listened to the wisdom within but also followed through and adapted the group activity in a way that made sense to her.

Paying attention to our inner wisdom, also known as *intuition*, is not typically addressed in early childhood education and care, but I think it is important to address it here because it is a critical part of being human. Intuition can be thought of as a knowing, feeling, or sensing. We are constantly noticing energy within us and all around us. Author Penney Peirce describes intuitive knowing in her book *The Intuitive Way* as "direct knowing—knowing without time-consuming, linear reasoning; knowing without external proof." Having coached business executives, political figures, scientists, and those interested in learning about intuition and related topics over the past thirty years, Peirce notes that we might forget to pay attention to our attention, but it is always with us.

Although the messages we receive from tuning into our intuition may not make sense to us at the time, this inner voice or wisdom is more readily available to us when we are present in the here and now. Jill Bolte Taylor, a Harvard-trained brain researcher, shares in her book *My Stroke of Insight* how she still relies on her intuition simply by focusing her attention and listening to how she feels in the present moment. As you read her personal reflection, notice specifically how she works with the left (logical) and right (creative, holistic) parts of her brain:

> Ever since the stroke, I steer my life almost entirely by paying attention to how people, places, and things feel to me energetically. In order to hear the intuitive words of my right mind, however, I must consciously slow my left mind down so I am not simply carried along on the current of my chatty storyteller. Intuitively, I don't question why I am subconsciously attracted to some people and situations, yet repelled by others. I simply listen to my body and implicitly trust my instincts.

Perhaps you were as amused as I was at Taylor's reference to the incessant noise in her mind as her "chatty storyteller." What resonated most with me was the absolute trust she places on her intuition; I now do the same thing. It has taken me many speed bumps and wrong turns over the years, but what I have learned is that intuition is 100 percent accurate, 100 percent of the time.

Listening to our intuition, which is very different from noticing the chatter in our minds, is not the same for everyone. Intuition can be experienced as a strong gut feeling or a subtle, soft, whisper-like sensation. I like to think of intuition as a personal navigational system (yes, a car reference again) because inner wisdom can always give us the best information about what we need in the moment. Just like mindfulness, intuition grows stronger as we practice.

So what does intuition have to do with teaching, learning, and early childhood? First, I do not think we pay enough attention to intuition during the early years because we do not pay enough attention to intuition in our adult lives, particularly for those living in Western cultures. Second, we could do a much better job supporting and nurturing the inner wisdom that children naturally possess. Consider the story about six-year-old Carla from Litany Burns's book *The Sixth Sense of Children: Nurturing Your Child's Intuitive Abilities*, which describes what happens when Carla insists that she feels something burning during family dinner. Even when her mother checks the appliances and reassures her that everything is fine, Carla persists. Note how her parents respond. Even though Carla's father is annoyed by the disruption to dinnertime, he gets up from the table:

> [He] checked all the electrical outlets, including those in the garage and the basement. Carla was told to finish her meal and get ready for bed. That night, while everyone was asleep, Carla woke up and ran into her parents' bedroom. "Daddy! Daddy! There's a fire in the house!" Although he smelled no trace of smoke, her father sleepily went down the stairs to inspect the house. When he reached the laundry room, he found the beginning of an electrical fire, which he quickly put out, ending the possibility of a disastrous blaze.

Although Carla's family might have been annoyed, they took her seriously. And that is the point: intuition is not necessarily linear or logical, and it can appear to be confusing or irrational. Therefore, teaching as well as learning to trust this inner knowing, even when it may seem puzzling, is at the heart of listening within. Trust plays a pivotal role when we are committed to teaching and learning mindfully. We must learn to trust ourselves and to teach children how much we trust them. If we want children to notice and respect their intuition, we must show them how much we trust what they have to share. I learned this lesson firsthand.

When Alyssa was about two years old, we had driven to the university where I worked. As we were getting ready to leave, I asked her to use the bathroom. She said she did not need to go. Knowing we had a forty-five-minute trip ahead (on the highway with no place to stop if we needed to) and that she was not consistently potty trained, I asked her again to use the bathroom. She refused. I became a little firmer and responded, "Lissy, you need to at least try to use the bathroom before we get in the car for a long trip home." At that point, she was clearly exasperated and exclaimed loudly for all my colleagues to hear, "My body is telling me I don't have to go to the bathroom!" I realized in that moment that I was sending my daughter a message not to trust her own body, so I backed off. I also realized that my repeated requests might have indicated to her that I did not trust her body's signals either. In case you were wondering, she did make it the entire way home, traffic and all, without incident.

Well-meaning adults can take control of all aspects of young children's lives without even knowing it, instead of encouraging them to tune into their body's feelings and signals. For example, we might pressure children to finish all of the food on their plates when they are no longer hungry, to stop crying when they get hurt, or to stay still when they have been sitting for a long time. Although these examples are not necessarily associated with intuition, when adults expect children to dismiss what they are feeling, youngsters learn not to listen to and trust their own bodies. This is not to be mistaken with giving in to children's pleas to stay up all night or to play unsupervised in a huge lake. Adults have a responsibility, to be sure, to provide safety and protection. At the same time, adults must support young children in gradually learning to take on more responsibility for their own safety and well-being.

As one way of nurturing children's intuition especially during the early years, adults must be present and prepared to listen. When it comes to helping children understand and preserve their own intuitive abilities, here are some ideas to consider:

- Encourage a young child to share her impressions, even if they seem illogical, unusual, or confusing to you.

- Refrain from rejecting, judging, or diminishing children or their experiences, especially if they are sharing something that makes absolutely no sense to you. Ask for clarification or more information, if needed.

- Be supportive and responsive when a child describes intuitive feelings, dreams, or other related experiences.

- Convey to young children that you can be trusted when they share their intuitive impressions, insights, sensations, and experiences. Trust strengthens between children and adults when we are active, nonjudgmental listeners.

- Invite children to creatively express themselves through singing, drawing, writing or scribbling, rapping, painting, photography, and dancing as ways to document their intuitive experiences.

- Encourage children to express what they are sensing in ways that are most natural and comfortable for them. Note that not every child will want to or have adequate language to explain what she is sensing.

Here is one more strategy that I created when Alyssa was very young that helped her to think critically, reflect honestly, and make informed decisions. My intention was for her to tune into her intuition by noticing how a person or situation made her feel. We called them the Three Questions, which were designed to be used anytime and anywhere and were especially helpful when Alyssa was facing a difficult situation such as being pressured by peers or dealing with uncertainty.

1. Is it safe?

2. Is it smart?

3. Is it kind?

We used these questions throughout Alyssa's adolescent years, since they seemed to offer the same clear guidance across different stages of life. Using the Three Questions at home or school is relatively easy, because we can first teach young children to ask the questions to themselves when in a new, confusing, or uncomfortable situation and then invite them to answer each question. If I could do it all over again, I might pose these questions in a slightly different way to encourage children to focus even more on their intuition and inner wisdom.

1. Does it feel safe?

2. Does it feel smart?

3. Does it feel kind?

Teaching mindfully is also about a profound awareness of the learning unfolding in the moment. There is immeasurable joy in the ever-turning cycle of teaching and learning. We cannot teach mindfully unless we are also learning mindfully. The practice of listening—both within and outside of ourselves—promotes a deeper sense of awareness so we can be fully present to what each moment has to offer. Young children are curious and love to explore, so let us follow as children lead us to where they want to go. Here is how one early childhood teacher in New York City ignited a spark about outer space by thoughtfully tuning in to what her three-year-old students wanted to learn:

> A year-long investigation of rocket ships and outer space began early in the school year, when many of the three-year-olds in my class noticed that the moon was out during the daytime. This fascination raised questions about why we can sometimes see the moon, where the moon goes, and how we could get there. As part of a Reggio-inspired school, my coteachers and I were eager to extend students' interest and inquiry and spark their curiosity on the subject. So we used our light projector to project images of the moon and outer space onto the walls of our classroom. We created a big rocket ship in the classroom using a large, recycled cardboard box, and we taped pictures of outer space and a mission-control deck inside and outside the box.
>
> By closely documenting and observing how the children interacted with the rocket ship, we developed a "rocket ship small group" with five students who had demonstrated a clear and continued interest in rocket ships and outer space. We decided as a small group to add to our existing rocket ship using recycled materials, so we enlisted the help of a former construction worker-turned-nursery school-teacher to guide us through the building process.

After a few months of expanding our rocket ship, I noticed my small group starting to get bored and uninterested in building. However, they were still fascinated by the parts of the rocket ship and how it blasted off into outer space. We began watching videos of real rocket ships blasting off, which I found on YouTube. These videos reinvigorated the small group's original interests, and they began asking very thoughtful, complex questions—many of which I couldn't answer.

Just as we had asked a construction expert to help us build the rocket ship, I knew it would be most valuable to have my students learn more about rocket ships from experts and real-life experiences. The small group and I researched "rocket ships in New York City" on the computer and found that the Intrepid Museum has a real space shuttle, *Enterprise*. The rocket ship small group was ecstatic about this finding and wanted to plan a trip there with our whole class.

We worked for months to plan our visit and spent hours researching *Enterprise* by watching videos of its flight and reading information from the Intrepid Museum's website. The rocket ship small group decided that since they were the rocket-ship experts of our class, they would be the ones to share their expertise with the other students and lead us on our tour of the space shuttle pavilion. In May, thirteen students from my class and ten adults spent the morning at the Intrepid Museum captivated by a real-life rocket ship as well as its intriguing features and history, as explained meticulously to us by five three-year-olds. This year-long investigation highlighted the importance of providing young children with real-life, authentic opportunities to take ownership and agency over their learning, as they often have so much more to teach us than we have to teach them.

This imaginative early childhood educator, Alyssa Blackman, is pursuing her graduate degree in education with an interest in young children with disabilities. In the spirit of full disclosure, she is also my daughter. She cocreated this captivating investigation together with young learners and fed their insatiable curiosity about their world and beyond. When children are thirsty to learn about people, places, and other worlds, the seeds of joy, mindfulness, and social action are implanted. In this way youngsters make connections to their own lives and beyond. When we help young children to genuinely care about these intersecting connections, they also learn how to care for others, including themselves. This caring is deeply rooted within the practice of being present.

Teaching Equitably

Even though they are closely interconnected, teaching equitably is different from teaching inclusively. Inclusivity is ensuring all children feel like they matter and belong. Conversely, teaching equitably is about inspiring young children to think deeply and critically, in ways that are meaningful for them, about people, land, history, and circumstances. When we teach equitably, we are acknowledging every child's unique genius, interests, learning styles, struggles, talents, preferences, fascinations, and experiences. To teach equitably is to teach about fairness.

Children are repeatedly told to pay attention but often are not taught how to do so. Mary Cowhey describes in her book *Black Ants and Buddhists* why children's attention is becoming shorter and how critical thinking and inquiry can promote sustained, engaged attention:

> In these days of fast food, instant messaging, music videos, call waiting, and fast cash, our society in general and our media in specific actively and aggressively shorten our attention span. As a teacher of critical thinkers, part of my job is to deliberately nurture sustained interest in questions over time. I want these children to grow into critically thinking citizens, not passive consumers of mass media fed by spin doctors. This kind of sustained attention is a process, not a hit-the buzzer, click-of-the-mouse reflex.

As educators, it is up to us to partner with families in remaining conscious about how children pay attention. Although young children are naturally curious, it is challenging for many of them to maintain prolonged attention, especially when there are so many competing distractions in our fast-paced, technological world. We can foster critical thinking right now at school and at home by minimizing distractions and eliminating multiple demands. Instead of feeding young children shallow bits of information or choosing projects that some adults see as cute but that do not engage children in active learning and inquiry, let's focus on teaching them how to be critical thinkers.

Teaching equitably is about encouraging critical thinking by supporting young learners' thirst for knowledge about the world in which they live. This happens when we encourage a profound sense of wonder by helping children to pose thoughtful questions and engage in serious inquiry and personal reflection.

As a mother, teacher educator, and researcher, Priya Lalvani raises some key points about the silence and lack of questioning that she observed, specifically when teachers describe how the students in their classrooms do not notice differences among their peers. As you read the following from Lalvani's 2015 article published in *Disability Studies Quarterly*, contemplate how you might address this issue about children's lack of questioning:

> In numerous conversations with my daughter's elementary school teachers over the years, when I have inquired about how they might introduce or discuss the topic of disability in the classroom, or how they answer questions from classmates about my daughter's differences, I have generally been assured that her classmates "don't notice anything different" or that "she blends right in, so nobody can tell." I am skeptical about these claims.

Lalvani goes on to question: Do young children actually not notice differences in the ways some of their peers communicate, learn, or move around? Are they not curious about the adaptive devices, the modified classwork, the occasional removal from the classroom, or the presence of professionals delivering specialized services? Should their lack of questioning be taken as indication that they are not curious about differences, or might this perhaps signal that they have learned to silence their curiosity?

Noticing differences, as well as similarities, is a natural part of being inquisitive and aware for young learners. As we become more conscious and aware in each moment, we also become better informed about what captivates every infant, toddler, and young child. Let us ignite the spark of curiosity during the early years and keep it brightly lit, so that children can deepen their interest about the multifaceted world in which they live.

As we encourage young children to think critically, we also teach them the importance of reflecting deeply on what they are learning. When we teach young children to engage in contemplation and critical inquiry, we ensure that each child's distinctive genius can shine brightly. Teaching equitably happens when frequent conversations, questions, and wonder, particularly related to diversity, are expected. Children's questioning ultimately produces new individual or collective investigations.

For example, in her article, Lalvani critically examines the meaning of disability and the nature of belonging with elementary-aged students. In this inquiry project, children engaged in thoughtful reflection, questioning, and the construction of new understandings about equity and justice. One of the students, Hannah, notes:

> If people with Down syndrome did not come to my school, I would never have met anyone with Down syndrome or disabilities. What a boring world it would be. . . People need all kinds of people in their lives, because otherwise, when they meet someone who is different, they won't have a clue.

Wendy, another student actively engaged in this project, articulates:

> I want to live in a world where all people are treated equally. . . I think inclusion is a good experience for everyone. Why should they be in separate rooms? Because a kid is a kid and there is no difference.

Another student, Minal, discusses her personal narrative:

> Disability means that you do things differently. You can get help or you can do things yourself . . . Some people are afraid of children with disabilities. That makes me feel upset . . . People who have disabilities are NOT from outer space. They are NOT aliens. We are all different. We are people.

Teaching equitably fosters a sense of genuine interest in the world through personal and careful contemplation, as Minal and her classmates so powerfully articulate. This kind of deep, thoughtful reflecting is a strong, elaborate thread woven through the tapestry of a mindfulness practice. In the spirit of full disclosure, Minal is a good friend of mine; you met her in chapter 3. When I told Minal I was writing a book and referring to the article she had been involved in, I invited her to share any new thoughts she had about fairness. Here is what Minal communicated to me through personal written correspondence:

> Some people don't care about people with disabilities. They think some people with disabilities should not be included in schools. That is called DISCRIMINATION. I think it is terrible. Everyone should be included in schools. One time I went to a protest about this. Everyone including people with disabilities should be equal. In fact, I made a speech about how people should be equal at my bat mitzvah. We all have the right and freedom to go to school with our friends. I go to school with many friends. I have friends from many countries and religion's and cultures. Some of them have a disability and some don't. It doesn't really matter. It only matters if you are a good person.
>
> I have a disability. It is Down syndrome. I have learning difficulties and I can't see well at night. It is hard for me to balance on stairs. I don't really like touching things like lotion or toothpaste. Yeah. You may think that's weird but this is who I am. People who have Down syndrome are basically normal. They do regular things like hanging with friends and work. They enjoy life. I don't care what people think about disabilities, because one thing I learned is that having a disability is normal. You should be proud of who you are and stay positive about yourself. Maya Angleu [sic] says that everyone is phenomenal in their own way. She also says it doesn't matter the way you look. All women are beautiful in their own way. Women have the POWER. Lady Gaga says: "There is nothing wrong with loving who you are." It doesn't matter if you're straight or lesbian or transgendered. She says: "Rejoice and love yourself today cause baby, you were born this way." I agree. I have a disability and nobody can mess with me. Don't Limit Me!!!! I love my self the way I am even when I have problems, because I WAS BORN THIS WAY.

We had not had this kind of conversation before because, in all honesty, I had never thought to ask. Even though I know Minal is intelligent, reflective, and knowledgeable about the world, we had never before engaged in a thoughtful inquiry about difference. As adults, we must be mindful to invest the time and effort to reach out to all the young people we know and engage them in a multitude of conversations and questioning about their beliefs and experiences about difference. We need more of these kinds of conversations in classrooms, homes, and other spaces to foster critical thinking and deeper inquiry.

In an effort to ensure that every child's perspectives are encouraged, we must be intentional about connecting with them. To ensure that their critical thinking and contemplation are genuinely valued, we must presume that every single child is worthy, capable, and smart. One way to do this is to ask ourselves, "Is the genius within this child flourishing in school and in life?" or "In what ways does this child thrive?" Questions like these lift the burden from the child to prove that he is smart, competent, and can "keep up" with his peers. This is another way of becoming more aware of deficit-oriented thinking and replacing it with a discourse of dignity.

One of my favorite quotes is by Ignacio Estrada, who is the director of grants administration at the Gordon and Betty Moore Foundation: "If a child is not learning in the way we are teaching, then we must teach in a way that the child can learn." Reaching and teaching all children happens when we are present in the here and now. We need to notice who is actively engaged, joyful, and appears to feel safe in the classroom—and who does not.

The notions of being smart or good at school are typically contextually driven by the educational environment and whether an individual seems comfortable in that environment. Beth Hatt explains this phenomenon in her 2012 article "Smartness as a Cultural Practice in Schools." She conducted a year-long ethnographic study in a kindergarten and discovered how being perceived as smart was closely associated with social positioning, power, and performing in a way the teacher deemed appropriate or desirable in class. Smartness and goodness, which went beyond simply obeying classroom rules, was closely linked to race and social class. Hatt describes how children of color or those who came from poor households "learn early on school is not a place where they belong or worth investing in, so they begin to disengage." In one example, Natalie, a White female student from a middle-class household, is perceived by classmates as the smartest in the class and a favorite student by the teacher. Jackson, a Black male student from a poor background, is identified as "not smart, and was the only child in the class who did not earn a sticker on the first day of school." Consider Jackson's kindergarten experience:

> Jackson has to move his car to yellow [a stoplight display in which each child has a car that moves off green when a class rule is broken] for repeatedly making "mouth noises." While moving his car, he begins to cry. Mrs. Daniels pulls him to the side and asks him if he has been making "good choices"—he nods his head, "Yes." Mrs. Daniels with frustration replies, "No, Jackson." She mentions if his car moves to red, a note will go home. Jackson says he gets a "whoopin'" when notes get sent home. He is then told to go back to the rug. He is told to "shut it off" and to "cry quietly." Jackson is unable to do so and placed in time-out. Mrs. Daniels says to Jackson, "You're in big school now and in big school we cry quietly." He is eventually allowed to leave time-out and told to make "good choices." Within the next hour, Jackson must move his car to red for moving around too much on the rug during story time. He is sent to time-out where he starts to cry. Mrs. Daniels tells him, "time-out starts all over if you start crying."

Remember, this investigation took place in a kindergarten, which is among the first experiences young children have with school. Additionally, this scenario played out on the first day of school. It seems as if the question "Is this child smart?" may have been the dominant narrative in that kindergarten classroom rather than "How is this child smart?" Review the scenario again, and identify all the messages that were conveyed to Jackson and all of his classmates who witnessed the exchange above about worthiness, smartness, and goodness. Think about what might be different if the climate in this classroom embraced an educational foundation of teaching equitably. If you were a master teacher, mentor, or coach in Jackson's class, what recommendations would you offer to uncover the genius within Jackson and to advance his genius at school, home, and community?

This is often a familiar experience at school for children from low-income backgrounds as well as for children of color, especially boys. This troubling discourse on race, gender, and economic status, similar to disability and other identity markers perceived as deficit oriented, is systemic in education during the early years. In 2018, in her article "Segregation of Technology: Disrupting Racist Frameworks in Early Childhood Education," Miriam Tager argues that systemic and structural injustice related to race and class are prevalent and are deeply rooted in early childhood education. Specifically examining technology inequities in school for young children, Tager warns how the unacceptable has become acceptable:

> It is also not acceptable practice for young Black children to be in classrooms with little to no technological equipment to help them in their learning. It is not okay for a district to tell teachers at a low-income non-White school that their children can go to the local library to get computer access while middle-class White children have personal iPads in their classrooms. Technology segregation still plays a huge role in the American schooling process.

Injustice along the lines of race, social class, gender, ability, religion, and ethnicity, among others, still prevails in the educational system. Teaching equitably is a powerful way of challenging biased paradigms and replacing unacceptable practices with respectful and fair ones. Showing young learners how to think critically about people, land, history, and circumstances fosters thoughtful inquiry about their own classroom and school communities as well as the world in which they live. At the very core of teaching equitably, children observe firsthand how to be highly respectful of and responsive to the genius inside every human being.

The Promise of Presence in Pedagogy

Next, we will examine how early childhood pedagogy can elevate well-being in young learners. This elevation begins with me and it begins with you—as we become more consistently present in each moment.

There are many family members, teachers, practitioners, researchers, and teacher educators, among others, who are deeply committed to reimagining early childhood education and care. As educators, we must take the initiative to transform narratives and discourses with young children that reflect a widespread and systemic focus on mindfulness. We can change the course of this generation and the ones to follow. It is about time that we come together as a collective voice to teach inclusively, mindfully, and equitably.

Here are some ideas about integrating mindfulness practices into early childhood pedagogy to better inform our teaching practice. These pedagogical suggestions are not necessarily new, but I present them here and in this way with the intention of framing all of our teaching practices within a lens of mindfulness.

Ten Diversity-Themed Tenets

The Irving Harris Foundation initially designed its *Diversity-Informed Infant Mental Health Tenets in Diversity-Informed Tenets for Work with Infants, Children, and Families* in an effort to embed the values of equity, inclusion, and diversity into the field of infant and early childhood mental health. These tenets were born out of "the persistent and urgent need to expand our professional capacity and deepen our work with families by increasing awareness and developing intentional action for individual, organizational, and systemic change." The tenets are recognized as a way of thinking and being, as well as a beginning of a conversation reflecting an ongoing, open-ended platform that will continue to grow. Just by reading the titles of the tenets, you can see how they echo many of the themes already discussed throughout this book.

1. Self-awareness leads to better services for families.

2. Champion children's rights globally.

3. Work to acknowledge privilege and combat discrimination.

4. Recognize and respect nondominant bodies of knowledge.

5. Honor diverse family structures.

6. Understand that language can hurt or heal.

7. Support families in their preferred language.

8. Allocate resources to systems change.

9. Make space and open pathways.

10. Advance policy that supports all families.

More information on each of these tenets is available through the Irving Harris Foundation at www.imhdivtenets.org

A Menu of Options to Replace Adaptations, Modifications, and Accommodations

When we speak about the need to modify an activity, expectation, or adapt teaching materials, there is an inherent message: there is one typical way children learn, and it needs to be altered in some way to "include" those students who are not capable of completing the task like everyone else. Instead, consider how the classroom could be transformed if we offer a menu of diverse options available to every child, so each child can select a way of approaching an activity in the way that feels most comfortable or meaningful. For example, there may be noise-canceling headphones in a classroom specifically for use by children who are sensitive to sensory overstimulation. We could offer the headphones to all of the children, so they may benefit from using them when they need to. Likewise, you may offer pencil grips, zipper toggles, knobbed puzzles, graphic organizers, large-print books, and other helpful supports to some children. However, what would happen if you were to provide a menu of options in the classroom? These and other resources could be available to every child in the class, whether they have an identified disability or not. A menu of options infused into our daily teaching practice would ensure that early childhood teachers are creating multiple pathways for young children to actively access, engage, represent, and interact with the classroom. The genius in every child would have multiple and diverse ways of thriving.

Howard Gardner, professor of education at Harvard University, introduced the theory of multiple intelligences, which confronted traditional thinking about intelligence, in his 1983 pioneering book *Frames of Mind: The Theory of Multiple Intelligences*. Gardner introduced new ways of understanding smartness, suggesting that people have a unique intelligence that is most representative of how they learn about and engage with the world. These intelligence categories reflect the broad scope of human potential and diversity: verbal/linguistic, logical/mathematical, auditory/musical, visual/spatial, interpersonal, intra-personal, bodily/kinesthetic, naturalist, and existentialist. When a wide menu of options is a natural part of how we teach, everyone's unique and individual intelligence can flourish.

 **Concluding Thoughts** ·····································

The key idea in this chapter is teaching inclusively, mindfully, and equitably. Well-being is the top priority in early childhood education and care, and it should be reflected in policy, practice, and pedagogy. The final chapter will explore the intersection between mindfulness and social justice with young children.

···

A Menu of Options for Teaching Inclusively, Mindfully, and Equitably

 **Children's Corner**

Baptiste, Barone. 2004. *My Daddy Is a Pretzel: Yoga for Parents and Kids*. Cambridge, MA: Barefoot.

Gates, Mariam, and Gates, Rolf. 2018. *Yoga Friends: A Pose-by-Pose Adventure for Kids*. Boulder, CO: Sounds True.

Ghannam, Katherine Priore. 2018. *Yoga for Kids and Their Grown-Ups: 100+ Fun Yoga and Mindfulness Activities to Practice Together*. Emeryville, CA: Rockridge.

Hoffman, Susannah. 2018. *Yoga for Kids*. New York: DK Publishing.

Parr, Todd. 2004. *The Peace Book*. New York: Little Brown and Company.

Verde, Susan 2015. *I Am Yoga*. New York: Abrams Books for Young Readers.

Willard, Christopher, and Daniel J. Rechtschaffen 2019. *Alphabreaths: The ABCs of Mindful Breathing*. Boulder, CO: Sounds True.

 Caregivers' Corner

If you would like to further explore StoryBook Yoga, here are some valuable resources on the integration of language, literacy, and movement.

Lederer, Susan Hendler. 2008. *StoryBook Yoga: An Integrated Literacy, Movement, and Music Program*. Audio CD and manual. Baldwin, NY: Educational Activities.

Lederer, Susan Hendler. 2018. "Mindful Attention Activities to Support Shared Book Reading." *Young Exceptional Children* 21(4): 216–227.

Lederer, Susan Hendler. 2012. "Storybook Yoga: Integrating Shared Book Reading and Yoga to Nurture the Whole Child." In *Translational Speech-Language Pathology and Audiology: Essays in Honor of Dr. Sadanand Singh*. San Diego, CA: Plural.

Take It to the Classroom

StoryBook Yoga

The following StoryBook Yoga Sample Script was conceptualized and developed for this book by Susan Lederer, professor of communication sciences and disorders at Adelphi University.

StoryBook Yoga makes shared book reading an active, whole-child experience. By infusing shared book reading with yoga poses and breaths, this approach nurtures language and literacy as well a physical and social-emotional development. The following lesson is based on instructions from *StoryBook Yoga: An Integrated Literacy, Movement, and Music Program.* You do not need any yoga experience to share this joy with your students.

Select a book that has animals and natural wonders featured in the story or pictures. Preview the book to identify the yoga poses and breathing practices you want the children to experience. Note that the poses listed in this example are based on the animals that appear in *The Peace Book* by Todd Parr (snake, elephant, and dog); you can change the poses to fit the book you choose.

Choose books with repetitive patterns, as opposed to narrative stories, since the story is interrupted every few pages. Add music if you wish.

See *StoryBook Yoga* for songs and instructions for twelve poses. The internet is a great source of illustrations and videos, so you can practice first.

Accept the children's interpretations of the poses and breaths. Linking breath with movement is what promotes mindfulness. And have fun!

1. Arrange the room with towels or yoga mats, preferably in a circle, and dim the lights.

2. Ask the children to take off their shoes and socks (optional) and sit comfortably with "pretzel legs."

3. Help them get ready to listen with a chime. Ask them to close their eyes, listen to the chime, and raise their hands when they no longer hear it.

4. Help the children get ready to look at the pictures by watching a glitter jar.

5. Begin with book yoga: Sit with knees up, feet on the floor. Inhale, open the knees, and make the soles of the feet touch. Exhale and close the knees like a book. Add a twist to turn your pages: Inhale and open the knees. Exhale and twist to the right. Inhale and turn back to the center. Exhale and twist to the left. Inhale and turn back to the center. Exhale and close the knees.

6. Read the first page of the book. Put down the book. Invite the children to rest on their bellies, arms by their sides. On the inhale, instruct them to raise their heads. Exhale and lower their heads. Inhale and raise their feet. Exhale and lower their feet. Inhale and raise both head and feet. Exhale lower the head and feet. Inhale and raise head and feet and use arms to swim. Exhale and lower head, feet, and arms. Allow children to rest for a few minutes and breathe. Invite them to return to "pretzel legs." (Note: This is not the traditional fish pose, which can be unsafe for developing necks.)

7. Resume reading. Invite children to return to a belly down position with hands under their shoulders. On the inhale, raise the upper body a little (baby snake), then exhale to lower. On the next inhale, rise a little farther (mommy snake), then exhale to lower. On the third round, inhale and rise even higher (daddy snake or king cobra), then exhale to lower. Children can hiss like a snake on each exhale as they sink back down

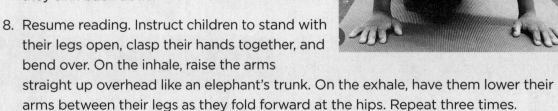

8. Resume reading. Instruct children to stand with their legs open, clasp their hands together, and bend over. On the inhale, raise the arms straight up overhead like an elephant's trunk. On the exhale, have them lower their arms between their legs as they fold forward at the hips. Repeat three times.

9. Continue reading. Children begin on all fours, hands under shoulders, knees under the hips (looks like you are ready to crawl). On the inhale, raise the hips to an upside-down V position (downward-facing dog pose). Hold for three to five breaths. On the exhale, lower knees and forearms, but keep the hips up for puppy pose. Invite the children to wag their puppy tails and even pant. Repeat the flow between downward dog and puppy. Finish in a child's resting pose.

10. Continue reading. On each page, teach the poses or breaths that fit the text.

11. The End! As children lie on their backs, play soft music.

12. Have the children roll up their mats and put them away for another day of StoryBook Yoga.

Breathing Exercises

Debby Kaminsky, founder of Newark Yoga Movement, developed these exercises. In schools, the most important thing we can teach educators, staff, and children is to breathe. Breath will center and self-regulate as well as energize. Try these exercises yourself, then share them with your students and colleagues. Feel the difference between these two breaths.

Focus Five

(from *Grounded Kids Yoga* https://groundedkids.com/)

We breathe an average of 16 breaths a minute, 960 breaths an hour, and 23,040 breaths a day. We can balance our nervous system and help reverse the fight, flight, or freeze response, as well as alleviate depression and anxiety. Breathing slowly and consciously turns on the vagus nerve that activates the parasympathetic nervous system. In just one minute, you can shift to a state of calm and relaxation.

Find a comfortable seat. You're invited to close your eyes or just soften your gaze.

Place the back of your hands on your lap, palms facing up.

Make two gentle fists with thumbs tucked inside.

Breathe in through your nose for the count of 5.

Breathe out of your nose for the count of 5.

Open your hands, leaving them on your lap.

Press your thumb and pinky finger together.

Breathe in through your nose for the count of 5.

Breathe out of your nose for the count of 5

Press your thumb and ring finger together.

Breathe in through your nose for the count of 5.

Breathe out of your nose for the count of 5.

Press your thumb and middle finger together.

Breathe in through your nose for the count of 5.

Breathe out of your nose for the count of 5

Press your thumb and pointer finger together.

Breathe in through your nose for the count of 5.

Breathe out of your nose for the count of 5.

Make two gentle fists once again with thumbs tucked inside.

Breathe in through your nose for the count of 5.

Breathe out of your nose for the count of 5.

Slowly open your hands and pause for a moment.

Notice. Have you felt a shift? Are you more relaxed?

Breath of Joy

This three-part breath coupled with movement gets energy flowing quickly, turning on endorphins and helping you feel uplifted.

Tell the children that this simple movement involves a three-part inhale through the nose (imagine sipping through a straw and then sipping some more and finally sipping in even more) and an exhale (like a long "Ha" sound) through the mouth.

Invite them to practice. Inhale through the nose and hold it. Then inhale a little more and hold it. Then inhale a little more. Breathe out through the mouth, making a long "Ha" sound.

Put the breathing together with arm movements. Remember the inhale is through the nose and the exhale is through the mouth.

Stand tall with feet planted firmly on the ground hip distance apart. Inhale and raise arms up in front of you at shoulder height. Inhale arms to your side parallel to the ground. Inhale arms up overhead with upper arms along your ears. Exhale out of your mouth (say "Ha") as your arms swing down to your side.

Repeat.

Inhale and raise arms up in front of you at shoulder height. Inhale arms to your side parallel to the ground. Inhale arms up overhead with upper arms along your ears. Exhale out of your mouth (say "Ha") as your arms swing down to your side.

Repeat as often as you want.

CHAPTER 8

Peace in the World: Where Does It Begin?

> **"Peace is our gift to each other."**
> —Elie Wiesel, Holocaust survivor, Nobel Peace Prize recipient, author, and lecturer

Together we have taken a journey about teaching and learning through a lens of mindfulness. Or perhaps being present is the journey, and teaching and learning with young children is simply a treasure we reap along the way. Either way, I believe that social justice is at the core. There can be no justice in the world unless we do our own part to acknowledge and protect the connections we have to ourselves, each other, and the spaces we inhabit.

Elie Wiesel's quote reminds me that spreading the gift of peace is among the greatest displays of presence, particularly when we give this to a young child. Even more powerful is when we are able to teach children how they can offer this priceless present generously and continually. Toward that end, the purpose of this chapter is taking care of people, places, and things in our lives and understanding how mindfulness practices are a pathway to becoming more conscious of these irreplaceable connections.

Diverse Voices on Teaching Mindfulness in Early Childhood

One of the best ways to understand how we can infuse mindfulness practices into the lives of young children is to examine what early childhood educators are already doing. Here is what Gabriella L. Gonzalez, who identifies as an Hispanic woman and is head teacher of three- and four-year-olds at St. Francis Academy in Union City, New Jersey, shares:

I have incorporated mindfulness meditation into my classroom routines. Teaching children that "me" time is important and taking a minute to breathe to calm our mind and body is something I will continue to do because children need be encouraged to understand their bodies, emotions, feelings, and how to positively express themselves. Children are growing up in a world full of technology and constantly being "on." Mindful meditation gives children the opportunity to "shut off" and listen to their own minds and bodies. Mindful meditation benefits not only the children but the teachers as well. Together as a community we can feel refreshed and focused. I have found that the children are more engaged during educational activities, have a kinder approach to communicating with one another, and have even taken these skills into their homes to share with their families.

As Gabriella points out, mindfulness transforms a classroom on multiple levels, including enhancing teachers' and children's physical and emotional well-being, deepening the sense of listening within and to others, improving concentration, feeling invigorated, as well as fostering connections to students' families.

A few years ago, I decided to conduct a small online study to see what was happening in classrooms to foster a sense of well-being with young learners. These findings provided a beginning point to understand what some early childhood teachers were thinking and how they were implementing mindfulness practices. Here are a few highlights from this 2017 article, "Being Present: An Exploratory Study on the Use of Mindfulness in Early Childhood," coauthored with Kim Robinson and David Aveta:

- Teachers identified a wide variety of reasons for using mindfulness in the classroom, with a majority of teachers using contemplative practices when they thought the class seemed restless. Teachers also chose to use mindfulness when it seemed as if students had been sitting for prolonged periods of time, when students requested it, and when transitions or unexpected changes in the routine occurred.

- More than half of teachers indicated that they used mindfulness practices when their young students exhibited signs of stress, and more than a third of teachers used mindfulness practices when they themselves felt stressed. More than one-third of teachers used contemplative practices to promote child well-being, and a quarter of teachers responded that mindfulness practices were a part of a scheduled classroom routine.

- No negative outcomes associated with the use of mindfulness practices were reported; the majority of teachers noted positive outcomes, such as physical, social, academic, and behavioral outcomes.

- Many of the teachers shared that they engaged in their own mindfulness practice. In their personal lives, meditation was the mindfulness practice teachers used most often; in the classroom, yoga was the mindfulness practice used most often with children.

What was striking to me is that many teachers had a consistent mindfulness practice in their personal lives and brought this knowledge and commitment to being present to their classrooms to share with young learners. In their own words, teachers who participated in the study describe how mindfulness practices in the classroom helped young learners to calm and center themselves, for example:

> I use yoga breathing to settle my children after active dancing/movement activities. We learn how to breathe and then the classroom expectation of when to use it is modeled. "Let's see who knows how to calm their bodies," and the class does yoga breathing. When a child is upset, we see her doing her yoga breathing and know this means to give her a private minute, and the entire class benefits from this. I tell the children they can teach this to their parents, and many have.

Early childhood teachers have unique preferences, styles, interests, and constraints, so it naturally follows that they implement mindfulness practices in their own classrooms in a wide variety of ways.

My sense is that as we deepen our own mindfulness practices as educators, we transform instruction as well as the classroom community. I believe the reason behind this is because when we are conscious, we can personally infuse a sense of wonder and awareness into the very spaces we inhabit. But how does this happen at a time when early childhood educators are facing enormous and unrealistic expectations each day? The growing pressures to increase academics and uniformity and to decrease play and creativity, among other irrational changes, may seem well beyond a teacher's sense of control. Or are they?

Unwrapping Presents: Experiencing Presence in the World Today

As a teacher educator, I have noticed over the years in my own university classroom a rapid increase in the number of students who seem overworked, overwhelmed, and underappreciated so early in their careers. I do not think my observation is an exception or an isolated experience. According to a 2018 report by the American Association of Colleges for Teacher Education, the number one reason for the steady drop in enrollment in university teacher-education programs in the United States is the belief that teaching is not a desirable profession. Findings in the report further note that almost half of teachers end up leaving the profession within the first few years of pursuing teaching as a career. Moreover, early childhood education is named among the most common teacher-shortage areas, suggesting this field is perceived as one of the least desirable careers. How can this be?

Salaries are still considerably insufficient, and the general lack of public understanding about what early childhood education is and is not are factors contributing to this perception. There must be a way that teachers can feel supported, empowered, and energized to do one of the toughest jobs in the world. Meena Srinivasan, an Indian

American educator respected worldwide for her work in mindfulness and schools, discusses her own feelings of emptiness and exhaustion that she felt during her first years of teaching until she pursued a mindfulness practice. In her book *Teach, Breathe, Learn: Mindfulness In and Out of the Classroom*, she describes a light-bulb moment when she realized that when she awoke in the morning irritable and frustrated, she subconsciously passed that on to her students, which made her feel even worse—and set in motion a cycle of negativity. She candidly shares the moment when everything became all too clear:

> In a flash, I learned that my emotional state is transmuted to my students regardless of the lesson I'm teaching. I know that a lesson absent of authentic, heartful interaction, however instructionally sound, would never create the connected, innovative, and loving classroom I had dreamed of. The demands placed on me to deliver high-quality instruction while covering massive amounts of content were immense. I felt empty. I was at the start of my career, but I already felt emotionally exhausted and incredibly tired from teaching.

There are many pearls of wisdom in this deeply honest reflection; the one that stood out to me was about the kind of classroom she imagined creating—a connected classroom. It seems to me that many teachers, and children too, are experiencing a disconnect from being present. Being present can return us to dreaming, imagining, and inspiring in the classroom and beyond. Srinivasan explains that mindfulness reconnected her to what was most important when she lost her way. She says that through mindfulness, she developed an awareness of the present moment both within herself and around her. This awareness and presence, she says, can promote well-being not only within herself but in her entire school community.

It does not matter whether we begin a mindfulness practice at home and bring it to our work or start our mindfulness practice with students in the classroom and then bring it to the many other parts of our lives. What matters is that we begin. And begin again. And again. When we stay connected to what we know to be precious and essential in our lives, we are simply being present in the moment.

Intersecting Connections of Being Present in the World

Given how technology has dramatically changed the way we interact with each other, many believe they are more in touch with others, but the truth is that in many ways we are more disconnected than ever. Renowned author and distinguished Massachusetts Institute of Technology professor Sherry Turkle is widely respected for her expertise about how technology influences the way we live. In her book *Alone Together: Why We Expect More from Technology and Less from Each Other*, Turkle explains the impact technology has had on our human experience: "We are increasingly connected to each other but oddly more alone: in intimacy, new solitudes. Given the isolation people may be experiencing despite the high frequency and massive volume of social contacts, it raises the question—what is it we are connecting to?"

When pondering this question, I wondered where being present fit in. I realized that when we live in a state of chronic mindlessness, the incessant chatter that floods our minds is nothing more than garbage. This toxic buildup of waste is like a raging river flooding our minds, continuing to surge, becoming greater and more forceful over time. And this, consequently, influences both the significant and minor decisions we make about how we choose to be in the world.

The Connection to Movement and Outdoor Spaces

How young children perceive and engage with the outdoors continues to be a neglected area of inquiry in early childhood education and care, particularly in the West. It's about time that adults acknowledge how curiosity and appreciation of the outdoors must hold the same value as a love of books does in the early years.

One of my dearest friends, Alan Berger, is founder and director of Peace through Play Nursery School in Chestnut Ridge, New York, a nature- and play-based, Reggio-inspired, and Montessori-infused early childhood school for preschoolers of all backgrounds, including those with various abilities. As you read about Peace through Play, consider how the outdoors serves as an extension of the classroom and the effect this has on children's learning and mindfulness.

> Weather permitting, we are outdoors most of the day (sometimes we only come indoors for naptime), but that means we come out in light rain, snow, and cold as we try to remember that children like all weather! We are fortunate to have two acres of woods with trails that the children can explore on their own. That means finding sticks, turning over rocks and logs, digging for worms, and trying to look up every once in a while and appreciate the tall trees and all they do with us. We practice fifteen minutes of yoga every day, and when we are outside that is where we practice. Yoga ends with two minutes of meditation, conscious breathing, and ringing of the chimes. The basic premise of our school philosophy is to infuse concepts of peace and humanity into our daily practice as a small community of children, teachers, and parents and to extend this to the larger community and world we live in. We do this through music, books, cooperative games, art, movement, and a myriad of nature-based materials that enhance learning and mindfulness.

The connection to the natural world is the cornerstone of this preschool, as it is in many early childhood programs around the world. This is in sharp contrast to the standard twenty minutes or so of playground time that children are allotted recess in many educational settings, particularly in publicly funded schools in the United States. Not all schools have playgrounds. One evening last year, Sandra, who teaches three- and four-year-olds in a large urban district, shared during a class discussion that there is no playground at the preschool where she works. Then another grad student chimed in to add that in her role as a mentor teacher in another large urban setting, nearly every early childhood school she visits regularly has no playground or outdoor space for young children. How is this even possible? This example highlights another perspective related to disparity and injustice in early childhood education and care.

Sandra shared with me in an email that she and her colleagues have been beyond frustrated around the lack of outdoor play space, and they have raised this issue at countless meetings over the past eighteen years—although the outcome has remained the same. Sandra recently emailed with an update: the school lease had not been renewed, and they were moving to a new district-owned school—with no playground! These realities are likely tied to race and class, as both districts represent a population of families with low economic resources and serve mostly children of color. Let us become more aware of and responsive to how the unacceptable has become acceptable. Let us transform our commitment to being present into a demand for justice.

The recommended readings and activities throughout this book offer practical ideas about the intersections between mindfulness and social justice, and how to begin. It's about noticing. It's about having conversations. It's about finding solutions with children when an injustice is detected. It's about taking care of ourselves, each other, and the land. It's about time.

The outdoor world is the ideal early childhood classroom with infinite possibilities for young children to learn about literacy, numeracy, science, history, communication, self-confidence, and so much more. Having some designated time for play, movement, and exploration outdoors is better than having no time to be outside. Nonetheless, the opportunities for outdoor play, exploration, and investigation are generally inadequate in early childhood education and care.

In addition to this the lack of attention to spaces, places, and time for outdoor play, the limited opportunities for children to enjoy and experience physical movement in school is also troublesome. The growing concern among teachers and families alike is that young children generally do not have ample time and space in school to stretch, run, jump, roll, dance, and move about, particularly as schools are requiring students to sit for longer periods of time for testing and increased academics.

There is a growing, widespread problem around the world: sedentary lifestyle. We are becoming a world that is sitting too much! The majority of articles from an online search on this topic focused on the negative effects of a sedentary lifestyle, such as chronic back pain, obesity, physical discomfort, behavioral challenges, and other health implications. There is growing concern and inquiry about this condition, and the outcomes of prolonged sitting and lack of movement appear grim. The serious, detrimental effects to body and mind, however, should not be the reason for us to move more or to encourage children to do the same. The reason young children should be moving is because our bodies were designed to move freely and regularly; humans were not built for inactivity. Young children learn about their bodies, others, and the world around them when they are actively engaging with people, places, and things through movement. Think about infants who put objects into their mouths to explore and enjoy them, or notice as toddlers see their moving shadow for the first time. There is wonder, curiosity, discovery, and joy when youngsters are moving, particularly in the world outside.

Although mindfulness is typically associated with silence and stillness, being present with intention can also occur when we are moving. Mindfulness and movement can go hand in hand. Greg McGrath, an elementary teacher, combined his personal interest in mindfulness with his enthusiasm for intense physical activity in the great outdoors. By integrating motion and mindfulness into the classroom culture, Greg guided his first-grade students to feel more focused and calmer by moving consciously and breathing. These mindfulness practices provided the class with indispensable cognitive, physical, and emotional breaks, among other benefits, throughout their busy day.

A Deeper Sense of Connection: The Natural World Is the Classroom

In the introduction, I note that the term *classroom* is simply a metaphor in this book. The natural world is the ideal classroom for young children and older ones too. Being present in nature enhances conscious awareness of the moment as well as our interconnectedness with the natural world. We are able to sense the relationship we have to all other living beings and more-than-human wonders, and the connection they have to each other.

Although I have visited numerous early childhood schools around the world, I have had the pleasure of spending time in several forest kindergartens in Australia, New Zealand, and Sweden. Everything about these schools revolves around nature and the outdoors, and mindfulness is so deeply embedded into the philosophy and practice in such a natural way. This excerpt from a 2017 article I wrote is based on visiting a couple of nature-based preschools in Australia:

> The natural outside world served as the curriculum, space, and materials that shaped children's investigations, inquiry, and discoveries. Wood blocks, which were handcrafted from trees in the local environment, and art materials were purposefully selected from local resources in the community. Stones, leaves, rocks, bark, dirt, water, glass, sticks, insects, and other living and nonliving items were brought from the outside in or were investigated directly in the natural habitat. There were no plastic or synthetic toys, games, books, or materials as far as I could tell.

This observation is representative of nature preschools in general, regardless of region or country. What is always striking to me is an almost exclusive use of locally sourced materials at every forest preschool, such as beautiful handwoven baskets and wooden boxes, which are a welcome alternative to the plastic bins filled with plastic, commercially produced toys typical of most preschools. Young children are typically responsible for designing and constructing handcrafted chairs, tables, benches, shelves, blocks, toys, bicycles, wagons, pillows, artwork, and outdoor obstacle courses, with some assistance and guidance from teachers or families.

Although the figure is greater worldwide, the number of nature preschools in the United States is growing rapidly. In 2017, the North American Association for Environmental Education (NAAEE) reported that there were more than 250 nature preschools and kindergartens in the United States, representing an increase of more 60 percent from the year before. According to Ken Finch and Patti Ensel Bailie, authors of "Nature Preschools: Putting Nature at the Heart of Early Childhood Education," nature or the outdoors is not a single topic, activity center, or theme in a nature preschool but is the central organizing feature "that intentionally ties together the preschool's philosophy, methodologies, classroom design, outdoor spaces, and public identity."

Aside from the obvious focus on where and how children spend their time, one theme I noticed across these schools is the unwavering commitment to ecological sustainability. For me, this acknowledgment is at the heart of mindfulness because it demonstrates a profound knowing and meaningful connection to the world in which we live. There seems to be an implicit understanding that to survive and thrive, the choices we make in each moment about how to live matter.

We make choices every day about the level of our commitment to preserve, protect, and take care of the natural environment, which we borrow during our time on earth. In the nature preschools I have visited, there is little, if any, waste. Every scrap of food, art supply, paper, or any other leftovers from a project or a meal is recycled or repurposed. Waste paper baskets or garbage cans are typically very small, if they are used at all.

In a conversation with one of the directors from an early childhood center, she confessed that she was feeling embarrassed about all the freshly washed sheets from children's nap time that were drying outside on clotheslines. She had decided to stop using the dryers at the school as another way of honoring the school's central commitment to sustainability—even though she didn't like the "messiness" it caused, especially when visitors came. I appreciated how thoughtful and serious this director was about closely aligning philosophy and practice when it came to the environment. A deep commitment to preserving the land in which we live often means confronting our own comfort levels related to convenience or accumulation.

There is one more impression about forest kindergartens that is worth noting: the beautiful sense of harmony that seems to permeate the atmosphere, a sense that is like a tangible energy or aliveness, an enchanting relationship with nature. I cannot think of a better way to explain this except placing it within the context of one of my favorite songs, Michael Franti's "The Sound of Sunshine." I love this cheerful melody because people typically see or feel rays of sun; however, through Franti's music, I can actually hear the magical sound of sunshine. It is the same when I ponder the sense of harmony in a forest preschool or nature-based school. This sense of harmony can be heard, felt, smelled, tasted, and seen as children engage in a joyful and intimate relationship with the outdoor world.

In nature or forest preschools, young children are regularly encouraged to explore water holes, mud and fire pits, forests, fields, rivers, streams, rock formations, and other outdoor worlds. They are also supported in taking risks in these environments. In this way, youngsters learn firsthand how to calculate and manage risk and discover resilience in experiences such as climbing trees or walking across boulders to cross to the other side of a stream. This is in stark contrast to Western thinking where compliance, rules, and regulations about safety determine how most schools operate and what teachers can and cannot do. Here is an insightful quote that eight-year-old Vera shared about her time in a forest camp in the United States:

> The best part about Forest Camp is Tree Alley. Tree Alley is a part of the forest where lots of trees have fallen down. We climb all over them. It's different than climbing in a playground, because every part of the tree is a little bit different. And I pay more attention to how I need to cross the tree than a ladder or something on a playground. And I am braver!

In addition to building confidence, competence, courage, and a sense of connection, there are other notable benefits that result when children are immersed in nature. Children can experience a sense of harmony through their school's herb, vegetable, fruit, plant, or rock gardens, which they often design, plant, and care for. For snack time, children help themselves to fruit served in large bowls and often eat lunch family- or buffet-style, with fresh, colorful salads, homemade vegetable soups, or other kinds of whole foods (never packaged, frozen, or canned). Nature preschools seem to have a cozy, warm, homelike feeling because of the deliberate focus on family, community, and the outdoors. I noticed a conscious awareness and deep interconnectedness with nature and outdoor worlds at every turn.

Nature-based practices are rooted in a long legacy of cultural traditions and native customs. Interestingly, a sense of accumulation represents how humans typically perceive nature. The common Western belief that we must take care of the Earth reflects a false sense of ownership or domination, as if humans actually own the land we inhabit. Tiokasin Ghosthorse—Cheyenne River Lakota Nation of South Dakota—is an international speaker on peace, Indigenous, and Mother Earth perspective. He reminds us how "we are not living on Earth but living *with* Earth." At the 2020 Inner Peace Conference Online, Ghosthorse further explained how it critical it is to take a serious look at language because of the predominant focus on words and ideas such as *domination, exclusion, authority, I,* and *mine*—all concepts that are nonexistent in Lakota, where the focus is on relationship.

Traditional Native understandings respect the interconnectedness among all living beings and nonliving things. These countless, sacred connections become crystal clear when people live in the present moment. When humans consistently engage in mindfulness practice, the Earth, sky, sun, and all beings appear much more interconnected as we realize the harmony and synchronicity have always existed and are literally everywhere.

After spending more than two decades in the forest industry in Germany, forester and best-selling author Peter Wohlleben describes in his book *The Hidden Life of Trees: What They Feel, How They Communicate—Discoveries from a Secret World* what he noticed in the woods when he became more present and more aware of just the tree trunks on his path:

> I began to notice bizarre root shapes, peculiar growth patterns, and mossy cushions on bark. My love of Nature—something I've had since I was six years old—was reignited. Suddenly I was aware of the countless wonders I could hardly explain even to myself . . . Every day in the forest was a day of discovery. This led me to unusual ways of managing the forest. When you know that trees experience pain and have memories and that tree parents live together with their children, then you can no longer just chop them down and disrupt their lives with large machines.

Being present, especially with nature and the outdoors, opens the doors to our senses. The unlimited intersections are suddenly alive and known to us as we better understand the profound and sacred connection between everyone and everything. How can this sense of knowing inform and influence our teaching practice with young children? When we are teaching and learning with young children in a state of mindfulness, the intersecting connections of the natural world echo the sound of harmony. This is the gift of presence.

What Does This Mean for You?

As we come to the last section of this chapter, I hope that you will have more questions when you close this book than when you first began. As we continue to contemplate the intersections of mindfulness and early childhood education and care, let us remain focused on the sacred intersections. Toward that end, one of my dear friends, Annie Bien, who is an English translator of Tibetan Buddhist commentaries, poet, meditation teacher, and yoga practitioner, shared this beautiful original writing:

> When we wake up in the morning until the time we go to bed at night, our minds get distracted, disturbed, our feelings skitter all over the place, up and down. We don't always notice what goes on with our bodies that makes us feel this way. But in between each waking up and going to bed, each dreaming or not dreaming, we are breathing.

We don't think about breath very much until we get sick or if something happens that makes it hard for us to breathe. Our breaths change when we're happy, sad, bored, troubled. Breath holds the key to bringing calmness in our lives, especially when a lot of things could disturb us. In Tibetan Buddhism, the word for meditation, *gom*, means "to familiarize, to cultivate our minds on a virtuous object" . . . focusing on something positive that doesn't harm others. Because your breath is always there while you are alive, you don't have to find a place to do breathing meditation. You can do it any time you don't feel calm; calmness will come to you.

Take a moment to refer to Take It to the Classroom at the end of this chapter for Breathing the Sky, a beautiful and original meditation Annie created just for this book. I appreciate the connections between where the sky meets the ocean or the sky meets the earth. This offers a perfect opportunity to meditate with young children about beautiful connections in the outdoor world.

Our mindfulness journey is an ongoing one filled with peaks and valleys, and we must return to the present moment again and again. In the spirit of inquiry, perhaps we can continue to ponder the question "How does my mindfulness practice inform my teaching practice?" Or perhaps the question is "How does my teaching practice inform my mindfulness practice?" It is up to each one of us to discover the intersections of our teaching and learning and the meaning that being present holds in our lives.

Returning to the quote by Elie Wiesel at the beginning of the chapter, I marvel at this gift of sharing peace. What a profound treasure to share. Only when we are fully aware and present in the moment can we share our full awareness and presence with another; this cannot happen in a state of mindlessness. I am reminded of Toni Morrison's touching words as she described how every time we greet a child, the look in our eyes must convey to that child that she is the most important thing in that moment and that she matters. Whether upon entering the classroom first thing in the morning or seeing a family member or caregiver after school, our eyes communicate whether we are present or not. The moment we are reunited with young children, they notice whether our eyes light up upon seeing them. If we are focused on other matters, such as texting, talking, and so on, they notice that too.

So how does this connect to peace? The way I see it—it is all about care. How do we take care of people, places, and things in our lives, including ourselves? I imagine most people would say they are in favor of peace in the world. But I doubt peace can ever be achieved on a global scale unless we have peace within. Thích Nhất Hạnh said it best in his *Peace Is Every Step*:

Consciousness exists on two levels: as seeds and as manifestations of these seeds . . . It is very difficult to us to be joyful at the moment the seed of anger manifests. Every time a seed has an occasion to manifest itself, it produces new seeds of the same kind . . . That is why we have to be careful in selecting the kind of life we lead and the emotions we express . . . Every time we practice mindful living, we plant healthy seeds and strengthen the healthy seeds already in us.

The seeds we planted yesterday will be harvested today. And the seeds that we plant today matter now and for the future. Let us be mindful of the seeds we plant with children and for them. By planting seeds of peace now, we are producing seeds of peace in our inner and outer worlds. Let us create a safe and peaceful world for children, and with them, a world in which justice and joy saturate the soil.

A Mindfulness Movement: Elevating Joy and Justice on the Planet

The notion of social justice is not new. There is, however, growing support for young children, as full citizens, to participate in social justice and in matters affecting their lives. There is an understanding that young children can and must be supported in making important decisions that affect them. In a 2010 article in the *Early Years*, Berit Bae, faculty at Oslo University College in Norway and distinguished scholar in early childhood education, advocates:

Contrary to what some may think if trapped in traditional views of children, the youngest children do not appear to be too "immature" to express their views or too young to influence their everyday lives. By meeting adults who are willing to challenge their own thinking and to interpret children's rights in local settings, children might have experiences in kindergarten that contribute to a sense of participating on one's own terms from very early in life.

This understanding, which recognizes and respects young children as competent and full participants in their own lives, has received worldwide attention within the last two decades. Early childhood teachers can foster a sense of connection and responsibility with young children so they learn either way that their voice or their silence makes a difference. What can educators do to promote a sense of social justice individually and collectively? Adults can critically examine together with young learners the early childhood curriculum, instruction, materials, and classroom culture. By teaching children to critically think, observe, research, question, reflect, and challenge, we are teaching them to stand up for themselves, each other, and the planet.

Elevating joy and justice through inquiry can happen at home, at school, and everywhere in between. Families, caregivers, and early childhood professionals must be active participants and valued partners to sow seeds of peace with young children. It is never too early to engage in conversations and inquiry with children about the world in which we live. Andrea Wesol, graduate student, wife, and parent of two small children shares this beautiful moment:

Two-and-a-half-year-old Sean and I were cuddled up next to each other on the couch, reading. In the course of the book, an anthropomorphic rabbit has a difficult time reacting to both the realization of a broken table and a lost remote control. The rabbit yells and throws things when circumstances are not what he expects. This is played for laughs in the book, but I was troubled by the assumption that this is a routine reaction to obstacles that we encounter in our lives. I paused in the reading and commented on the rabbit's response. I wondered aloud, "What else could the rabbit have done?" Sean took a deep breath and started counting!

Whether reading together, at the dinner table, or riding in the car or bus, we can all reflect with young children about inner peace and peace in the world.

In the absence of respect or dignity, there is a discourse rooted in deficit-oriented and disapproval thinking. Teaching equity is like teaching mindfulness—they both represent an ongoing process in which reflection and questioning are constant. My sense is that when we traverse the path of mindfulness, social justice naturally happens. Creating a better-educated world happens when adults take the time to listen, learn, and locate where we can do a more mindful job. When we work in partnership with young children to become better educated and informed, we are elevating justice in the world and maintaining discourses of dignity.

Creating a better-educated world starts with me and with you. We will find our own unique voices and individual avenues to engage young children, but it does begin with practice. One of the toughest questions many teachers face is how to infuse mindfulness practices into the classroom when they are new teachers, not tenured, or are expected to follow a prescribed curriculum. These are excellent questions. There is no one recipe for success because every school is different just as every teacher has his or her unique circumstances that will determine how best to address mindfulness and discourses of dignity within a system that has not fully embraced these values. The common variable is to have a network of support as we navigate through mindfulness and social-action connections. Find just one other individual, a small group, or a large community, and within these supportive and safe spaces collectively pursue social justice and strengthen a culture of mindfulness. Consider inviting families, administrators, early childhood professionals, community leaders, and university students pursuing teacher education who hold shared visions and experiences around social justice to your school or classroom. It might also be beneficial to engage those who do not have the same ideas but might be open or curious.

Here are some strategies to find the courage to explore intersections of mindfulness and social justice in educational environments where there may be limited awareness or support:

- Bring a group together frequently to discuss solutions to systemic issues. Choose real-life situations, children's quotes, books, or journal articles to spark a conversation.

- Go with the flow at school and in the classroom, without being insubordinate or contentious, but provide the kind of climate and space that children need to thrive.

- Think outside the box and offer creative ways to troubleshoot or problem solve that offer a win-win situation for everyone.

- Invite guest speakers or identify other kinds of resources to provide inspiration and resources that can be influential in bringing about change.

- Attend a workshop to stay inspired and informed, or offer to provide a professional development for your school, district, or community.

In Norway, there was a massive, collective response from early childhood practitioners, families, teacher educators, retired professionals, among others, to change the mindlessness discourse in early childhood education and care. This movement, which was organized by early childhood educator Kari Eide and known as the Kindergarten Uprising, prevented the standardization and testing of language skills in all kindergartens and influenced child-teacher ratios. Through the use of social media, thousands across Norway who were deeply concerned about the early childhood system shared stories and demanded social change using the hashtag #unjustifiable. Change is possible. Banding together and standing up for the rights of young children sends a powerful message about what is unacceptable and what is not.

Spotlight on Planting of Seeds with Children: Social Justice and Mindfulness Now

There are many ways to engage in partnership with young learners to transform classroom culture, practice, and policies, and to make a difference on a much grander scale. Here is one example of a small group of graduate students in one of my courses who decided to work as a team to complete a final assignment related to social justice with young children. They chose to teach mindfulness practices to the young learners in their classrooms and then support these learners to teach the practices to other students at the school. Initially, when this idea was presented at staff and grade-level meetings at each school, not every teacher was receptive. One teacher commented, "I'm not sure how it's going to go . . . but I don't anticipate they'll have a genuine understanding of the point." Another noted, "I guess I wonder why meditation. I just don't picture them meditating." However, after the project was underway, teacher feedback was overwhelmingly positive with comments such as, "It is simple and it worked," "I felt like I was tuned in with my inner self," and "[Children] look forward to it! Now they're letting me know how they'd like to do it."

The reflections from the young children themselves are also noteworthy. Here are just a few highlights:

- **Prekindergarteners and kindergarteners:**

  - "When I am sad or mad that means I breathe and I feel better."

  - "When I grow up I want to do meditation."

  - "I feel like I hear bubbles like I'm the ocean."

  - "I feel happy. Mama is going to be happy."

- **First graders:**

  - "It makes me feel like I was flying in the wind."

  - "If you're kind of mad but not mad, it calms you down."

  - "It makes me feel like I have more energy."

- **Second graders:**

  - "It makes me feel good and nice. I feel sleepy and warm inside."

  - "It makes me feel comfortable."

  - "I'm going to teach my mom what she can do when she's yelling."

  - "I like moving my body out of my desk. Usually we're told to sit down in class."

- **Third, fourth, and fifth graders:**

  - "It made me feel normal. It made me feel comfortable in my own skin."

  - "It made me feel relaxed. And calm."

  - "It made me ready for the day."

In an effort to infuse mindfulness into their own classrooms and to teach others at the school to do the same, this initiative elevated well-being at each school and made a lasting, positive impact. The graduate students wrote in their final paper: "The biggest takeaway from this social action plan is that it is not over. It has truly just begun. Social change is a process not a product. While we have received the type of results we intended by implementing our mindfulness action plan, this does not mean we are simply done." Social justice with young children is possible and it is happening. Figuring out with children what problem to solve or issue to address is the first step in creating a world of joy and justice. The power of presence is now.

●●● Concluding Thoughts ·······································

As we come full circle, let us return to the notion of a mindfulness movement. We have learned throughout this book how educators are already making a profound impact in the lives of young children through the practice of mindfulness. In its simplicity, this practice is about taking care of ourselves, each other, the planet, and other worlds. We begin a practice by maintaining inner peace in our own lives. When we turn again and again to being present, we are more authentic and better equipped to practice mindfulness with children. There are endless opportunities to plant seeds of peace into the lives of young children so they in turn can do the same. The seeds of peace are the same seeds of social justice, because when we care about the world and other beings, we take care of each other. World peace begins with me. How about you?

Not too long ago, my daughter, Alyssa, and I were discussing some of her fondest childhood memories. She talked about how we ran outside during a rain shower, no shoes on, and laughed and played and splashed around in a puddle. I remember that magical moment vividly, but I was surprised to learn this made her absolute favorite list. I started to wonder whether, if we had jumped in puddles more often, it would have become mundane. I doubt it—puddles are meant for splashing.

···

A Menu of Options for Teaching Inclusively, Mindfully, and Equitably

 Children's Corner

Byers, Grace. 2018. *I Am Enough*. New York: Balzer + Bray.

Engle, Margarita. 2015. *Drum Dream Girl: How One Girl's Courage Changed Music*. Boston: HMH Books for Young Readers.

Hoose, Phillip M., Hannah Hoose, and Debbie Tilley. 1998. *Hey, Little Ant*. Berkeley, CA: Tricycle.

Littlechild, George. 1997. *This Land Is My Land*. New York: Children's Book Press.

McDaniel, Breanna. 2019. *Hands Up!* New York: Penguin Random House.

Reynolds, Peter. 2019. *Say Something*. New York: Orchard Books.

Yousafzai, Malala. 2017. *Malala's Magic Pencil*. New York: Little, Brown Books for Young Readers.

 Caregivers' Corner

Baglieri, Sue, and Priya Lalvani. 2019. *Undoing Ableism: Teaching about Disability in K–12 Classrooms*. New York: Routledge.

Hanscom, Angela J. 2016. *Balanced and Barefoot: How Unrestricted Outdoor Play Makes for Strong, Confident, and Capable Children*. Oakland, CA: New Harbinger.

Larimore, Rachel A. 2019. *Preschool Beyond Walls: Blending Early Childhood Education and Nature-Based Learning*. Lewisville, NC: Gryphon House.

Louv, Richard. 2008. *Last Child in the Woods: Saving Our Children from Nature-Deficit Disorder*. Chapel Hill, NC: Algonquin.

McGurk, Linda Åkeson. 2018. *There's No Such Thing as Bad Weather: A Scandinavian Mom's Secrets for Raising Healthy, Resilient, and Confident Kids (from Friluftsliv to Hygge)*. New York: Touchstone.

Sampson, Scott D. 2015. *How to Raise a Wild Child: The Art and Science of Falling in Love with Nature*. New York: Houghton Mifflin Harcourt.

Sapon-Shevin, Mara. 2010. *Because We Can Change the World: A Practical Guide to Building Cooperative, Inclusive Classroom Communities*. 2nd ed. Thousand Oaks, CA: Corwin.

Websites on Building Social Justice Starting in the Classroom

Teaching for Change

https://www.teachingforchange.org

This first-rate website, designed for teachers and families, offers practical "tools to create schools where students learn to read, write and change the world." There are well-conceptualized, clearly organized, and easy-to-access sections on parent organizing, teaching resources, book lists and reviews, and much more. An indispensable resource for every school or home.

Using Their Words

http://www.usingtheirwords.org

This is an excellent resource for young childhood and early elementary educators working to incorporate justice action into their classrooms. Montclair State University professor Bree Picower uses the website to post viable, visible ways to work with young people in social justice platforms. The informative and well-crafted site includes important lesson plans, recommended children's literature, and elements of social justice education. One of the best parts of this website is that teachers' voices are prominently featured.

 Take It to the Classroom

Breathing Exercise

by Annie Bien

Pick a comfortable position for sitting down. You can sit on a cushion with your legs crossed, your back straight, and your hands on your knees. You can sit also in a chair. The most important thing is that you're comfortable so you won't get distracted.

Place your hands on your knees.

Look down the tip of your nose onto the floor about two feet away from you and begin to notice your breath.

Breathe gently in.

Breathe gently out.

Feel your breath come to an end before you start to breathe in again.

Can you do this five times without losing count?

If you lose count, start again. It might be tricky to do at first, but it gets easier gradually.

Between each breath, give yourself a chance to rest your mind. Let your mind relax.

Imagine you can see the sky. Now see where it meets with the ocean.

Imagine the horizon where sky meets earth.

Let all your worries get so small that they turn into tiny flecks of dust and disappear.

If you find your eyes have closed, gently open them.

Now stand up. Give yourself a big stretch, and reach your arms up and your legs out. Take a deep breath, let your breath go, and smile.

Partner Poses

Partner poses are a great way to build fun into your yoga routine at home or on the go. Children love partner poses because they are interactive and leave more room for connecting and giggling during yoga. They are a simple way to bring focus, teamwork, and empathy. Use these poses to practice other nonverbal skills, such as eye contact (when possible) and nodding. Be sure to demonstrate a sense of humor as you get into the partner poses so everyone knows it's okay to laugh and be silly. Just remind children to breathe and concentrate so no one gets hurt.

For three-year-olds, it's best to practice all the partner poses with an adult. Children ages four and up can practice these poses with a sibling, friend, or an adult.

Double Tree

Double tree is a simple partner pose for grown-ups and children of all ages that improves balance and encourages eye contact (if possible). Children can easily do this one together and will have fun pretending to be various kinds of trees in different places.

1. Start in tree pose. Lift one foot and press it against the inside of the opposite thigh, then place palms together at the chest, facing each other. Mirror poses so one partner is balancing on the right leg and the other partner is balancing on the left leg.

2. Partners raise their arms and press their hands together at the top of the tree. (If one partner is significantly taller, she can simply meet the hands of the smaller person.)

3. Take a few deep breaths and make eye contact as both partners stand tall in tree pose.

4. To release, both partners set their elevated foot down next to the standing foot and lower their arms.

5. Repeat on the other side.

6. For more fun, try waving your "branches" in the wind while holding the pose. Call out different places and weather patterns for your tree in which to be.

Partner Seated Twist

This is a soothing, supported stretch through the upper body and an accessible partner pose that doesn't require any acrobatics or balance. If little ones are distracted, this is a great pose for kicking off partner work or your daily practice.

1. Both partners sit cross-legged, facing one another with knees touching.

2. Both people reach their right arm around their lower back.

3. Each reaches their left hand out to grab the other's right hand. If it's hard to reach hands, one partner can hold a towel and each person can grab one end of the towel.

4. Keep twisting together, possibly grabbing each other's wrists for a deeper stretch.

5. Repeat on the second side.

Double Boat

Go on an aquatic adventure. This pose teaches teamwork and fires up the core to release energy. It also requires balance and knowing your limits. If there is a big size difference between the partners, straight legs might not be possible. Just take it as far as you can and have fun in the process.

1. Partners start by sitting on the ground, facing each other. Each partner has their knees pulled in and up toward the ceiling and feet flat in the floor.

2. Partners press the soles of their feet into their partners' feet, creating leverage in the legs. Partners can grab each other's hands for a deeper connection.

3. Continue pressing the feet together, keeping the knees bent, as each person lifts and lengthens through the spine.

4. As the partners maintain their connection in the hands and the feet, they slowly begin to straighten their knees as far as is comfortable.

5. If straightened knees are not possible, partners can stay in the pose with their knees bent. As they hold the pose, partners take a few deep breaths together, maintaining eye contact and maybe even smiling.

6. To release, each partner lowers their feet to the ground and releases their hands.

From *Yoga for Kids and Their Grown-Ups: 100+ Fun Yoga and Mindfulness Activities to Practice Together* by Katherine Priore Ghannam, published by Rockridge Press. Copyright© 2018 by Callisto Media. All rights reserved.

The Power of Presence

Discovery Meditation

This discovery meditation, which is more involved and open ended than the other guided meditations in this book, is great for encouraging imagination, intuition, and independence. This can be used as a tool to strengthen children's awareness and appreciation for the powerful connections to people, other living beings, the land, and themselves. In preparation, here are some things you may want to consider before you begin:

• Let children know they will be using their imaginations to visit a special place that is their very own.

• Dim or turn lights low. You may also close the blinds or curtains.

• You may have gentle, soft music, or nature sounds in the background, but this is not necessary.

• Use a soft voice. You can also record this meditation and have it for future use.

• Provide visual displays of scenic and beautiful places such as majestic mountains, the African bush, a tropical island, rain forests, sandy beaches, blossoming gardens, or any other beautiful, serene landscape to offer children ideas of possible places to "visit," perhaps also including relevant audio. You might even show these photos to children before the activity, and let them know they can "visit" one of them in this guided meditation, if they choose to do so.

• Help children to find a comfortable and clean space to lay down (or seated if they prefer).

1. Close your eyes. Feel your eyelids touch.

2. Now take a deep breath through your nose. Breathe it out through your mouth.

3. Take another deep breath in. And then breathe it out. Keep breathing like this, slowly, naturally.

4. Keep your focus on your breath as you breathe in and out. Let's breathe this way for ten seconds. (Count slowly to ten.)

5. Now keep breathing like that, keep your eyes closed, and open your imagination.

6. Picture in your mind a beautiful magic carpet. It is your very own. Perhaps it is colorful. Maybe it is soft. Your magic carpet welcomes you to take off on a fun adventure.

7. Now step onto your magic carpet and sit down getting ready for takeoff. You feel relaxed because you feel safe and also excited to travel to a faraway place in your imagination.

8. Your magic carpet takes off and goes higher and higher into the sky. You are smiling because you know you are completely safe and protected, and a wonderful adventure lies ahead.

9. Your magic carpet now goes even higher above the clouds. You can picture this in your imagination.

10. The magic carpet is taking you to a most beautiful and peaceful place. It can be somewhere you have been or somewhere new. It's totally up to you.

11. Your magic carpet is about to land in a magical and peaceful place. It might have a lake, mountains, gardens, or rainbows. You decide. It is the most beautiful and peaceful place you could ever imagine.

12. Your magic carpet is now landing, and you can see everything more clearly. When you have landed, take a moment to look around and notice what you see. Perhaps you see a waterfall? Maybe trees or flowers? Let your imagination show you this beautiful, peaceful place. (Pause.)

13. You are ready to step off your magic carpet. Imagine how the ground feels under your feet.

14. Imagine the wonderful smells in your beautiful, peaceful place. (Pause.)

15. Now imagine how you feel being here in this magical and peaceful place. You may feel relaxed, strong, healthy, brave, peaceful, or happy—it is up to you. The most important thing is that you feel really good. (Pause.)

16. As you explore more of this peaceful and magical place, what else do you notice? Take a moment to observe how it feels, how it smells, and how it tastes. Experience it all. (Pause.)

17. Take a big breath in and out. Feel a deep connection to the land and the natural beauty that surrounds you. (Pause.)

18. Now take a moment to invite any visitors into your space. In your imagination, see what kind friends or loved ones come to your beautiful, peaceful place. These visitors could be animals or they could be one person you know or even a group of people. They may be imaginary friends. Or you might decide you would like to be alone—it is totally up to you. (Pause.)

19. If there are special visitors, what do they say or do? Do they have a special message for you? (Pause.)

20. Before it is time to go, you decide to find a quiet place to rest. What do you see? What do you hear? Use your imagination to find a lovely space in your magical and peaceful place to lie down. As you lie down and get comfortable, feel the earth beneath you. You feel very relaxed, calm, and filled with peace. Imagine this wonderful feeling filling up your whole body. This wonderful feeling is inside you. This wonderful feeling is also all around you. (Pause.)

21. It is almost time to leave and get back on your magic carpet. You can visit this peaceful place again another time. You can take this feeling of calm and peace with you.

22. Now it is time to get back on your magic carpet. Imagine yourself getting ready for takeoff. Your magic carpet lifts off and now heads for the sky. You notice the fluffy clouds. You will be back in this room in a moment. (Pause.)

23. Your magic carpet is now landing back where it took off. You have returned safely and are now back in this room. Keeping your eyes closed, take a moment to breathe deeply. You can even start to slowly move or gently stretch your body. (Pause.)

24. When you feel ready, begin to open your eyes. Just remember this beautiful, peaceful place because you can go there using your imagination.

The Power of Presence

APPENDIX

Deepening a Daily Mindfulness Practice

Just by living in the world today, life can be seen as one big classroom and maintaining presence an ongoing lesson. We can't expect to live a peaceful life or in a peaceful world if we don't have inner peace. Whether you are beginning a mindfulness practice or have been a longtime student of a contemplative practice, whether you are an educator or are caring for a child at home, this section is an invitation to maintain a daily practice. Here are some ideas to get you started or to serve as guideposts to deepen or expand your practice.

Getting Ready

- **Let the practice find you:** See what kind of mindfulness practice really speaks to you. There are many different ways to practice so start with the one that calls out to you. You don't have to choose a mindfulness practice; it chooses you.

- **Realize this is a practice:** Mindfulness is not the destination but the path. It is ongoing with many peaks, valleys, and speed bumps along the way. Being present and returning to present moment is the practice. So be gentle with yourself and let go of judgments, expectations, and goals. It's just practice.

- **Stay the course:** This is part of our daily routine, and sticking to it no matter what else is going on in our lives is part of practice. We don't typically forget to brush our teeth, because brushing is just a natural part of our routine each day. It is exactly the same with a mindfulness practice—it becomes a natural part of our daily lives. We simply show up, especially when we really don't want to and have a thousand excuses not to.

Getting Set

- **Where to practice:** Find a quiet, private, and pleasing space where there are no distractions. Although you can practice anywhere, the familiarity of a pleasant space that you return to each day will help maintain consistency.

- **When to practice:** Determine the best time of day to practice. Although you can practice anytime, it is often recommended to practice the same time every day. Many people, myself included, practice in the morning as a way to enter the day, but some prefer to practice in the evening to let go of the day (both are excellent choices!). You might even decide to practice upon awakening and before bedtime. This is such a personalized experience, so practice anytime that works best for you.

- **How long to practice:** Since there is no one way or even a correct way to practice, this is really up to you. Many people like to start out with a five-minute mindfulness practice, although you can begin with a one-minute practice if it is difficult to get started. The main thing is to show up every day. You will sense when the time is right to expand your mindfulness practice.

- **What to practice:** There are countless paths to increase awareness in the present moment, so it is best to see which one(s) speaks to you. If you find yourself drawn to a particular practice, search for a well-respected teacher to guide you or connect with a community as you engage in a deeper and fuller experience. Here are just a few options you may want to explore:

  - **Seated practice:** This is a traditional way to bring awareness to the present moment as you sit in a comfortable cross-legged position on a cushion or the floor or sit comfortably in a chair with feet flat on the floor. Start by using your senses to notice things—the noise outside, the tick of a clock, tension in your jaw, clothes touching your skin, and so on. Eyes can be closed or turned downward as you become aware of your surroundings but not intensely focused on them. Simply notice and let go. You can also bring your attention to your breath as you inhale and exhale over and over and over again. Just breathe freely. If your mind wanders (and it will) gently bring your focus back to noticing your breath.

  - **Walking meditation:** This is perfect when you have nowhere to go. It is a movement meditation although you are not walking to get to a specific destination. As with all other types of practice, quieting the mind is where you want to focus your attention so it is best not to be in a high-traffic area where thinking about safety and navigation are constantly required. You can bring awareness to your breath or use all of your senses to tune into the surroundings. Refrain from any judgment, commentary, or interpretation.

- Body scan: This is very useful to restore awareness and appreciation for your physical body and to strengthen the connection between body and mind. Find a quiet space and be comfortably seated or lying down. You might start by tuning into your body without judgment. With eyes closed, if comfortable, focus on your toes as you say to yourself "toes relax." Alternatively, you can say to yourself "toes at ease." Then bring awareness to each body part as you "scan" moving from the bottom of your body (toes) to top (head) saying quietly to yourself, "ankles relax," "feet relax," "legs relax," "knees relax," and so forth until you recognize each part of the body. This focused attention in each moment can bring a sense of inner stillness and relaxation to your overall body.

- Yoga: There are many traditions and styles of yoga so, if this is of interest, the first step is to find a good fit for you. Look for and select a qualified teacher with whom you trust and respect. Yoga, which has been around for thousands of years, is often defined as "union" or "concentration." It is recommended to study with one teacher or at one yoga school so your inquiry of yoga can expand over time. Learning directly from an experienced, knowledgeable teacher, particularly one who has a steady practice, is encouraged.

- Guided meditation: There are countless options to engage in a guided practice given the availability of apps and other resources. They will generally guide you through visualizations or provide auditory experiences, usually set in nature. These can be helpful tools to quiet the mind and return to the present moment. I generally do not use apps but many people seem to like them.

Keep Going

There are many pathways to becoming more mindful and reflective in our work with young children. One graduate student, who is also a first-grade teacher, commented recently how she is observing a noticeable presence (forgive the pun) in mindfulness now that she has started her own contemplative practice. More books, conversations, and other references to mindfulness started crossing her path. This is likely no accident. When we become more aware of being present in the moment, we are more open to and welcoming of similar experiences. Like attracts like.

Maintaining a daily practice is an important way to ensure consistency and accountability in our roles as teachers as well as learners. In one of my graduate courses, students document their experiences in a contemplative journal. This is not an accounting of the day but rather a space to record all questions, insights, and reflections related to a personal daily mindfulness practice. This is a private space to include observations or connections between a mindfulness practice and inside and outside the classroom. A contemplative journal is a perfect place to note any changes, challenges, contradictions, or confusion.

I invite you to keep a mindfulness or contemplative journal to determine if this is a tool that you want in your life. Many people, myself included, have found this type of documentation brings a greater sense of clarity, comfort, guidance, and inner wisdom. Feel free to play with metaphors, images, poems, visual maps, raps, quotes, or anything else that holds meaning for you by including these in your contemplative journal. It can be quite useful to read all of the entries from previous weeks and take note of insights or reflections you observe across all of entries, including times when you feel stuck or off track. I have personally found that maintaining a written record is an excellent way to more clearly understand my own practice, especially small or subtle shifts, which can often get lost when the mind is full of chatter. A mindfulness practice is a personalized journey and there are many paths to (re)mind us to return to the present moment. The portal of presence is always open. Now is the time to begin. And begin again. And again. And again. It's about time.

References and Recommended Readings

Adair, Jennifer Keys, and Lilly Bhaskaran. 2010. "Meditation, Rangoli, and Eating on the Floor: Practices from an Urban Preschool in Bangalore, India." *Young Children* 65(6): 48–52.

Alahari, Uma. 2017. "Supporting Socio-Emotional Competence and Psychological Well-Being of School Psychologists through Mindful Practice." *Contemporary School Psychology* 21(4): 369–379.

Altman, Roberta, Susan Stires, and Susan Weseen. 2015. *Claiming the Promise of Place-Based Education*. Occasional Paper Series 33. New York: Bank Street College of Education.

American Association of Colleges for Teacher Education. 2018. "With Declining Enrollment, Teacher Colleges Recalibrate." *Education Week* 38(1). Washington, DC: American Association of Colleges for Teacher Education.

Ames, Louise Bates. 1946. "The Development of the Sense of Time in the Young Child." *The Journal of Genetic Psychology* 68(1): 97–125.

Angelou, Maya. 1986. "Wonder." *Maya Angelou Poems*. New York: Bantam.

Australian Government, Department of Education and Training. 2009. *Belonging, Being and Becoming: The Early Years Learning Framework for Australia*. Canberra, Australia: Department of Education and Training. https://docs.education.gov.au/node/2632

Bacon, Jessica. 2019. "Pursuing 'Radical Inclusion' within an Era of Neoliberal Educational Reform." In *The SAGE Handbook of Inclusion and Diversity in Education*. London, UK: SAGE.

Bae, Berit. 2010. "Realizing Children's Right to Participation in Early Childhood Settings: Some Critical Issues in a Norwegian Context." *Early Years* 30(3): 205–218.

Beach, Ralph. 1996. "Our Children Are Getting the Wrong Message." In *Putting Children First: Visions for a Brighter Future for Young Children and Their Families*. Baltimore: Paul H. Brookes.

Beneke, Margaret, et al. 2019. "Practicing Inclusion, Doing Justice: Disability, Identity, and Belonging in Early Childhood." *Zero to Three* 39(3): 26–34.

Bishop, Rudine Sims. 1990. "Mirrors, Windows, and Sliding Glass Doors." *Perspectives* 6(3): ix–xi.

Bogdan, Robert. 1988. *Freak Show: Presenting Human Oddities for Amusement and Profit*. Chicago: The University of Chicago Press.

Burns, Litany. 2002. *The Sixth Sense of Children: Nurturing Your Child's Intuitive Abilities*. New York: New American Library.

Burton, Neel. 2017. "The Joy of Solitude." *Psychology Today*. https://www. psychologytoday.com/us/blog/hide-and-seek/201711/the-joy-solitude

Campbell, Emily. 2014. "Mindfulness in Education Research Highlights." *Greater Good Magazine*. https://greatergood.berkeley.edu/article/item/mindfulness_in_education_ research_highlights

Children's Defense Fund. 2017. *The State of America's Children*. https://www. childrensdefense.org/reports/2017/the-state-of-americas-children-2017-report/

Christakis, Erika. 2016. *The Importance of Being Little: What Preschoolers Really Need from Grownups*. New York: Viking.

Costa, Gerard, and Kaitlin Mulcahy. 2018. "Talking with Young Children about the Tree of Life and Other Tragedies." Montclair, NJ: Center for Autism and Early Childhood Mental Health, College of Education and Human Services, Montclair State University.

Cowhey, Mary. 2006. *Black Ants and Buddhists: Thinking Critically and Teaching Differently in the Primary Grades*. Portland, ME: Stenhouse.

Dachyshyn, Darcey M. 2015. "Being Mindful, Heartful, and Ecological in Early Years Care and Education." *Contemporary Issues in Early Childhood* 16(1): 13–41.

de Becker, Gavin. 1999. *Protecting the Gift: Keeping Children and Teenagers Safe (and Parents Sane)*. New York: Dell.

Delpit, Lisa. 2006. *Other People's Children: Cultural Conflict in the Classroom*. New York: The New Press.

Deringer, S. Anthony. 2017. "Mindful Place-Based Education: Mapping the Literature." *Journal of Experiential Education* 40(4): 333–348.

Derman-Sparks, Louise. 2008. "Why an Anti-Bias Curriculum?" In *Rethinking Early Childhood Education*. Milwaukee, WI: Rethinking Schools.

Derman-Sparks, Louise, and Julie Olsen Edwards. 2010. *Anti-Bias Education for Young Children and Ourselves*. Washington, DC: National Association for the Education of Young Children.

Devcich, Daniel, et al. 2017. "Effectiveness of a Mindfulness-Based Program on School Children's Self-Reported Well-Being: A Pilot Study Comparing Effects with an Emotional Literacy Program." *Journal of Applied School Psychology* 33(4): 309–330.

DiNicolantonio, James J., and Amy Berger. 2016. "Added Sugars Drive Nutrient and Energy Deficit in Obesity: A New Paradigm." *Open Heart* 3(2): e000469. https://doi-org/10.1136/openhrt-2016-000469

Droit-Volet, Sylvie. 2013. "Time Perception in Children: A Neurodevelopmental Approach." *Neuropsychologia* 51(2): 220–234.

Duhn, Iris. 2012. "Places for Pedagogies, Pedagogies for Places." *Contemporary Issues in Early Childhood* 13(2): 99–106.

Edwards, Carolyn, Lella Gandini, and George Forman, eds. 1993. *The Hundred Languages of Children: The Reggio Emilia Approach to Early Childhood Education.* Greenwood, NY: Praeger.

Elkind, David. 2006. *The Hurried Child.* 25th anniversary ed. Cambridge, MA: Da Capo.

Erwin, Elizabeth J., ed. 1996. *Putting Children First: Visions for a Brighter Future for Young Children and Their Families.* Baltimore: Paul H. Brookes.

Erwin, Elizabeth J. 2017. "Transparency in Early Childhood Education: What the West Can Learn from Australia's Focus on Well-Being." *Global Education Review* 4(3): 56–69.

Erwin, Elizabeth, and Kimberly Robinson. 2015. "The Joy of Being: Making Way for Young Children's Natural Mindfulness." *Early Childhood Development and Care* 186(2): 268–286.

Erwin, Elizabeth, Kimberly Robinson, and David Aveta. 2017. "Being Present: An Exploratory Study on the Use of Mindfulness in Early Childhood." *The International Journal of Holistic Early Learning and Development* 4: 1–17.

Erwin, Elizabeth, et al. 2015. "'It's Like Breathing In Blue Skies and Breathing Out Stormy Clouds': Mindfulness Practices in Early Childhood." *Young Exceptional Children* 20(2): 69–85.

Farquhar, Sandy. 2016. "Time in Early Childhood: Creative Possibilities with Different Conceptions of Time." *Contemporary Issues in Early Childhood* 17(4): 409–420.

Felver, Joshua, et al. 2013. "Mindfulness in School Psychology: Applications for Intervention and Professional Practice." *Psychology in the Schools* 50(6): 531–547.

Ferri, Beth, and David Connor. 2006. *Reading Resistance: Discourses of Exclusion in Desegregation and Inclusion Debates.* New York: Peter Lang.

Fetell Lee, Ingrid. 2018. *Joyful: The Surprising Power of Ordinary Things to Create Extraordinary Happiness.* New York: Little, Brown Spark.

Finch, Ken, and Patti Ensel Bailie. 2015. "Nature Preschools: Putting Nature at the Heart of Early Childhood Education." In *Claiming the Promise of Place-Based Education.* Occasional Paper Series 33: 95–104. New York: Bank Street College of Education.

Fincham, Emmanuelle. 2016. "Words and Bodies." In *Disrupting Early Childhood Education Research: Imagining New Possibilities.* New York: Routledge.

Fine, Michelle. 1992. *Disruptive Voices: The Possibilities of Feminist Research.* Ann Arbor, MI: The University of Michigan Press.

Flook, Lisa, et al. 2010. "Effects of Mindful Awareness Practices on Executive Functions in Elementary School Children." *Journal of Applied School Psychology* 26(1): 70–95.

Flook, Lisa, et al. 2015. "Promoting Prosocial Behavior and Self-Regulatory Skills in Preschool Children through a Mindfulness-Based Kindness Curriculum." *Developmental Psychology* 51(1): 44–51.

Fox, Jeremy, et al. 2012. "Preventive Intervention for Anxious Preschoolers and Their Parents: Strengthening Early Emotional Development." *Child Psychiatry and Human Development* 43(4): 544–559.

Freire, Paulo. 1998. *Pedagogy of Freedom: Ethics, Democracy, and Civic Courage*. Translated by Patrick Clarke. Lanham, MD: Rowman and Littlefield.

Gallwey, W. Timothy. 1997. *The Inner Game of Tennis: The Classic Guide to the Mental Side of Peak Performance*. New York: Random House.

García-Campayo, Javier, et al. 2017. "How Do Cultural Factors Influence the Teaching and Practice of Mindfulness and Compassion in Latin Countries?" *Frontiers in Psychology* 8: 1161. https://doi.org/10.3389/fpsyg.2017.01161

Gardner, Howard. 1983. *Frames of Mind: The Theory of Multiple Intelligences*. New York: Basic Books.

Ghannam, Katherine Priore. 2018. *Yoga for Kids and Their Grown-Ups: 100+ Fun Yoga and Mindfulness Activities to Practice Together*. Emeryville, CA: Rockridge.

Gibbons, Andrew. 2016. "Do 'We' Really Live in Rapidly Changing Times? Questions Concerning Time, Childhood, Technology and Education." *Contemporary Issues in Early Childhood* 17(4): 367–376.

Groves, Betsy McAlister. 1996. "Growing Up in a Violent World: The Impact of Family and Community Violence on Young Children and Their Families." In *Putting Children First: Visions for a Brighter Future for Young Children and Their Families*. Baltimore: Paul H. Brookes.

Hamm, Catherine. 2015. "Walking with Place: Storying Reconciliation Pedagogies in Early Childhood Education." *Journal of the Canadian Association for Young Children* 40(2): 57–67.

Hạnh, Thích Nhất. 1991. *Peace Is Every Step: The Path of Mindfulness in Everyday Life*. New York: Bantam Books.

Hạnh, Thích Nhất. 2015. *Silence: The Power of Quiet in a World Full of Noise*. New York: HarperOne.

Hard, Louise, Frances Press, and Megan Gibson. 2013. "'Doing' Social Justice in Early Childhood: The Potential of Leadership." *Contemporary Issues in Early Childhood* 14(4): 324–334. https://journals.sagepub.com/doi/10.2304/ciec.2013.14.4.324

Haskins, Cathleen. 2010. "Integrating Silence Practices into the Classroom: The Value of Quiet." *Encounter: Education for Meaning and Social Justice* 23(3): 15–20.

Haskins, Cathleen. 2011. "The Gift of Silence." *Montessori Life* 23(2): 34–39.

Hatt, Beth. 2012. "Smartness as a Cultural Practice in Schools." *American Educational Research Journal* 49(3): 438–460.

Higashida, Naoki. 2013. *The Reason I Jump: The Inner Voice of a Thirteen-Year-Old Boy with Autism*. New York: Random House.

Hinton, Devon, et al. 2013. "Acceptance and Mindfulness Techniques Applied to Refugee and Ethnic Minority Populations with PTSD: Examples from 'Culturally Adapted CBT.'" *Cognitive and Behavioral Practice* 20(1): 33–46.

Honig, Alice Sterling. 2010. *Little Kids, Big Worries: Stress-Busting Tips for Early Childhood Classrooms*. Baltimore: Paul H. Brookes.

Hursh, David. 2007. "Assessing No Child Left Behind and the Rise of Neoliberal Education Policies." *American Educational Research Journal* 44(3): 493–518.

Hyland, Nora. 2010. "Social Justice in Early Childhood Classrooms." *Young Children* 65(1): 82–90.

Irving Harris Foundation. 2018. *Diversity-Informed Tenets for Work with Infants, Children, and Families*. Chicago: Irving Harris Foundation. https://diversityinformedtenets.org/the-tenets/english

Junger, Alejandro. 2009. *Clean: The Revolutionary Program to Restore the Body's Natural Ability to Heal Itself*. New York: HarperOne.

Kabat-Zinn, Jon. 2005. *Wherever You Go, There You Are: Mindfulness Meditation in Everyday Life*. 10th anniversary ed. New York: Hachette.

Kabat-Zinn, Jon. 2012. *Mindfulness for Beginners: Reclaiming the Present Moment—and Your Life*. Boulder, CO: Sounds True.

Kabat-Zinn, Jon. 2013. *Full Catastrophe Living: Using the Wisdom or Your Body and Mind to Face Stress, Pain, and Illness*. New York: Bantam.

Keller, Julia, et al. 2017. "'Your Brain Becomes a Rainbow': Perceptions and Traits of 4th-Graders in a School-Based Mindfulness Intervention." *Journal of Research in Childhood Education* 31(4): 508–529.

Khalsa, Sat Bir Singh. 2019. "The Multiple Mechanisms of the Multiple Practices in Yoga: Putting It All Together." Lecture presented at the Yoga and Science: The Mechanisms of Yoga and Meditation Conference, Brooklyn, NY, January 19–20.

Klatt, Maryanna, et al. 2013. "Feasibility and Preliminary Outcomes for Move-Into-Learning: An Arts-Based Mindfulness Classroom Intervention." *The Journal of Positive Psychology* 8(3): 233–241.

Klingbiel, David, and Tyler Renshaw. 2018. "Mindfulness-Based Interventions for Teachers: A Meta-Analysis of the Emerging Evidence Base." *School Psychology Quarterly* 33(4): 501–511.

Knaus, Marianne. 2009. "Childhood Today Explored through Notions of Being and Time." *New Zealand Research in Early Childhood Education Journal* 12: 123–129.

Knaus, Marianne. 2015. "'Time for Being': Why the Australian Early Years Framework Opens Up New Possibilities." *Journal of Early Childhood Research* 13(3): 221–235.

Koenig, Kristie, et al. 2012. "Efficacy of the Get Ready to Learn Yoga Program Among Children with Autism Spectrum Disorders: A Pretest-Posttest Control Group Design." *American Journal of Occupational Therapy* 66(5): 538–546.

Lalvani, Priya. 2015. "'We Are Not Aliens': Exploring the Meaning of Disability and the Nature of Belongingness in a Fourth-Grade Classroom." *Disability Studies Quarterly* 35(4): 1–22.

Lalvani, Priya, and Jessica Bacon. 2019. "Rethinking 'We Are All Special': Anti-Ableism Curricula in Early Childhood Classrooms." *Young Exceptional Children* 22(2): 87–100.

Lim, Xinyi, and Li Qu. 2017. "The Effect of Single-Session Mindfulness Training on Preschool Children's Attentional Control." *Mindfulness* 8(2): 300–310.

MacDonald, Elaine, and Richard Hastings. 2010. "Mindful Parenting and Care Involvement of Fathers of Children with Intellectual Disabilities." *Journal of Child and Family Studies* 19(2): 236–240.

Malik, Rasheed. 2017. "New Data Reveal 250 Preschoolers Are Suspended or Expelled Every Day." *Center for American Progress*. https://www.americanprogress.org/issues/early-childhood/news/2017/11/06/442280/new-data-reveal-250-preschoolers-suspended-expelled-every-day/

Meikeljohn, John, et al. 2012. "Integrating Mindfulness Training into K–12 Education: Fostering the Resilience of Teachers and Students." *Mindfulness* 3(4): 291–307.

Moss, Peter, et al. 2016. "The Organisation for Economic Co-operation and Development's International Early Learning Study: Opening for Debate and Contestation." *Contemporary Issues in Early Childhood* 17(3): 343–351.

Moss, Peter, and Urban, Mathias. 2019. "The Organisation for Economic Co-operation and Development's International Early Learning Study: What's Going On." *Contemporary Issues in Early Childhood* 20(2): 207–212.

Nagasawa, Mark, Lacey Peters, and Beth Blue Swadener. 2018. "The Costs of Putting Quality First: Neoliberalism, (Ine)quality, (Un)affordability, and (In)accessibility?" In *Reconceptualizing Early Childhood Education and Care—A Reader: Critical Questions, New Imaginaries, and Social Action*. 2nd ed. New York: Peter Lang.

Napoli, Maria, Paul Rock Krech, and Lynn Holley. 2005. "Mindfulness Training for Elementary School Students: The Attention Academy." *Journal of Applied School Psychology* 21(1): 99–125.

Neece, Cameron L. 2013. "Mindfulness-Based Stress Reduction for Parents of Young Children with Developmental Delays: Implications for Parental Mental Health and Child Behavior Problems." *Journal of Applied Research in Intellectual Disabilities* 27(2): 174–186.

Nepo, Mark. 2011. *The Book of Awakening: Having the Life You Want by Being Present to the Life You Have*. Gift ed. Newburyport, MA: Conari.

New Zealand Ministry of Education. 2017. *Te Whāriki: He whāriki mātauranga mō ngā mokopuna o aotearoa: Early Childhood Curriculum*. Wellington, New Zealand: Ministry of Education. https://www.education.govt.nz/assets/Documents/Early-Childhood/Te-Whariki-Early-Childhood-Curriculum-ENG-Web.pdf

Nitecki, Elena, and Helge Wasmuth. 2017. "Global Trends in Early Childhood Practice: Working Within the Limitations of the Global Education Reform Movement." *Global Education Review* 4(3): 1–13.

North American Association for Environmental Education (NAAEE). 2017. *Nature Preschools and Forest Kindergartens: 2017 National Survey*. Washington, DC: NAAEE.

Palmer, Parker J. 1998. *The Courage to Teach: Exploring the Inner Landscape of a Teacher's Life*. Hoboken, NJ: John Wiley and Sons.

Parker, Gail. 2019. "Healing the Wounds of Racial Distress: What's Yoga Got to Do with It?" Lecture at the Yoga and Science: The Mechanisms of Yoga and Meditation Conference, New York University Tandon School of Engineering, Brooklyn, NY, January 19–20.

Parker, Keith. 2006. "Debate: Should Technology Be Used in Every Classroom?" National Education Association. http://www.nea.org/archive/14111.htm

Parnell, Will, and Jeanne Marie Iorio, eds. 2016. *Disrupting Early Childhood Education Research: Imagining New Possibilities*. New York: Routledge.

Paugh, Patricia Cahill, and Curt Dudley-Marling. 2011. "'Speaking' Deficit into (or out of) Existence: How Language Constrains Classroom Teachers' Knowledge about Instructing Diverse Learners." *International Journal of Inclusive Education* 15(8): 819–833.

Peirce, Penney. 2009. *The Intuitive Way: The Definitive Guide to Increasing Your Awareness*. New York: Atria Books.

Porges, Stephen W. 2011. *The Polyvagal Theory: Neurophysiological Foundations of Emotions, Attachment, Communication, and Self-Regulation*. New York: W. W. Norton and Company.

Porges, Stephen, W. 2019. "Ancient Wisdom Meets Contemporary Neuroscience." Lecture at the Yoga and Science: The Mechanisms of Yoga and Meditation Conference, New York University Tandon School of Engineering, Brooklyn, NY, January 19–20.

Rameka, Lesley. 2016. "Kia whakatōmuri te haere whakamua: 'I Walk Backwards into the Future with My Eyes Fixed on My Past.'" *Contemporary Issues in Early Childhood* 17(4): 387–398.

Randoph, Brenda. 2008. "I Didn't Know There Were Cities in Africa! Challenging Children's—and Adults'—Misperceptions about the African Continent." *Teaching Tolerance* 34. https://www.tolerance.org/magazine/fall-2008/i-didnt-know-there-were-cities-in-africa

Rapp, Whitney H., and Katrina L. Arndt. 2012. *Teaching Everyone: An Introduction to Inclusive Education*. Baltimore: Paul H. Brookes.

Razza, Rachel, Dessa Bergen-Cico, and Kimberly Raymond. 2013. "Enhancing Preschoolers' Self-Regulation via Mindful Yoga." *Journal of Child and Family Studies* 24(2): 372–385.

Rechtschaffen, Daniel. 2014. *The Way of Mindful Education: Cultivating Well-Being in Teachers and Students*. New York: W. W. Norton and Company.

Reid, Denise. 2009. "Capturing Presence Moments: The Art of Mindful Presence in Occupational Therapy." *Canadian Journal of Occupational Therapy* 76(3): 180–188.

Roeser, Robert, et al. 2013. "Mindfulness Training and Reductions in Teacher Stress and Burnout: Results from Two Randomized, Waitlist-Control Field Trials." *Journal of Educational Psychology* 105(3): 787–804.

Rogers, Fred. 2018. *Won't You Be My Neighbor?* Directed by Morgan Neville. Los Angeles: Tremolo Productions.

Rogoff, Barbara. 2003. *The Cultural Nature of Human Development*. Oxford, UK: Oxford University Press.

Sahlberg, Pasi. 2016. "Professional Autonomy, Trust, and Collaboration in Educators' Work." Presentation at the Annual Conference of the Philosophy of Education Society of Great Britain. New College, Oxford, UK, April 2.

Saltzman, Amy. 2014. *A Still Quiet Place: A Mindfulness Program for Teaching Children and Adolescents to Ease Stress and Difficult Emotions*. Oakland, CA: New Harbinger.

Salzberg, Sharon. 1995. *Lovingkindness: The Revolutionary Art of Happiness*. Boston: Shambala.

Schonert-Reichl, Kimberly, et al. 2015. "Enhancing Cognitive and Social-Emotional Development through a Simple-to-Administer Mindfulness-Based School Program for Elementary School Children: A Randomized Control Trial." *Developmental Psychology* 51(1): 52–66.

Shahmoon-Shanok, Rebecca, and Howard Carlton Stevenson. 2015. "Calmness Fosters Compassionate Connections: Integrating Mindfulness to Support Diverse Parents, Their Young Children, and the Providers Who Serve Them." *Zero to Three* 35(3): 18–30.

Showers, Paul. 1991. *The Listening Walk*. New ed. New York: HarperCollins.

Singh, Nirbhay, et al. 2010. "Mindfulness Training for Parents and Their Children with ADHD Increases the Children's Compliance." *Journal of Child and Family Studies* 19(2): 157–166.

Sorrels, Barbara. 2015. *Reaching and Teaching Children Exposed to Trauma*. Lewisville, NC: Gryphon House.

Srinivasan, Meena. 2014. *Teach, Breathe, Learn: Mindfulness In and Out of the Classroom*. Berkeley, CA: Parallax.

Stern, Eddie. 2019. "The Breathing App." https://eddiestern.com/the-breathing-app/

Stern, Eddie. 2019. *One Simple Thing: A New Look at the Science of Yoga and How It Can Transform Your Life*. New York: North Point.

Swedish Environmental Protection Agency. 2019. "This Is the Right of Public Access." Swedish Environmental Protection Agency. http://www.swedishepa.se/Environmental-objectives-and-cooperation/Swedish-environmental-work/Work-areas/This-is-the-Right-of-Public-Access/

Tager, Miriam B. 2018. "Segregation of Technology: Disrupting Racist Frameworks in Early Childhood Education." *Critical Education* 9(16): 5–16.

Taylor, Jill Bolte. 2009. *My Stroke of Insight: A Brain Scientist's Personal Journey*. New York: Plume.

Tenfelde, Sandi, Lena Hatchett, and Karen Saban. 2018. "'Maybe Black Girls Do Yoga': A Focus Group Study with Predominantly Low-Income African-American Women." *Complementary Therapies in Medicine* 40: 230–235.

Thierry, Karen, et al. 2016. "Two-Year Impact of a Mindfulness-Based Program on Preschoolers' Self-regulation and Academic Performance." *Early Education and Development* 27(6): 805–821.

Turkle, Sherry. 2017. *Alone Together: Why We Expect More from Technology and Less from Each Other*. New York: Basic Books.

Turnbull, H.R., and Ann Turnbull. 2000. "Accountability: Whose Job Is It, Anyway?" *Journal of Early Intervention* 23(4): 231–234.

Turner, Bret. 2019. "Teaching First-Graders about Microaggressions: The Small Moments Add Up." Teaching Tolerance. https://www.tolerance.org/magazine/teaching-firstgraders-about-microaggressions-the-small-moments-add-up

United Nations Educational, Scientific, and Cultural Organization (UNESCO). 1994. *The Salamanca Statement and Framework for Action on Special Needs Education*. Salamanca, Spain: UNESCO. http://www.unesco.org/education/pdf/SALAMA_E.PDF

United Nations Office of the High Commissioner for Human Rights. 1989. *Convention on the Rights of the Child*. New York: United Nations. https://www.ohchr.org/Documents/ProfessionalInterest/crc.pdf

Urban, Mathias, and Beth Blue Swadener. 2016. "Democratic Accountability and Contextualised Systemic Evaluation: A Comment on the OECD Initiative to Launch an International Early Learning Study (IELS)." *International Critical Childhood Policy Studies* 5(1): 6–18.

Viglas, Melanie, and Michal Perlman. 2017. "Effects of a Mindfulness-Based Program on Young Children's Self-Regulation, Prosocial Behavior and Hyperactivity." *Journal of Child and Family Studies* 27(4): 1150–1161.

Von Lob, Genevieve. 2017. *Five Deep Breaths: The Power of Mindful Parenting*. New York: Random House.

Waller, Tim, et al., eds. 2010. "The Dynamics of Early Childhood Spaces: Opportunities for Outdoor Play." *European Early Childhood Education Research Journal* 18(4): 437–443.

Watson, Karen. 2017. *Inside the 'Inclusive' Early Education Classroom: The Power of the 'Normal.'* New York: Peter Lang.

Wohlleben, Peter. 2016. *The Hidden Life of Trees: What They Feel, How They Communicate—Discoveries from a Secret World*. Vancouver, Canada: Greystone.

Wright, Travis. 2018. "Contesting Hegemony: Re-Imagining Masculinities for Early Childhood Education." *Contemporary Issues in Early Childhood* 19(2): 117–130.

Zenner, Charlotte, Solveig Herrnleben-Kurz, and Harald Walach. 2014. "Mindfulness-Based Interventions in Schools: A Systemic Review and Meta-Analysis." *Frontiers in Psychology* 5: 603. https://doi.org/10.3389/fpsyg.2014.00603

INDEX